MARGARET DIBBEN'S SMART QUESTIONS

MARGARET DIBBEN'S
SMART
QUESTIONS
TO ASK ABOUT
MONEY

How to Get What You Really Need and Want

ORION
BUSINESS
BOOKS

First published in Great Britain in 1999 by
Orion Business
An imprint of The Orion Publishing Group Ltd
Orion House, 5 Upper St Martin's Lane, London WC2H 9EA

A CIP catalogue record for this book
is available from the British Library.

ISBN 0 75282 109 1

Designed by Staziker Jones

Printed and bound in Great Britain
by Bath Press

To Geoff, who read the text with
a sub's eye and a reader's head,
and provided unstinting moral
support and sustaining meals.

Contents

Introduction   xii

1 STARTING POINTS   1
Making your own investment decisions   2
Investing ethically   3
Investing for retirement   6
Investing for children and grandchildren   7
You and your partner   9
About tax   11
Setting up a trust   25
Complaining about a financial services organisation   27
Computers and your finances   30

2 GETTING ADVICE   33
Advice on investments   33
What advisers must do   35
Dealing with independent financial advisers   37
Choosing an independent financial adviser   41
Talking to a tied adviser   48
Getting advice from a stockbroker   50
Getting investment advice from an accountant   54
Getting investment advice from a solicitor   55
Discount brokers   56

3 BUYING INVESTMENTS – BASIC PRODUCTS   58
Savings accounts   58
National Savings   64
Unit trusts   65
Open-ended investment companies (oeics)   73
Investment trusts   74
Individual Savings Accounts (ISAs)   81
Personal Equity Plans (PEPs)   86
Tax Exempt Special Savings Accounts (TESSAs)   87
Guaranteed equity bonds   88
Offshore investments   90
Shares   93
Gilts   100

4 BUYING INVESTMENTS – LIFE INSURANCE   103
Life insurance and tax   106
Endowment policies   106
Traded endowment policies   112
Whole-life insurance policies   114
Single-premium insurance bonds   116
Friendly society policies   121
Minimising inheritance tax on life insurance proceeds   123

5 PENSIONS   124
The state pension   125
Company pensions   128
AVCs and FSAVCs   134
Personal pensions   136
Future government plans for pensions   143
Annuities   144
Getting advice on personal pensions and annuities   148
Having enough money to live on when you retire   150
Retiring early   151
Retiring gradually   152
Pensions and divorce   153
Pensions and tax   154

6 MORTGAGES   155
Basic questions about mortgages   155
Mortgage intermediaries   163

Questions to ask a lender or broker before taking a mortgage   164
Information you have to provide before getting a mortgage   167
Getting a mortgage when you have a poor credit record   168
Raising money from your home when you are retired   168
Different types of mortgages available   170
Interest rate choices   173
Mortgage jargon   174
The Mortgage Code   174

7 OBTAINING CREDIT   176
The basics of credit   177
Credit cards   179
Store cards   184
Charge cards   185
Personal loans   185
Hire purchase   187
Secured personal loans   188
Credit reference agencies   188
Credit scoring   191
Getting credit if you have a poor credit record   192
Repaying a loan early   194
The Lenders' Code of Practice   194
Actions to take before obtaining credit   195

8 BANK ACCOUNTS   196
Questions to ask yourself before opening a bank account   196
New-style banks versus traditional   198
Cheque accounts   199
Plastic cards   211
Access to your money while abroad   214
Student accounts   217
The Banking Code   218

9 GENERAL INSURANCE   219
House insurance   221
Car insurance   232
Holiday insurance   236
Legal expenses insurance   243
Extended warranties on goods   245
Pet insurance   247

Lloyd's of London   248
The ABI Code of Practice   249

10 LIFE AND HEALTH INSURANCE   250

Term insurance   251
Insurance to provide money when you are ill   256
   – Income protection insurance   257
   – Loan protection insurance   259
   – Critical illness insurance   263
   – Long-term care insurance   265
   – Private medical insurance   269
   – Health cash plans   275
   – Dental plans   275
   – The ABI Code of Practice on Genetic Testing   277

APPENDIX   278

   Index   283

Acknowledgements

Many people have given their time generously to help me prepare this book. They checked the facts and they suggested more questions that customers ought to ask. I know just how long this has taken.

In particular, my heartfelt thanks go to Steve Bee of Scottish Life, Brian Capon at the British Bankers' Association, Martyn Ingram of The Investors Partnership, David Oliver of Arthur Andersen, John Patrick at the Consumer Credit Trade Association and Stuart Valentine at the Securities Institute.

Many more organisations have contributed invaluable advice: the staff at Annuity Bureau, Apcims, Association of British Insurers, Association of Friendly Societies, Association of Investment Trust Companies, Association of Unit Trusts and Investment Funds, Barclays, Baronworth, Benefits Agency, CGU, Chase de Vere, DAS, Denplan, Experian, Financial Services Authority, Grant Thornton, Halifax, Holden Meehan, IFA Promotion, Legal & General, Norwich Union, Nursing Home Fees Agency, Opas, PolicyPlus, ProShare, Scottish Mutual, Standard Life, the Stock Exchange. And the Ombudsman's offices, where they see the results when things go wrong: Banking, Building Societies, Insurance, Investment, PIA and Pensions.

I am enormously grateful to you all for your patience and enthusiasm.

Introduction

Why should I read this book?

Finance is a complicated subject. Even the experts in the business admit to being confused, and they spend all day working on nothing else. There is small hope, then, for people who occasionally buy investments and insurance to understand enough to judge them with any confidence. The problem with so many financial products is that you cannot know for sure whether you have bought the right one until many years later, when you cash in the investment or claim on your insurance policy.

This makes it vitally important that you ask the right questions before you buy – and that you ask all the questions that might affect your decision. What advisers or salespeople do *not* tell you, unless you ask the right questions, is just as important as the information they volunteer. Marketing literature never highlights the negative points. Remember: what the big print gives you, the small print takes away.

This book answers the questions you already have and suggests many more questions that you ought to ask before choosing financial products. It cannot provide all the answers, though it should:

- show how many questions you need to consider
- warn you not to take answers on face value, and
- give you the confidence to ask, ask and ask again.

Everyone involved in personal finance has a duty to explain what you are buying in words that you can understand. Those who use jargon probably do not understand it themselves. You do not have to put up with poor explanations. However helpful someone has been, if you are not satisfied, go elsewhere. You do not have to give any reasons or excuses, and there are plenty of good people who are keen for your business. You would not buy a house, a car or even a pair of shoes just because a salesperson had gone to a lot of trouble. Apply the same rule to your financial dealings.

I know it is simple to tell people how they ought to go about buying personal finance and quite another thing to put it into practice. If you feel uncomfortable cross-questioning a salesperson or adviser face to face, write down your questions and ask for a written reply. With the increasing use of e-mail, communication is getting even easier. Indeed, now that so many financial transactions are conducted by telephone, getting answers and agreements in writing is becoming more critical. Telephone selling has simplified shopping around, but you have no proof of what the salesperson has promised.

So you need another checklist:

- Get it in writing.
- Read all of a contract before you sign it.
- Keep all the paperwork.
- Check that the document you are due to sign says what you were expecting. If not, ask why not. Never assume that it probably means what you thought it did – it won't. Contracts are put in writing to set down the situation as agreed by both parties, and so you cannot complain about the terms of a contract after you have signed it.
- If you disagree with the contents, you can refuse to sign. You can even cross out the statement you disagree with and write in your own understanding of what you were told; if the company does not like this, it will soon let you know.
- Don't allow anyone to rush you.

Always remember that *you* are the customer, *you* are paying and so *you* have the right to make demands.

You have more protection today than ever before when you buy financial products or take advice on them. But beware, because there are still loopholes. Not all financial transactions come within the

Financial Services Act; products outside the rules include bank and building society savings accounts, term insurance, health insurance and house insurance. Reputable organisations quite rightly extend the same degree of care to all their products. Others do not.

No financial institution, even the best, acts with your individual best interest at heart. Banks, building societies, insurers and investment firms are commercial companies; they suggest you take certain actions or buy particular products because that is what they have to sell. They are not paternalistic organisations, and you cannot take it for granted that what they are suggesting is best because it's for you. You have to make the effort to check for yourself that you are making the right choice. You have to ask the searching questions.

Finally, a word about how this book is structured, for it is clear that there are different types of questions you will want to ask.

There are questions you need to ask and have answered before you even approach the professionals, so you have a good background knowledge of what you, and they, are talking about. And there are the questions you should ask directly of the salesperson or adviser to make sure you are getting what you want. There are sometimes questions that you have to answer yourself to clarify exactly what you need. Each type of question is distinguished in the text, with my comments on them shown in italic. The 'tips' highlight important points you need to know.

I believe this book provides the facts and the advice you need to take control of your finances. I hope it will give you the confidence to insist on getting the best.

Now get asking!

1 Starting Points

Questions to ask before you start organising your money

No one spends time sorting out finance for fun; there is nothing enjoyable about filling in forms and worrying about tax. At certain times of our lives, though, we are forced to think about money – most outstandingly with birth, marriage and death.

But at times of crisis you should not rush into making financial decisions. You will make better use of your money if you plan ahead, and you should always start with the fundamentals:

- deposit money in a savings account so you can cash it in quickly if necessary
- contribute to a pension
- if other people rely on your earnings, buy life insurance
- invest at the safer end of the stock market.

Once you have a basic strategy in place, you can start thinking about more ambitious investments and more detailed financial planning.

Making your own investment decisions

Most of us save because we need more money:

- for the short-term – extra holiday money
- for the medium-term – our children's education
- for the long-term – retirement

Being clear about even this simple point makes investment easier to understand. You can cut through more of the complexities of financial planning if you first answer the questions below – and come back to this checklist whenever you think about buying investments:

ask yourself

- Do I have some special occasion, or some special person, in mind for the proceeds of this investment?
- Am I saving for extra regular income, or for capital growth to create a larger lump sum?
- How much can I afford to save?
- Over what period do I want to save?
- Shall I invest a lump sum or make regular savings?
- How quickly might I want to cash in my investment?
- Can I afford to lose any of the money I invest? (*This is risk: you take the risk that your investment might go down in value in the hope that, given enough time, it will go up by more than investments where there is no risk.*)
- What rate of tax am I paying now, and might pay in the future? (*Your tax rate makes some investments better value than others.*)
- Does this investment take inflation into account? (*If your capital stays the same, it in fact loses value because inflation means you can buy in the future less with the same amount.*)
- Do I understand how this investment works? (*If you can't understand how you will make money, don't buy that type of investment. If the return seems too good to be true, it almost certainly is.*)
- Do I want to make my own investment decisions or leave them to someone else?

Even if you use a financial adviser to choose your investments, with a little understanding of your own added in, you will be able to ask more searching questions, and be confident that the adviser is making the right decisions.

The broad investment choice is between bank and building society savings accounts, where the money you invest remains the same, earning interest; and investments linked to share prices, where your money goes up and down in value as stock markets move, and where that money earns dividends. As well as shares, stock market investments include unit trusts, insurance policy investments and your pension.

tip

The terms 'saving' and 'investing' can be used interchangeably, but usually saving means putting money aside for the short term, in bank and building society savings accounts, whereas investing refers to the longer term – several years at least in investments linked to share prices.

Investing ethically

Many people are concerned about the environment and the damage done by big business. By investing ethically, you can invest your money confident that you are not contributing to the harm.

ask Margaret

What type of investments are sold as ethical investments?
Investments labelled as ethical are mainly unit trusts and Individual Savings Accounts (ISAs), although you can find a few life insurance policies, personal pensions, mortgages and bank accounts that claim to be ethical. Or, you can buy shares in individual companies that you believe behave ethically.

What makes an investment ethical?
There are two definitions. One is the negative approach of avoiding areas that you may find objectionable, such as:

- nuclear power
- animal experiments
- armament manufacture
- repressive regimes

- gambling
- alcohol
- pornography
- genetic engineering.

The other approach is positive, investing in companies whose activities you believe help:

- the environment
- conservation
- recycling
- pollution control
- their local community
- staff relations.

Ethical funds try to combine both aspects. But there is a further sub-division between ethical funds and environmental, or 'green', funds that invest in companies in the business of protecting the environment by water treatment, recycling, waste collection and disposal, renewable energy, and energy conservation.

Do all ethical or green funds use the same criteria for deciding where to invest?
They all differ.

How can I choose which ethical investment to buy?
You want a fund that most closely matches your priorities. You can either ask a specialist financial adviser or contact a fund manager directly: fund managers produce detailed information about companies they invest in and which they avoid.

tip

> **The Ethical Investment Research Service (Eiris) monitors individual companies and ethical investments. Its address is given in the Appendix.**

Do ethical unit trusts perform as well as ordinary ones?
As with any unit trust, the performance of one fund can be vastly different from another. Overall, ethical funds perform reasonably well compared with average UK shares, but they are always handicapped by being able to invest in only a limited number of companies. Many well performing UK companies do not pass the ethical test.

You can establish your attitude to ethical investment by asking yourself these questions.

ask yourself

- How ethical do I want to be? (*It is extremely difficult to be totally pure. For example, would you invest in a supermarket that treats its staff well and donates large amounts to charity but builds on greenfield sites? Would you invest in a packaging manufacturer that helps the local community but makes cigarette packets – or a glass manufacturer that makes whisky bottles? Do you object to animals being used for medical experiments, or only by cosmetics manufacturers? The more stringently ethical you want your investments to be, the greater the risks, because you are restricting the number of companies in which you can invest.*)
- Do I want an ethical investment or an environmental one?
- Do I want all my investments to be in UK companies, or do I want some investments overseas? (*It is sensible to spread your investments more widely than the UK, even when you are investing ethically.*)
- Am I prepared to accept a lower return by keeping to a strictly ethical code?

tip

> **All ethical investment funds produce a list of where they are willing to invest and where they won't. You can ask for a copy of that list before investing. Do not expect to find a fund that exactly matches the areas you feel strongly about, but you should find one close enough.**

Questions to ask a financial adviser before buying an ethical investment.

get the facts

- Do you have specialist knowledge of ethical investments?
- Can you tell if the investment I am interested in has matched up to its ethical claims? (*This is difficult because there is no research into this aspect.*)
- What is the investment fund's investment record? (*Investing ethically is a comparatively recent idea and some funds won't have a long track record; if not, look at any parent company's record.*)

tip

> **Eiris has a list of independent financial advisers who advise on ethical funds. See the Appendix for Eiris's address.**

Investing for retirement

It is natural to assume that investing for your retirement means buying a pension. Pensions, with the advantage of tax relief on contributions, certainly form a substantial part of retirement planning, but they are not the only way of providing income after you stop work. You can invest in ISAs, and buy property to rent out.

When planning your finances for retirement, ask yourself these questions.

ask yourself

- How many years are there left before I retire? (*The nearer you are to retiring, the safer your investments need to be.*)
- Do I want to retire before the official retirement age? (*You need to pump as much as you possibly can into a pension and still check whether you can afford to retire.*)
- Is my job likely to last until I'm ready to retire?
- Do I have a company pension? (*Ask your employer how much you are likely to get.*)
- Am I paying into any other pension plan? (*Get an illustration from the insurance company showing how much this might pay out.*)
- Have I paid into any other company pension in the past? (*If you have lost contact with the firm, write to the Pension Schemes Registry, whose address is given in the Appendix.*)
- How much state pension will I get? (*Ask the Benefits Agency for an estimate; pick up form BR19 from your local Benefits Agency.*)
- Will I be entitled to any other state benefits?
- Is my spouse planning to retire at the same time? (*Get similar quotations for his or her pensions.*)
- Will the children be off my hands by the time that I plan to retire?
- Will my mortgage be paid off?
- Will I look for a part-time job when I've retired?
- After deducting my estimated bills from the income I expect in retirement, is there any shortfall? (*If there is a shortfall, you need to start saving more.*)

Investing for children and grandchildren

Parents and grandparents always want to give their youngsters a good start, from a few pounds in the piggy bank to the deposit for a house. Whatever your intention, you need to choose the appropriate form of saving.

Can I give any type of investment to a child?

Any investment that doesn't have a minimum age limit. For example, no one under 18 can hold ISAs.

Should I keep the investments in my name or put them in the child's?

Children can hold some investments (shares, unit trusts and investment trusts) only through a parent or guardian until they reach a certain age. When investments are in its own name, or designated with its initials, the child can use its own tax allowance and, if you died, the money is already safely with the child. However, if you have more children, you need enough money to give them all the same; and if one child's investments outperform the others, this can cause jealousy.

What happens if I invest for my grandchildren in my name but die before giving them the money?

You should make your wishes clear in your will.

Which is the best way to save for university costs?

It depends how long there is to go before you need to start paying. If you start saving when the child is born, so there are 18 years to go, you can afford to take some risk and an equity-linked investment such as unit trust or investment trust is suitable. With around ten years to go, you should take less risk: there is still time for a unit trust or investment trust to build up adequately, but you should choose a fairly safe fund. Within five years, you have no time to take risks and a safe unit trust or a savings account is better. If the money is due now, you will have to pay out of your current earnings or savings, or borrow the money, perhaps through a second mortgage.

Here are questions to ask yourself.

ask yourself

- Why am I saving for the children? Is it for spending money, perhaps for a school trip, for new clothes, for a nest egg for an eighteenth birthday, or to see them through university? (*Remember that you need to choose different investments when investing for different periods of time.*)
- Am I investing a one-off lump sum, a little each month, or as and when I can afford it? (*If this is your first child or grandchild, assume it will not be your last. Whatever you are planning now, be prepared to do the same for all future children.*)
- Do I want the child to have access to the money?
- How long do I want the money tied up?
- Do I want it to pay out on a certain date?
- Do I want a safe, moderately safe or risky investment?
- Do I want the children to know about it?
- Do I want the parents to know about it? (*Someone else should know about the investment in case you die suddenly.*)
- Are the parents receiving state benefits? (*Money you give your grandchild reduces the parents' benefit. It might be better to buy the children's school clothes or equipment instead, but first check what the DSS will allow.*)
- Do I want to keep the investments in my name or the child's?

THE EFFECTS OF TAX

Parents who give money to their children need to understand the tax position. The rules apply only to parents, not to grandparents or anyone else giving money to children:

- Parents have to pay tax on the interest or dividends from any money they give their child, once that income exceeds £100 a year. Two children can earn £100 each; each parent's gifts can earn £100 before tax is due.
- Tax is paid on all the income, not just the amount above £100.
- The parent who gives the money is taxed at his or her highest rate.
- The limit applies to unmarried parents and their own children or step-children, and to divorced parents.
- Parents can largely overcome the tax drawback by choosing investments for their children that provide capital growth but pay no income.

You and your partner

REORGANISING YOUR FINANCES WHEN YOU MARRY OR SET UP HOME WITH A PARTNER

When you marry or set up home with a partner, try to stay cool-headed. Obviously you trust each other and plan to stay together for ever, but that is no reason to avoid the mundane matter of money.

Joint accounts

ask Margaret

Should we put all our assets into our joint names?
This is to some degree a personal decision about how much you each want to run your own finances. But:

- Having at least some money in a joint bank account enables the survivor to continue withdrawing money when the other dies - a widow with no money in her own name might not even be able to buy groceries until probate is granted.
- If you rely on the income from your savings, put your savings accounts into joint names for the same reason.
- You can often earn a higher rate of interest by combining your savings and having a larger amount on deposit.
- The Inland Revenue taxes joint accounts as though each partner owns half. If you want more of the tax burden to fall on the one who pays a lower rate of tax, tell the Inland Revenue how the account is split – although you might avoid argument with the Inland Revenue if you keep the money in separate accounts.
- You can hold joint assets as either joint tenants or tenants in common, whether it is a savings account, investments or a property. Joint tenants both own the whole asset, so that, when one dies, that person's share automatically passes to the other. Between married couples, there is no tax to pay but, if the joint tenancy is between unmarried people, the deceased's share is counted for inheritance tax purposes. Instructions in a will cannot stop this happening, although the recipient could then pass the money on to someone else. As tenants in common, each partner owns a share of the asset in his or her own

right, in whatever proportions the couple decides. You must leave instructions in your will about whom you want to inherit your share because it does not automatically go to your partner. You can leave your share to whoever you want. Joint accounts are automatically set up with the account holders as joint tenants, unless you ask other-wise.

tip

> WARNING: **Gifts made for tax-saving reasons, like any other gifts, must be made without strings attached. Whatever money you give your spouse, that person does not have to invest it the way you want, or even invest it at all.**

tip

> **From the outset, you will probably find it better to keep your own sep-arate bank accounts and set up one joint account into which you both pay an amount each month for household bills.**

REORGANISING YOUR FINANCES WHEN YOU SEPARATE OR DIVORCE

If you possibly can, untangle your finances in a co-operative frame of mind. Confrontation only costs you money and stress. The impli-cations of divorce for pensions are set out in Chapter 5.

ask Margaret

Is everything divided fifty-fifty?
You may agree to that; but if you can't agree on a share-out, a court and the Child Support Agency will decide how your assets and income are to be split.

How can I stop my spouse selling investments to reduce the amount I could receive?
You can apply to the court for an injunction to stop this happening. Act immediately you are suspicious; do not wait until you have proof.

Am I responsible for my partner's debts?
It depends what type of debts they are. You are responsible for your spouse's unpaid:

- council tax to the date your spouse leaves
- joint mortgage payments

- joint personal loan payments
- credit card spending, if you are the main cardholder.

What happens to jointly held life insurance policies when we divorce?

You can keep them going. This is preferable to cashing them in because you would get poor value. If you have no life insurance, you might want to take a policy out on the life of the one making maintenance payments.

Joint bank accounts – and untangling them

ask Margaret

What ought I to do if my partner and I have a joint bank account but split up?

Ask the bank to close the account and open two separate ones instead. The bank will want to see that you have made adequate arrangements for standing orders and direct debits to continue being paid. Keep a written record of what you have agreed with the bank and with your ex-partner.

Can one partner pull out of a joint account without the other agreeing?

Yes. When you set up the account, you both sign a mandate authorising the bank to honour cheques signed by either of you alone. Either of you can cancel that mandate which means that, from then on, both of you have to authorise every transaction.

What if my partner keeps taking money out of the account but stops paying money in?

Assuming the account allows either of you to sign cheques, the bank honours all cheques until you tell them to stop. You are both equally responsible for joint bank accounts and so, if your partner pushes the account overdrawn and refuses to put any money in, the bank expects you to pay up.

tip | **You need to make out new wills when you divorce.**

About tax

Tax is a crucial part of your financial planning.

ask Margaret

How many different types of tax might I pay?
Several:

- Income tax, payable on income you earn from working, on interest and dividends from investments, and on rent you receive from renting out property
- capital gains tax (CGT), payable on profits that you make from selling assets or on the notional profit on possessions you give away; there is no capital gains tax payable when you die
- inheritance tax, payable by your beneficiaries or estate, on what you leave behind when you die which can include gifts made during your lifetime
- insurance premium tax, payable on house, motor, loan protection, private medical and holiday policies
- value added tax (VAT), payable on most goods and services that you buy
- stamp duty, payable when you buy shares or property
- National Insurance contributions, payable on your salary
- council tax.

PERSONAL TAX

ask Margaret

How much can I earn before I pay tax?
With income tax, everyone can earn a certain amount before tax is due; the figure changes each year and is set in the Finance Act following the Budget. For CGT, you can make a certain amount of gains each year before tax is due, although some investments are free of capital gains tax. Inheritance tax is payable only once your estate reaches a certain figure.

Is it legal to pay as little tax as I can get away with?
Yes. You do not have to pay any more than is due and you can rearrange your finances (known as 'tax avoidance') to make sure that you pay the minimum amount of tax. Nevertheless, when avoiding tax you must be honest; you must not reduce your tax bill by concealing information, which is 'tax evasion' and is a criminal offence.

How can I be sure I am paying the right amount of tax?
You can try working it out for yourself, with the help of a tax guide or tax software. You can – as well or instead – pay a tax adviser to check the calculations.

tip

> April 5 is the last day of each tax year; a new tax year starts on each April 6. A pension, or ISA, contribution made on April 5 therefore comes under the old year's allowance.

What is a tax allowance?

A tax allowance is a sum of money that you can earn before you start paying income tax. The higher the allowance, the less tax you pay. A 'tax break' is a loose term for any scheme or rule that results in you legally paying less tax.

What can I do if I haven't told the Inland Revenue about money I should have paid tax on for several years?

Contact your local tax office and explain the situation. You will not be the first person to do this and, if you co-operate, the staff there will help you sort yourself out. If the Inland Revenue discovers by its own means that you have been evading tax, it will treat you more harshly than if you own up. It will be really severe if you say you have disclosed all your sources of income but it finds that you have kept some hidden.

If I come clean, will I have to pay tax on the past years?

You will have to pay all the tax you owe for the previous years plus interest and a penalty. But the longer you leave it, the more it will cost.

How do I pay income tax?

If you are employed, through the PAYE (Pay As You Earn) system, by which an appropriate amount of tax is deducted by your employer from your pay. But any other earnings, any income that is not taxed at the right rate before you receive it, and any capital gains, are taxed through the self-assessment scheme.

SELF-ASSESSMENT

Unless all your income is taxed at source, or you earn too little to pay tax, you have to complete a tax return under the self-assessment system.

ask Margaret

What does self-assessment mean?

You tell the Inland Revenue how much tax you think you ought to be paying.

Can I pick any figure I like?

You must calculate the amounts based on your actual income and gains. And, to support your figures, you must keep records of the transactions so that, if you are asked, you can prove everything you have written on your tax return.

What is to stop me underestimating the tax due?

Your tax return must be honest and should be based on accurate, not estimated, figures. The Inland Revenue will notice if your bill is substantially lower than last year's, and it will investigate further if it is suspicious. If there are genuine reasons why your tax bill is far lower one year than the previous, use the blank space at the end of the self-assessment annual return to explain the circumstances.

What if I don't produce accounts?

You do not need a formally drawn-up set of accounts in order to complete a self-assessment form, but you must by law keep records and receipts for everything you claim.

What records do I have to keep?

There is no definitive list, but broadly your records should include:

- documents containing information used in completing your tax return
- documents you might need for a future tax return – perhaps for a capital gains tax calculation
- proof of your income
- proof of the expenses you claim
- any social security payment slips.

tip

It is useful to have a system – even just a shoe box – to store the records you will need, such as building society vouchers or dividend slips, as they turn up.

What if I can't produce all these pieces of paper?

You could pay more tax if you cannot prove the figures on your annual tax return, but the Inland Revenue says it takes a commonsense view in the absence of paperwork. You could be fined, though, if you deliberately destroy records to sabotage an enquiry.

How can I tell if I ought to get a tax return?

If you pay basic-rate tax, which is all deducted by your employer through PAYE, or your income is no more than the basic state pension, you will not get a tax return. But you should fill in a tax return if you:

- are a higher-rate taxpayer
- are self-employed
- are a company director
- have any other jobs
- make capital gains on your investments
- take in lodgers
- own property that you rent out.

If I get a tax return, will I get one every year even if my circumstances change and I don't need to send one in?

Once you are on the system, you are likely to keep getting a tax return but, if this is no longer necessary, you can ask your tax office to take you off the list.

If the Inland Revenue doesn't send me a tax return, does that mean I don't have to fill one out?

You must contact the Inland Revenue whenever you have income, or made gains, that it does not know about. The onus is always on you to inform the Revenue about tax that you ought to be paying.

tip

> **You can telephone or write to your tax office to check any points you are unsure about involving tax. They welcome calls. Keep a note of the name of the person you spoke to, and the date.**

Have I anything to fear if my tax return is honest and accurate?

You will not be fined but you could still be investigated or, as the Inland Revenue describes it, 'called for enquiry'. The Revenue picks around 8,000 tax returns a year at random for a full enquiry, in addition to any it thinks might be wrong.

What does an investigation involve?

A full enquiry goes into your whole tax return and you will have to substantiate every item that you have claimed. A partial enquiry looks at one or more particular aspects of your return, and the Revenue's questions might be sorted out by correspondence alone.

What happens if the Inland Revenue finds something wrong?

You will be called in for a meeting, with your accountant if you have one, and a tax inspector will explain why the Inland Revenue thinks that you owe more tax than you have declared.

When will I know if I'm being investigated?

The Inland Revenue has to decide within 12 months of the date when the return was due, which is the January 31 following the end of the tax year in question.

If I send in my tax return at the last minute, am I less likely to attract an enquiry as there is less time in which to be picked?

No. The Revenue still has the next 12 months in which to decide to investigate.

tip

> You cannot usually claim from the Revenue any extra fees that your accountant charges for an enquiry, but you should ask to have the costs refunded if the Revenue turns out to have made a serious mistake.

If I fill out the tax return myself but make a small mistake in the calculations, will Inland Revenue staff notice?

Probably. They check your figures to some degree.

What happens if I pay the tax I think I owe, but it was not enough?

You will pay interest on the shortfall, whatever the reason for not paying the right amount.

What happens if I pay too much tax?

You will receive interest on the overpayment.

What are the interest rates charged or paid by the Inland Revenue?

The Revenue sets its own official rate – one for charging taxpayers and a lower one for paying them – and each changes from time to time.

Can I claim the money back if I don't discover the overpayment for a couple of years?

You can claim a refund up to six years later.

Can the Inland Revenue, then, also chase me for unpaid tax for six years?

If they suspect you have deliberately avoided paying tax, there is no limit to how far back they can delve.

How much do I have to tell the Revenue about my investments?

You do not need to tell the Inland Revenue when you buy investments, but you must disclose the income you receive from them and how much you sold them for if they are liable to capital gains tax.

How much time do I have to send back each annual tax return?

You must send in the return by the 30 September following the end of the tax year if you want the Revenue to calculate your tax bill for you, or by the following January 31 if you work it out yourself or use an accountant to do it.

What happens if the return is late?

You will be fined £100 automatically.

Is there any reason why I shouldn't leave it right to the last minute?

Not in terms of being fined. But you risk suffering a last-minute crisis that prevents you getting the return in on time – for instance, the return could be delayed in the post. The sooner you complete the tax form after the events, the easier it is to remember what happened, the more time you have to put together all necessary documents and, if the Inland Revenue comes back with any queries on your tax return, you still have time to provide the extra information.

Can I send my details to the Inland Revenue on a printout from my computer?

No. You have to fill in the tax return provided. However, the Inland Revenue is moving towards computerisation and provides a disk called the Electronic Version of the Return (EVR) – telephone 0645-000404 for a free copy. You can use this disk to fill in your return and print it out with the calculations done automatically, unless your return includes income from:

- self-employment
- partnerships
- share schemes
- property
- trusts
- overseas
- capital gains.

Before you post your tax return

- go through all your bank and credit-card statements to ensure you can account for all the receipts on the statements
- look at all your investments and check how much income they produced
- compare the figures you put on this year's tax return with last year's, because that is what the Revenue will do – and if any large sums of money have appeared, or disappeared, make sure you can explain why
- check your figures one last time, and make sure that net and gross figures are in the right boxes
- check that you have signed your tax return and dated it.

Getting someone else to fill out your tax return for you

ask Margaret

Now I'm taxed under self-assessment, do I need an accountant?

Theoretically you should be able to fill out the form yourself, but a lot of people find it difficult. Or they simply do not have the time to do it themselves.

If I need help with my tax return, do I have to use an accountant?

There are no rules to say who can or who can't help with your tax affairs; it could just be a well-meaning friend. The more complicated your affairs, the more likely you are to need a qualified adviser, but it does not have to be a chartered accountant – there are other grades of accountant, and people called tax advisers, some charging a fixed fee, who need not be qualified accountants at all.

tip

> **Whoever helps you with your tax, you remain the person responsible to the Inland Revenue for getting your return in on time and paying the right amount of tax. And if your accountant or tax adviser is blaming the Inland Revenue for being slow or making mistakes, phone the Revenue yourself: your adviser could be right but might be making excuses.**

Are cut-price tax return services any good?

They can be, but only if your tax affairs are straightforward. Most firms offering a cut-price service do no more than feed your details into a computer and let the software work it out; they do not ask you any questions or give you any advice on minimising your tax bill. Some dubious firms are known to the Inland Revenue as persistently giving suspect advice. If you employ one of these, and the Revenue recognises the name, it might look more closely at your tax return.

Should I steer clear of unqualified accountants?

Not necessarily. There are many tax advisers around, often ex-Inland Revenue employees, who provide a good service for straightforward accounts at a modest price.

If tax advisers use computer software to fill in my tax return, can I do the same?

Yes. There are several computer programs on sale.

What do tax advisers do and what will they charge?

Different advisers offer different services, from completing a simple tax return to helping with inheritance tax planning. Charges by accountants and advisers vary enormously and depend on the complexity of your affairs.

If I use a qualified accountant, is the Inland Revenue more likely to accept my figures without too much scrutiny?

All accountants must take reasonable steps to satisfy themselves that their clients have provided all the information they should for accurate tax returns. But you are not safeguarded from a random enquiry.

Will an accountant make sure I pay my tax on time?

An accountant should do so, but do not assume that yours will chase you to be prompt.

Can I be blamed if I get all the information to my accountant in good time but the accountant is slow and misses the Inland Revenue January 31 deadline?

You still have to pay the fine. You could try asking the accountant to reimburse you, but it is entirely your responsibility to make sure your tax is paid on time.

Questions to ask before choosing an accountant

get the facts

- Do you charge a fixed fee or an hourly rate?
- How much will you charge?
- Will you fill out my tax return?
- Will you chase me if it is getting close to a tax deadline?
- How long do you take to complete a tax return?
- Do you have other clients in my line of business? (*It is helpful if your accountant is familiar with your type of work.*)
- Will you handle my tax yourself or will it be someone else in the firm?
- Do you give investment advice? (*Those who do so must be authorised under the Financial Services Act.*)

Questions to ask a tax adviser who is not a qualified accountant

get the facts

- Do you have professional indemnity insurance? (*You want an adviser with insurance so that, if you lose money, you can claim compensation.*)
- Do you have qualifications? And if so, what are they? (*Tax advice is a comparatively new career, and so you want someone who is committed to the point of taking exams.*)
- Do you belong to a trade association?
- How much will you charge?
- What do I get for my money?
- Will you charge extra if my accounts turn out to be more complicated than you expected?
- By what date will you have finished the work on my behalf?

DATES IN THE TAX CALENDAR

You must pay tax by:

- January 31: payment of outstanding income tax and capital gains tax for the year that ended in the previous April; and the first instalment of tax due for the tax year you are currently in, ending next April – assume this will be half of last year's total income tax bill unless your circumstances have changed
- July 31: the second instalment for the tax year that ended the previous April.

Dates by which tax returns must be sent back:

- September 30 if you want the Inland Revenue to calculate the bill for the tax year that ended the previous April
- January 31 if you work out the tax due yourself for the tax year that ended in the previous April.

For employees, important times of the year are:

- January: if your circumstances have changed, a PAYE coding notice will be sent to your employer for the tax year starting in the following April
- May 31: the latest date by which your employer must issue you with form P60 showing how much you earned and how much tax you paid in the tax year that ended in the previous April
- July 6: the latest date by which your employer must issue Form P11D showing the employee benefits and expenses you received in the year ended the previous April.

Penalties for missing deadlines

- For missing January 31: if you have sent in no tax return for the year that ended the previous April you will be fined £100, which is fixed and automatic. Interest will be charged on any tax unpaid from the previous tax year.
- At February 28: if you still owe tax from a year earlier, there is an extra 5 per cent surcharge on top of the interest and tax you owe.
- For missing July 31: if you still have not sent in a tax return for the year ending the April of the previous year, another £100 fixed penalty applies and interest continues to be chargeable on any unpaid tax. If you still owe tax from 18 months earlier, a 10 per cent surcharge on the unpaid tax applies and the Inland Revenue can start legal proceedings against you.

ask Margaret   **Will the Inland Revenue accept an excuse for sending in the return late?**
It accepts only really good excuses, such as:

- you didn't receive the tax return (*and you must genuinely not have received it*)
- the return was lost in the post going back to the Inland Revenue (*but the Revenue will probably accept this only if there was a known flood, fire or strike at the Post Office*)
- you lost your records through fire, flood or theft
- you have suffered coma, a serious heart attack, stroke or mental condition (*although being in hospital for a long stay is not on its own an acceptable excuse*)
- a close relative is seriously ill and has taken up a great deal of your time (*although you must have started preparing your tax return*)
- a close relative has died just before the deadline.

Excuses the Inland Revenue will not accept include:

- 'I'm too busy.'
- 'I'm too stressed.'
- 'I had flu.'
- 'The tax return is too difficult.'
- 'I lost the tax return.'
- 'I've been on holiday.'
- 'My job took me abroad.'
- 'My accountant let me down.'
- 'I can't find the information I need.'
- 'The tax office didn't remind me.'
- 'I can't afford the tax I think is due.'
- 'I didn't realise I'd forgotten to sign the cheque.'

YOUR LOCAL TAX OFFICE

Your local tax office can be a help if you have any questions.

ask Margaret

Where can I find my local tax office?

Look in the phone book under 'Inland Revenue'. You can phone, write or call in person with or without an appointment.

If I contact the local tax office, will the staff there want to know about all my tax affairs?

Not if you do not want to tell them. They will be willing to answer one or two specific questions or, if you want more detailed help, someone can look more closely at your file. If you think you will want the tax office to look up your file, be ready to quote your National Insurance number.

If I call at a tax office, will I have to give my name and address?

Not if you do not want to.

Will the local tax office help me fill out my annual tax return?

They will help to the extent of explaining the form and telling you what needs to go in; but they will not fill in the figures for you.

If I try to fill out my tax return myself but find it confusing, can I ask the Inland Revenue for help?

Yes, you can telephone or call in to your tax office as often as you like to ask questions. The staff there can go through precise details with you if you need them to.

Will the tax staff show me how I can save tax?

No. They will give you factual advice only, which might result in paying less tax, but they will not point out action you could take to avoid tax.

I receive income from the state pension and two company pensions, all dealt with by different tax offices. Can I have my records moved to the same place?

This might be possible. Ask whichever seems to be your 'main' tax office.

THE PAYE SYSTEM

ask Margaret **How does my employer know how much tax to deduct under PAYE?**

The Inland Revenue issues every taxpayer with a PAYE code number and sends it to employers; through this number, your employer can tell how much tax to deduct.

What does my PAYE reference number indicate?

It reflects the tax allowances you can claim. If you want more details, the Inland Revenue publishes a leaflet entitled *Understanding your Tax Code*.

tip

The Inland Revenue publishes dozens of free leaflets on specific aspects of the tax regime. You can pick up copies at your local tax office and Citizens Advice Bureau, or sometimes you can find them in your local library.

TAX-SAVING TIPS

There are a number of ways in which you can legitimately minimise the tax you pay.

- Make sure you claim all the allowances to which you are entitled. Do not assume the Inland Revenue knows which ones you should have.
- If you are a non-taxpayer, or know children who are, make sure you claim bank and building society interest gross rather than net of tax. Ask at the branch for form R85.
- If you have two or more jobs, check that you are receiving one set of allowances. By mistake, the Revenue might give you none, so you pay too much tax, or two, so you pay too little – which it will eventually ask you to pay.
- If you are married, and one partner pays tax at a lower rate than the other, as a couple you can save tax by putting investments in the name of one who pays at the lower rate. Co-habiting couples can do the same, although tax is payable on gifts between them.
- If you do not have enough money to pay a tax bill, you can ask for it to be postponed, although you will pay interest on the money you owe.
- Giving away money during your lifetime leaves less in your estate when you die, and so there is less likelihood of inheritance tax; but you should worry more about yourself than your beneficiaries – never give away money to save tax if it leaves you financially vulnerable.
- When someone dies, any inheritance tax bill must be paid before probate is granted. Ask building societies and banks to release money from the deceased's account to pay inheritance tax or funeral expenses.

THE INLAND REVENUE TAXPAYER'S CHARTER

The Taxpayer's Charter sets out the following aims for the Inland Revenue in its dealings with the public:

- to be fair
  - settling your tax affairs impartially
  - expecting you to pay only what is due by law
  - treating everyone with equal fairness
- to help you
  - get your tax affairs right
  - understand your rights and obligations
  - by providing clear leaflets and forms
  - with information at enquiry offices
  - by being courteous at all times
- to provide an efficient service
  - settling your tax affairs promptly and accurately
  - keeping your private affairs confidential
  - using the information you provide only as allowed by law
  - keeping to a minimum your costs
  - keeping down the Revenue's costs
- to be accountable for its actions
- to tell you how to complain if you are not satisfied.

Setting up a trust

A trust is a device that allows you to give an asset to someone else without losing control over it.

ask Margaret

How can trusts help me?

They enable you: to pass your assets to whoever you want, but prevent them squandering the money until they are old enough to be sensible; to let someone enjoy the income from your asset without owning the capital; and sometimes to save on inheritance tax.

How do trusts work?

Trust law allows two people to own the same asset: one is the trustee who is the legal owner; the other is the person benefiting from the asset, the beneficial owner.

If I put my assets in trust, am I the trustee or the beneficiary?

You can be both.

Who can be trustees?

Anyone you nominate can be a trustee – friends, family members, a bank or a solicitor; you can be a trustee yourself, but not the only one. Beware that the professionals charge for their services.

Can trustees do what they like with the money?

They have a legal duty to look after the assets on behalf of the beneficiaries; they can't use the money for themselves unless they are also beneficiaries.

Who can be beneficiaries?

Anyone you nominate.

Can I give my house away to my children during my lifetime to avoid inheritance tax?

You can give your house to your children during your lifetime but this would overcome inheritance tax only if you stopped living there or you paid them full rent.

Can I give my house away to reduce my assets when the local authority assesses me for a nursing home?

No. See p.265 in Chapter 10 for more on paying for long-term care.

How do I go about setting up a trust?

You can either set up a trust during your lifetime to take immediate effect, or you can include instructions in your will for a trust to take effect on your death, called a 'will trust'. To do that, you need a solicitor with experience of setting up trusts. And you have to decide which type of trust you want:

- A 'bare' trust, or simple trust, where the beneficiary actually owns the assets and it is taxed as theirs. This is the trust you need when you want to invest money for children, in their names, using their tax allowances.

- An interest-in-possession trust (called a life-rental trust in Scotland), where the income goes to a named beneficiary but the capital can eventually go to someone else. This is the trust you need when you want a spouse to receive income from your investments after your death, but not sell them, so they eventually go to your children, a charity or whomever you choose.
- A discretionary trust, where the trustees decide who gets the income, and how much. You need a 'general discretionary trust' when putting assets aside for children, including those not yet born, for they have no rights to any money and handouts are entirely at the trustees' discretion. You need an 'accumulation and maintenance' trust when you want trustees to give children income, when needed, but for the children to become entitled to the income and capital at age 25.

Once I've set up a trust, can I close it?

Only with extreme difficulty and only if all the trustees and all the beneficiaries agree.

Where can I find a trust specialist solicitor?

Contact the Society of Trust and Estate Practitioners (Step) for a list of members in your area. The address is given in the Appendix.

tip | **You can easily put life insurance policies in trust so that, on your death, your beneficiaries receive the money faster and you minimise the likelihood of paying inheritance tax. See p.123.**

Complaining about a financial services organisation

All financial institutions must have a customer-friendly complaints procedure, at least for products and services falling within the Financial Services Act. You have no grounds for complaint, though, if your investments lose value.

Whatever the product or service you are unhappy with:

- First, write or talk to the person you were dealing with.
- If that gets you nowhere, contact the firm's head office. Ask branch staff or the telephonist for the name of the person to contact.
- If you are still dissatisfied, try a trade association that the company belongs to.
- Alternatively, you can take your complaint to the appropriate Ombudsman. All Ombudsman schemes are free to complainants, and so never pay a solicitor to approach an Ombudsman on your behalf.

The separate Ombudsmen for investments and insurance are being amalgamated into one mandatory Financial Services Ombudsman with one point of contact. Until then, if you contact the wrong Ombudsman, your complaint will automatically be redirected to the right place. The addresses are given in the Appendix. The separate Ombudsmen are:

- *Banking Ombudsman*: deals with banking business with all the major banks, including those that used to be building societies, except for investments, which are handled by the PIA Ombudsman
- *Building Societies Ombudsman*: covers savings accounts and mortgages with all building societies, but not investments, which are handled by the PIA Ombudsman
- *Insurance Ombudsman*: for complaints about general insurance bought from companies and members of Lloyd's that have chosen to join the scheme
- *Investment Ombudsman*: handles disputes about investments with investment managers, unit trust managers and pension fund managers if they are regulated by the Investment Management Regulatory Organisation (IMRO)
- *PIA Ombudsman*: deals with complaints about companies belonging to the Personal Investment Authority (PIA) – independent financial advisers and investment firms selling life insurance, personal pensions and unit trusts
- *Pensions Ombudsman*: handles complaints about company pensions and personal pensions but not state pensions, although most personal pensions complaints are dealt with by others – usually the PIA Ombudsman – and before approaching the

Pensions Ombudsman you must take your complaint to the Occupational Pensions Advisory Service (OPAS)

- *Adjudicator for Inland Revenue, Customs & Excise and Contributions Agency*: deals with complaints about these government departments.

COMPENSATION SCHEMES

Banks and building societies

The Deposit Protection Scheme is activated if a bank or building society ceases trading.

- It guarantees to repay 90 per cent of the first £20,000 (or €22,000) that each customer has in a building society, UK bank or UK branch of a foreign bank.
- The maximum guaranteed in each bank or building society is £18,000.
- Joint accounts have a double limit, but if someone has two accounts with the same bank, they are covered only once.
- The protection includes interest earned to the day the bank ceases trading.

Insurance

If an insurance company collapses, customers may be compensated under the Policyholders Protection Scheme. The maximum guaranteed is 100 per cent of a car claim and 90 per cent of any other general insurance claim in progress; with life insurance, another insurer is required to take on the policyholders and, when a policy matures, the customer is guaranteed to get 90 per cent of any payment that was guaranteed under the original policy.

Investments

If a person loses money on investments because an insurance company crashes, the Investors Compensation Scheme pays the first £30,000 that is lost and 90 per cent of the next £20,000, a total of

£48,000. This covers products regulated under the Financial Services Act, and includes unit trusts, pensions and life insurance.

Company pensions

If anyone steals from a company pension scheme, the employer has to make good the loss. If the employer is no longer in business, other pension funds will pay, through the Pension Compensation Scheme, to compensate those who have lost money.

Personal pensions

If someone loses money from a personal pension because an insurance company collapses, the Investors Compensation Scheme pays the first £30,000 and 90 per cent of the next £20,000 – a total of £48,000.

Computers and your finances

There are a number of computer software programs to help you keep track of your finances or to organise your share portfolio, and others to help you work out your tax bill.

BANKING BY COMPUTER

Increasingly, banks are setting up systems that allow customers to access their accounts through computers and through the Internet; check with your bank for the latest information. As this is a new area, many banks make no charge for the service, although this might change in the future.

The advantage is being able to access your bank account at any time – day or night – and from anywhere in the world to check statements, pays bills, change standing orders, cancel direct debits, or transfer money between accounts.

FINANCIAL PRODUCTS THROUGH THE INTERNET

The Internet is a convenient way of buying financial products – certainly straightforward ones that you can choose for yourself without professional advice. You can call up information, make comparisons, and choose in your own time. But, as the Internet is unregulated, there is enormous scope for unscrupulous people to set up scams. Before buying anything through the Internet, you need to make sure that the company you intend dealing with is authentic. Find its geographic address, not just its website address, because it could be based anywhere in the world. To be quite sure, telephone to check that it is what it claims to be.

ask Margaret

How can the Internet help with financial planning?

You can visit websites of companies whose shares you might want to buy, financial institutions for details of their products, and brokers and financial advisers. Some websites show no more than a company name, address and telephone number, and perhaps the glossy brochure they normally send by post; others provide frequently updated information about the company and its products, with general financial advice thrown in free; a few go a stage further and enable you to buy their products via the website.

You can also visit the websites of online information companies that provide share prices, statistical information and performance tables for various financial products, covering most of the companies that sell them. Sometimes this information is free; sometimes companies make a service charge, particularly for up-to-the-minute information.

Which products can I find out about on the Internet?

- mortgages
- credit cards
- personal loans
- savings accounts
- bank accounts
- shares
- unit trusts
- investment trusts
- individual savings accounts (ISAs)
- house and car insurance
- travel insurance

- life insurance
- personal pensions.

What financial products can I buy through the Internet?

So far, car insurance, house insurance, shares and individual savings accounts (ISAs).

What else can the Internet do?

It can:

- hold, and constantly update, your investment portfolio – or, if you like, a pretend portfolio so you can test how the investments perform
- compare your investments against an index
- calculate how much loans cost at various interest rates and over different timescales
- provide investment news
- provide investment research
- publish personal finance advice
- check bank account balances and pay bills.

Is it cheaper to buy financial products through the Internet?

Sometimes it is, but not usually.

How do I pay when I buy through the Internet?

That depends on the arrangements set up by the provider. With a few, you give your credit card number on the screen, otherwise you post a cheque.

tip

> **When buying through the Internet, check the security mechanisms of the service provider – you will find plenty of links giving up-to-date information. Financial institutions are preparing for the latest technological breakthrough – digital TV – when you will be able to organise your finances through your television set.**

2 Getting Advice

You can be more confident today that financial advisers are competent, trustworthy and knowledgeable because the Financial Services Act 1986 has largely cleaned up the industry. But that does not mean that you can assume all advisers are equally qualified or experienced, or that they all offer the same quality service.

The only way to find out is to ask them. There is no need to feel embarrassed; it is your money at stake and there is no reason why you should take the risk of buying inappropriate or poorly performing investments because the adviser is inadequate. You can find a good adviser if you ask the right questions.

Advice on investments

There are two categories of investment advisers. The important difference between them is that some can advise on, and sell, only the investments produced by the company they work for (known as 'tied' advisers); others (independent financial advisers) can advise on, and sell, products from any company. All advisers must take the same care with the advice they give and comply with the same regulations.

ask Margaret

Who provides 'tied' financial advice?

Tied advisers, company representatives and appointed representatives. These people can be:

- individuals working directly for a financial services company
- individuals working outside a company
- firms of advisers
- insurance companies
- unit trust groups
- banks
- building societies.

Who provides independent financial advice?

- independent financial advisers (IFAs)
- stockbrokers
- banks, through their IFA subsidiaries
- building societies, if they have IFA subsidiaries
- some solicitors
- some accountants.

Where can I find a tied adviser?

Contact the company whose products you want to buy.

How can I find an independent financial adviser?

Ask friends, relatives and colleagues if they can recommend anyone. Check whether your employer has an arrangement with a financial adviser as a staff perk. You can also contact IFA Promotion and ask for the names of IFAs in your area, or the Institute of Financial Planning or *Money Management* for their names of registered fee-based advisers. Addresses for each of these organisations are given in the Appendix. If these methods fail, look for names in *Yellow Pages* under 'financial advisers', or search the Internet.

tip

> **The names provided from all these sources come with no seal of approval. You still need to make your own choice.**

Which is better: independent advice or tied advice?

Independent advice has to be better because it gives you a wider choice of investments.

Do I have to pay for financial advice?

You always pay for advice, but it can be done in one of two ways: either paying a fee, or letting the adviser earn commission from the company whose investment you buy. Fees are charged on an hourly rate, whether you take the advice or not. Commission is paid by investment companies and that money is then deducted from your investment, as a percentage of the amount you invest or pay in premiums, regardless of how much time the adviser takes. Some advisers give you the choice, but all must confirm at the outset which it will be.

Which is preferable: fees or commission?

Advisers who earn commission are paid by the companies whose products they sell and not by the person who is buying the investment. Commission can work out cheaper if you are investing just a few thousand pounds, or you know without advice where you want to invest and are able to negotiate a discount. Paying a fee is better if: you want a complete overhaul of your finances but probably do not intend buying any investments; you want investments that pay no commission, such as National Savings; or you want to be quite confident that the adviser is not in any way influenced by the amount of commission paid.

What advisers must do

The law says that advisers must:

- find out enough about you so that they can give you the most appropriate advice possible, through a questionnaire called a 'fact find'
- recommend investments that are most suitable for your situation but only if you need them
- tell you whether they are tied or independent advisers
- provide you with reasons why they are recommending the investments they suggest

- provide you with quotations specific to your circumstances
- hand you a booklet called a 'Key Features' document produced by the product provider, which shows the commission and charges you have to pay, how risky the investment is, and what the product is designed to do
- give you a client agreement letter setting out the terms of business for the proposed contract
- take exams and become qualified

ask Margaret

Can I take advice from an adviser without buying an investment?

Certainly. You are never under any obligation to buy.

How can I tell if an adviser is any good?

All advisers must be regulated under the Financial Services Act and comply with minimum standards of behaviour, including honest dealings and a certain level of knowledge. But, to get reliability and good service, you also want an adviser who works hard on your behalf, understands your particular attitude to investing, makes sensible decisions from the personal information you provide, keeps up-to-date with developments, and enjoys the work.

Can I assume that all advisers are properly authorised?

It is a criminal offence to give financial advice without authorisation, but you should still confirm that the person you intend dealing with has that authorisation. Telephone the Financial Services Authority (FSA) to ask – the number is given in the Appendix – and the adviser will not find out that you have checked up. FSA staff can tell you immediately whether someone is on its list of authorised personnel and the level of advice that that person is allowed to give (which varies with how qualified the adviser is).

tip

> **You should be wary of 'broker funds', where advisers pick a selection of unit trusts and package them under their own names. Advisers are unlikely to make more money for you this way, and it usually adds another level of charges.**

Dealing with independent financial advisers

Some advisers cover all types of investing, while others specialise in:

- pensions
- retirement planning
- annuities
- ethical investments
- home income plans
- advising expatriates.

For choosing a specialist pension adviser, see p.149 Chapter 5.

ask Margaret

Don't I need to be rich to use an independent financial adviser?

Not at all, although the more money you have, the more time they are likely to spend with you. You could have difficulty finding an adviser willing to take you on if you can afford to invest only, say, £20 a month.

tip

If you are investing less than £40 a month, turn to page 47 for a tip on execution-only buying, or consider a bank or building society savings account (see p.58).

How do I choose an independent financial adviser?

You could trust to luck and put yourself in the hands of the first one you find – perhaps the office that is closest. Preferably, though, you should take time to visit several and get a feel for what they do and how they operate.

How will advisers react to being interviewed to see whether I want to place my business with them?

Their initial reaction is a useful indication of whether they are any good or not. They should welcome the opportunity to talk to you, without charge, for about half an hour. If you sense you are getting a cool reception, strike them off your list.

There is no need to feel nervous about interviewing advisers. If it helps, you can get used to the idea by seeing one or two just for the practice. You are under no obligation to sign up and need give no reasons for going elsewhere.

What do I say to a financial adviser?

You do not need to worry about awkward silences, because financial advisers do plenty of talking. Indeed, none of the answers you get will be as succinct as they appear here. Nevertheless, do not just sit there and listen. Your questions are more important than the sales talk, and so make sure you get the information you want. Take a notebook with you, and a written list of questions that you want to ask; tick them off as you get answers. You will appear knowledgeable, and the adviser will think carefully before speaking.

Do I have to go to the adviser's office or will an adviser come to my home?

It is more efficient for the adviser if you do the travelling, but some will meet you wherever it is convenient. In any case, looking round the adviser's office is useful, because you can check that it is well organised with helpful, efficient staff. If an adviser does not appear to have an office, take that name off your list.

Can I get comprehensive advice from two or three advisers and compare what they recommend?

Certainly you can, if you are paying a fee for the advice, although it will be extremely expensive. You can also have in-depth meetings with several commission-earning advisers, but it would be fair to tell them at the outset that you are talking to more than one.

If I take recommendations from several advisers, do I have to buy something from each?

You are under no obligation to buy anything.

tip

> Many independent financial advisers give discounts on their commission, and not just those that call themselves 'discount brokers'. Ask the financial adviser to share the commission with you – there is no need to be shy, for many clients do it. Sometimes investment providers will agree a special price for extra-large investments, say £200,000. Tell your adviser to negotiate this for you.

Can I have, say, two advisers and give some business to one and some to another?

You can, and this might be preferable if one adviser specialises in, say, retirement planning and another in offshore investments. Or you might prefer to have all your money looked after by one person (or firm) that knows about all your finances.

Once I've chosen an IFA, can I change to another?

You can switch advisers at any time.

What happens to any commission that an IFA is earning from me when I move to a different adviser?

Commission paid when you bought an investment stays with the original adviser. The investment company might agree to switch renewal commission (see p. 43) to the new adviser, or might even stop paying it.

tip

> **You can ask an investment company not to pay renewal commission if you feel the adviser has not earned it. The company might agree with you, but you will not be any better off because the company keeps the money for itself.**

How can I tell if the amount of commission an adviser earns has influenced the choice of investment?

You can't, unless the adviser is unable to produce a convincing reason why it is a good choice. The rules say IFAs must not be influenced by commission, but not all advisers are sticklers for rules. If you are not convinced, do not go ahead; you are under no obligation. And be wary if you suspect an adviser is recommending an investment simply because it is fashionable: when you make a long-term investment, there is no reason to buy on the basis of what is popular at the moment.

Why does my adviser encourage me to buy ISAs just before the end of a tax year?

Because it is a selling opportunity. April 5 is the last day on which you can use that tax year's ISA allowance. Salespeople will also be active throughout April because they want to sign you up for the new year's ISA allowance.

tip

> WARNING: **Remember that every time you cancel one investment and buy another, you pay charges to start again.**

How can I trust financial advisers when they mis-sold personal pensions to workers in company schemes?

Interview several and rely on your judgement. You can ask about their pensions mis-selling record.

I already have a selection of investments. Will I have to hand them all over to the adviser?

It is entirely up to you how much business you give an adviser – from your whole life savings to investing in one unit trust.

Do advisers provide ongoing advice year after year, or do I just get one session?

You are entitled to ongoing advice; that is part of the service. If your adviser doesn't provide it, go elsewhere.

If my financial adviser moves to another firm, can I move too?

The adviser's contract probably bans poaching of business on transfer, but there is nothing to stop you switching if you know where the adviser has gone.

tip

> **Before signing any agreement given to you by an adviser, read it through. Take it home to study, if need be, for there is no need to rush. Ask the adviser to explain anything you do not understand. And being advised not to do something is just as important as a recommendation to invest. If an adviser says you can ignore a certain action, ask why and get the answer in writing. Keep all the paperwork you get from a financial adviser for several years. In any case, you might need it for your self-assessment tax return.**

Do I have the right to see the information the adviser holds on me?

Under the Data Protection legislation, you can see anything held about you on computer and, depending on the filing system and when the information is stored, on paper.

tip

> WARNING: **You might receive a mailshot out of the blue from an independent financial adviser who has bought your name and address from a mailing list agency. The letter will be addressed to you personally, and even signed 'with best wishes' or something similar. But if you buy an investment recommended in the mailshot, even though it is from a financial adviser, you are buying on an 'execution-only' basis (see p. 50) so you can't later complain that you were given bad advice.**

> **WARNING:** **Never act on financial advice from friends, relatives or casual acquaintances unless they are authorised financial advisers acting in a professional capacity. Personal finance is a highly complex subject and your money is too important to treat casually.**

Choosing an independent financial adviser

Answers to the questions in this section will give you a comprehensive picture of an IFA. The complete list of questions is too long for a preliminary meeting but, once you have agreed to use a particular adviser, you should expect answers to as many of these questions as you want to ask.

Get the niceties out of the way quickly so that you can start asking your questions. The adviser may have already provided some of the answers in introductory remarks, but it does not matter if you ask the same questions again; if the adviser shows any signs of impatience, go elsewhere.

QUESTIONS YOU WOULD LIKE TO ASK

You will not get the relationship off to a good start if you ask the next questions as bluntly as expressed here – there are more polite ways of finding the answers – but they are certainly questions you are likely to have in mind, and you would want your IFA to answer them.

get the facts

- Are you recommending this investment because it pays more commission than most?
- Do you know what you are talking about?
- Are you honest?
- Are you likely to run off with my money?
- Are you trying to sell me more insurance than I need?

THE KEY QUESTIONS

get the facts

- Are you independent or tied?
- Do you take commission or charge a fee?
- Are your charges negotiable?
- How do you do your research? (*Large firms have in-house staff; small ones should subscribe to a research company.*)
- What qualifications do you have? (*Everyone giving financial advice must now have passed exams. Advisers who say they do not need qualifications because they have been doing the job for years are breaking the law. Report them to the Financial Services Authority.*)
- Are you authorised to handle clients' money? (*If not, always write cheques directly to the investment company whose product you are buying.*)
- What investments are you authorised to advise on? (*Some advisers are restricted to life insurance and unit trusts, which may be enough but, if not, you need a more qualified adviser.*)
- How long have you worked for your company? (*You want to see signs of stability. And check that they are indeed still employed by the same company.*)
- Are you computerised? (*An adviser who has not caught up with new technology cannot be any good.*)

A COMPREHENSIVE LIST OF QUESTIONS

get the facts

- You do realise that I'm seeing several advisers before choosing one and that I am taking it for granted that this is a free interview?
- Are you independent or tied? (*You already know the answer because you deliberately picked an independent adviser. If by some chance the answer is 'tied', explain that you really want independent advice and leave; or go ahead knowing that the recommendations will come from only one company's range of products.*)
- Will you be looking after me yourself, or will it be someone else? (*If it is someone else, make sure you meet that person as well. You want to make sure it is someone you can work with, and you want to hear their answers to these questions.*)
- Will one person be assigned to my business or several? (*Ideally, the same person will look after you at all times, with a back-up for when he or she is away.*)
- What happens to my file if the adviser looking after me is ill, on holiday or dies?

- Do you charge a fee for advice or take commission? (*Most earn commission. Some work out the fee, compare this with the commission they will earn on the investment you intend to make, and charge whichever costs you less. If any adviser tries to suggest that investing costs you nothing, go elsewhere because this is quite untrue.*)
- How many hours will you spend sorting out my finances? (*In reality, advisers do not know until they have finished, but they should be able to give a close estimate based on past experience. Note that a complete overhaul of your financial situation is likely to take around 10 hours; an annual review thereafter, around two hours.*)
- If you charge a fee, how much is it? (*Rates start at around £100 an hour.*)
- If I pay a fee, what happens to the commission that the investment company pays? (*The adviser should refund it to you. Be wary of words like 'offsetting', because this might mean you are getting only some of it back; if you are paying a full fee, you should get it all.*)
- Will you refund all the commission even if this comes to more than I would have paid in fees? (*If the agreement with the IFA says you will get the commission refunded, you should get it all.*)
- Will you keep the renewal commission? (*This is a subject that advisers do not talk about much. Investment companies often pay renewal commission – may be 0.5 per cent of the value of your investment – to the adviser who sold you the product for every year that you keep the investment. This pays for future advice. The adviser will keep the renewal commission even if you do not ask for ongoing advice, so make sure you do.*)
- What will you do for the money you earn each year from my invesments? (*You should at least get an annual review.*)
- Are your charges fixed, or can we negotiate? (*Charges are often negotiable. Commission-based advisers can agree to rebate some of their commission to you, either as a cash refund or by adding it to your investment. It is always worth asking for such a rebate, although advisers are more likely to agree if you have a lot of money to invest or appear a good prospect for the future. Fee-based advisers might reduce their hourly rate, but beware that they could increase the number of hours to compensate. See also discount brokers on p.56.*)
- Might you recommend an investment that doesn't pay commission? (*Advisers must recommend the best investment for you, whether it pays commission or not, although the practice might be different.*)
- Can you recommend several investments, for me to make a choice?
- Will you contact me if you think I ought to sell any of my investments? (*Advisers should contact you, although many don't. If they do, you need to*

check that the adviser is not 'churning' – encouraging you to buy and sell more often than is necessary, simply for the adviser to earn extra commision.)

- Will you contact me if the stock market crashes?
- Will you let me know what is going on when interest rates come down?
- How large is your firm?
- Do you have any other offices?
- How long has your company been in business?
- Are you part of a network? (*Advisers pay networks to take over time-consuming office work, to help them with research, and to comply with the regulations of the Financial Services Act.*)
- How do you do your research? (*The old method, which some still use, is to stick to the products of a handful of companies that they like, even though they should investigate the whole range. Computers, though, have made the job easier and there are software firms that sell investment analyses to financial advisers. Larger firms and networks undertake their own research: some select from the entire range; others create a panel of a dozen or so companies that perform consistently well. Products from a panel should be good, but they will not necessarily be the best for you, even though the advice should be cheaper.*)
- How many companies' products do you recommend?
- How much investment experience do you have? (*Someone newly qualified can be up-to-date and enthusiastic; or, in contrast, they might just be more familiar with theory than with real life. Alternatively, an adviser who has been around a long time can have accrued some common sense – or to be out-of-date and jaded.*)
- Do you specialise in any particular area, such as pensions or ethical investments?
- How much do you know about investment trusts? (*Advisers who are knowledgeable about investment trusts are likely to have a wider understanding of investments as a whole.*)
- Can you help me choose individual shares to buy? (*Almost certainly not. That is a job for stockbrokers. Some IFAs can put you in touch with a local firm of stockbrokers with which they themselves do business.*)
- What is the full range of services you provide? (*You might be looking just for investment advice, but your financial well-being also involves a pension, life insurance and health insurance. If you want even wider advice, large firms can provide tax advice and help with writing wills.*)
- Are you happy to work with my accountant and solicitor? (*Of course, the adviser will say 'yes', but at least you have put the question on the record.*)
- How does my financial situation compare with your other clients? (*Some firms*

specialise in wealthy clients, or older people, or expatriates. You will do better if the adviser's expertise is appropriate to your needs; if the other clients are a lot wealthier than you, for instance, you might get less attention.)

> **Does the adviser look the sort of person to understand and be in tune with your lifestyle? A young adviser might not understand the worries of an older person. But if you are young, you might prefer dealing with someone of your own age. A woman might be more comfortable talking to a female adviser, of which there are many nowadays. If you take a dislike to an adviser's dress sense, that alone is a good enough reason to look for another: you need to trust, and feel comfortable with, your adviser.**

> WARNING: **If an adviser starts telling you anecdotes about other clients, go elsewhere. You could be the butt of the next story.**

- Can I call you from time to time to check up on my investments? (*The answer should be yes, although some advisers discourage this from the fear that you will be on the phone every week. The more money you are investing, the more likely they are to make themselves available.)*
- Will you send me a regular statement of my finances? (*Investment companies send half-yearly statements, but these are often difficult to understand. Ask the adviser to amalgamate the list for you.)*
- What should I do if I'm not happy with anything you have done? (*The adviser should not be affronted. All advisers must have a structured complaints procedure and give you the name of the person in the firm who handles complaints.)*
- Can I see your complaints record? (*It is possible, but unlikely, that no one has ever complained about the adviser. Advisers have to keep records of complaints, which the regulator checks, so the IFA's firm should be able to produce this information for you.)*
- What is your 'persistency' record? (*You are not asking how often the adviser pesters people to buy investments; 'persistency' is the length of time clients keep the investments and policies that they buy. This, too, is information that advisers must log, and you are looking for a high persistency rate, meaning that clients hold their investments for a long time.)*
- Can you help with capital gains tax and inheritance tax? (*Advisers must have a basic knowledge of the tax system because it affects all investment recommendations. But if you want detailed tax advice, you need an accountant, and the adviser might be able to recommend a contact.)*

• Can I see testimonials from some of your other clients?

QUESTIONS TO CHECK AN IFA'S KNOWLEDGE

You can include a few questions that will reveal whether advisers really know what they are talking about.

• What is the name of the manager of this fund you are recommending?
• How long has this person managed the fund?
• What size is the fund?
• What is the benchmark for the fund? (See also p.51.)

And, if you are feeling bold:

• Is the style of management top down or bottom up? (*The 'top down' strategy assesses the broad outlook, such as whether Europe is a good place to invest; the 'bottom up' way looks at the prospects for each company within the portfolio.*)

tip

Ask for clarification if the adviser uses phrases like: 'This could be to your advantage in the long term.' Talking about the 'long term' is a great get-out because nobody knows what will happen to investments in the future. If you were cynical, you might think it meant: 'Don't come back for at least ten years to complain that your investment has fallen because, by then, the chances are I won't be around.'

tip

Don't believe advisers who claim to have inside information: 'Interest rates are coming down next month.' They have done no more than read the same newspaper reports as you have. Indeed, much investment advice is no more than someone's considered opinion, albeit backed by advisers' knowledge and experience. But your opinion is just as valid, and you can disagree with their recommendations.

tip

WARNING: If the adviser says you must sign up for an investment immediately or it will cost you more, let it go. It is better to miss an opportunity than find yourself locked into a bad investment. Do not be pressured into handing, say, your redundancy cheque to a particular adviser because your colleagues have already done so – they could all be wrong.

QUESTIONS FOR YOU TO ANSWER: THE FACT FIND

Once you have picked the adviser you want to do business with, you will need to arrange a longer meeting to discuss your financial situation. This time you will have to answer questions. The questionnaire, or fact find, is designed to find out your current financial position, your family situation, and your financial needs for the future.

You can refuse to answer any of the questions in the fact find questionnaire, but the adviser can do a better job if you provide comprehensive information. If you refuse to answer any questions, you will have to sign a statement confirming this.

tip

> **If you really dislike answering questions, you should go for an execution-only service. Instead of recommending investments, the adviser simply carries out your instructions. But you are not taking advice, so you can't later complain that you bought the wrong investment.**

By the time the fact find is completed, the IFA should have a good understanding of your current finances and your prospects, and can make various recommendations:

- Do nothing, because your finances are in good shape already. (*Possible but unlikely.*)
- Sell some or all of your existing investments. (*You want to be convinced that this is the right course of action. If it involves selling life insurance policies, you should be suspicious, because that is almost certainly the wrong thing to do.*)
- Buy new investments, insurance policies and pensions. (*The adviser will probably say you ought to buy something, but he or she has to give you reasons for every recommendation.*)

QUESTIONS TO ASK BEFORE BUYING INVESTMENTS THAT AN ADVISER RECOMMENDS

get the facts

- Why have you picked this particular company's investments? (*Some investment groups have a name for selling consistently good products and many are average. Some are known to sell expensive products that perform badly; they are expensive because they pay high commission and a bad adviser will be tempted to recommend them to earn more money. Ask for details of several different products.*)

- Why have you chosen this particular investment?
- Is this a 'regulated' product? (*'Regulated' products give you protection under the Financial Services Act.*)
- How much will you earn from selling me this investment? (*They are obliged to tell you.*)
- What is the downside to the investment you are recommending?
- Am I committing myself to regular payments?
- For how long is my money tied up?

tip

> **Warning: Never feel obligated to advisers, however much trouble they take over your modest investments. That is their job. Do not invest unless you are convinced you are doing the right thing. Never invest because you feel guilty for letting them down.**

QUESTIONS TO ASK YOURSELF BEFORE GOING AHEAD

ask yourself

- Do I understand how my money is going to be invested? (*If not, don't sign the contract.*)
- If it is a regular-savings investment, can I afford to keep up the payments?

Talking to a tied adviser

ask Margaret

Do tied advisers have to comply with the same regulations as independent financial advisers?

Yes. The only difference is that they can recommend only products sold by the company they work for.

How can I tell if the product sold by a tied adviser is any good?

If the company has a good reputation, its products are likely be good enough.

How do I know if the company has a good reputation?

Don't ask the salesperson. Read personal finance magazines and the personal finance pages in newspapers, and you will see that some companies are recommended more often than others.

Will tied agents always be able to find the right investment for me?

No company can create enough different products to be certain that they have one that is best for every potential customer. If the company doesn't sell a product that is appropriate for you, or the one it sells is not right in your circumstances, company salespeople are required to say so; they must not try to sell you anything inappropriate or next-best.

Do I have to pay for advice from a company salesperson?

If you listen to the advice but don't buy anything, you pay nothing. You pay when you buy an investment, although you will not write out a cheque because the charges are deducted from the money you invest.

How are tied salespeople remunerated?

Company salespeople can be paid in different ways: by salary with bonuses; by salary plus commission on sales; by commission only; or by being self-employed and earning commission through sales.

QUESTIONS FOR THE COMPANY SALESPERSON OR TIED ADVISER TO ANSWER

The questions you should ask a tied adviser are most of the same questions you would ask an independent adviser, plus certain others.

get the facts

- Which company do you work for? (*There ought to be little doubt, for it should be blazoned across the literature.*)
- How long have you worked for the company? (*The longer the better.*)
- Where did you work before? (*It is probably a bad sign if the adviser worked for several other investment companies; a good salesperson might be headhunted by a rival company but it would be for a senior position. Advisers who previously worked outside financial services, perhaps as a teacher or policeman, may be more mature in their outlook and approach.*)
- Why did you leave your previous job? (*The reason should sound convincing, although no one is going to admit that they could not meet their sales targets.*)
- How long do you expect to be staying in this job? (*You want continuity but a good salesperson is likely to be promoted.*)

Getting advice from a stockbroker

You need a stockbroker to advise on dealing in shares.

ask Margaret

What sort of services do stockbrokers provide?
There are three levels:

- 'Execution-only' is the most basic, and therefore the cheapest. The stockbroker simply carries out your instructions to buy or sell shares without giving any advice or comment. You cannot ask any questions about the shares or your decision to invest. You pay commission on each deal.
- An advisory service, when you can ask for the stockbroker's opinion and advice before dealing. You pay commission on each deal.
- A discretionary service, which means that the stockbroker takes control of your investments, making all the decisions to buy and sell without discussing it with you beforehand. You can pay either commission on each deal or an annual fee. It is cheaper than an advisory service but more expensive than execution-only.

tip

> **If you are paying for an advisory service, make sure you use it. If you are not taking advantage of your stockbroker's advice, you might as well pay the cheaper cost of execution-only. The cheapest service is from discount stockbrokers, who do nothing but take execution-only orders over the telephone.**

Are stockbrokers interested in people with only a few hundred pounds to invest?
With that amount of money, they are more likely to suggest you buy unit trusts or investment trusts.

How do I find a stockbroker?
Ask if friends can recommend someone. Or contact the Association of Private Client Investment Managers and Stockbrokers (Apcims), which will send you a complete list of private-client stockbrokers including their areas of expertise. Alternatively, you can contact the London Stock Exchange. The addresses of both are given in the Appendix. Ask several stockbrokers for their brochure so you can see how they vary; then phone two or three for an introductory meeting.

Do I have to use a stockbroker to buy shares?

Mostly, because only stockbrokers have access to the stock market. The exceptions are buying shares when they are first issued; or buying directly from a friend.

Do I have to use a stockbroker to sell shares too?

You can sell shares without using a stockbroker if you already know someone prepared to buy them. Complete a stock transfer form (see p.95).

Can I buy shares through my bank?

You can if your bank has a stockbroking subsidiary. At the very least, branch staff should be able to take your order. Some banks have in-branch dealing where, through a computer, you can buy or sell on the spot. Some building societies offer stockbroking services, either through a stockbroking firm that they own or by arrangement with an outside firm.

Is my money safe if I hand it to a stockbroker?

Stockbrokers do go bankrupt occasionally but, if they have been complying with their regulator's rules, clients' money is ring-fenced from the firm's money and should be safe. If clients' money were stolen, the Investors Compensation Scheme steps in (see p.29).

How can I check that my stockbroker is managing my portfolio as well as possible?

Portfolio managers set themselves a target – or 'benchmark' – against which they measure their performance. Ask which benchmark is used for your investments.

How do benchmarks work?

They show how an average portfolio is performing, so that you can see whether yours is on target, above average, or below average. There is one benchmark particularly relevant to small investors: the Private Investor Index published in the *Financial Times*. It has been constructed as a typical, average-risk portfolio for UK investors and is divided into three targets: income portfolio; growth portfolio; and balanced portfolio.

Do I have grounds for complaint if my broker has done worse than the benchmark?

You should certainly raise the issue, but it is not that clear-cut. The precise make-up of your portfolio makes an enormous difference – for instance, you might have a growth portfolio and have agreed to take high-risk investment decisions, but the same benchmark is used for comparatively safe growth portfolios.

What should I do if I am not happy with the way my stockbroker is handling my portfolio?

Ask for a meeting and state clearly that you are dissatisfied. There is no need to feel embarrassed about doing this, and you will not be the first client to complain. The stockbroker will try to explain why your fears are unjustified, but will find it harder to argue if the performance is below the benchmark.

tip

> **Remember, when choosing a stockbroker, that you need someone you feel comfortable with. You do not need to give any reasons why you reject one or accept another.**

Can I switch stockbrokers if I'm not happy?

You can, but it is easier with some services than others. With an execution-only service, there is no continuity and you can deal through a different broker each time; with an advisory broker, you can move to another unless your shares are in the firm's nominee account. If your shares are in the stockbroker's nominee account, whether you are an advisory client or a discretionary client, transferring to a different broker can be expensive.

Where can I find cut-price share-dealing services?

They often advertise in newspapers and specialist magazines.

Can I use both an execution-only stockbroker and an advisory stockbroker?

Certainly.

Can I call a telephone-based broker and buys shares immediately?

They will check out your creditworthiness before you deal for the first time; then they will give you a password and after that you can telephone orders whenever you want.

QUESTIONS TO ASK WHEN CHOOSING A STOCKBROKER FOR ADVICE

get the facts

- How much commission do you charge? (*Specify the amount of money you want to invest, or number of shares you want to sell, because costs vary depending on the size of the deal.*)
- What is the minimum commission? (*This is important, because a high minimum works out expensive when you are dealing in small quantities of shares.*)
- Is there a maximum commission? (*This is useful if you are dealing in large amounts.*)
- Would the commission be any lower if you handled my whole family's business? (*The stockbroker should be prepared to negotiate a lower fee.*)
- What do you charge for holding my shares in a nominee account?
- Is your transaction charge lower if I use your nominee account? If not, why not?
- Will I receive the shareholder perks for shares I hold in the nominee account, and if so, will you charge extra for passing them on? (*They might pass them on. See nominee accounts, p.97*)
- Are there any other charges I could face?
- Will you be looking after me, or will it be someone else in the firm? (*If it is someone else, ask to meet that person as well.*)
- Can I buy and sell through the Internet? (*Some stockbrokers take orders over the Internet; a few also allow you to deal through the Internet.*)
- When you carry out my instructions, will you act immediately or wait until later in the day when you have orders from several clients buying or selling the same shares?
- Can I instruct you to buy only below a maximum price and sell only above a minimum? If so, can I leave an order with you for a period of time, and for how long?
- Which benchmark do you use to measure the performance of clients' portfolios?
- Do you offer financial planning and tax advice?
- Do you send a newsletter to clients, including share recommendations?
- Will you send me copies of your research into companies?
- Who owns this stockbroking firm? (*It might be independent or owned by a bank or foreign institution.*)
- Do you have insolvency insurance?
- Where will you deposit any of my money held in cash? (*This should be in a reputable bank.*)
- Are your staff paid a salary, or do they rely on commission?

QUESTIONS TO ASK WHEN CHOOSING AN EXECUTION-ONLY STOCKBROKER

get the facts

- Do you have Financial Services Authority authorisation?
- Do you have a freephone or low-cost telephone number?
- During which hours can I place orders?
- How quickly will you execute my order?
- Can I deal through the Internet?

QUESTIONS TO ASK YOURSELF BEFORE CHOOSING A STOCKBROKER

ask yourself

- What level of service do I want?
- Do I want to deal entirely over the phone or through the Internet – or might I want to visit the stockbroker's office?
- Do I want the stockbroker's office close to my home, or near my work, or in London?
- Do I want to deal with a small firm or a large one?
- What investments do I already have? (*Stockbrokers can give better advice if they know where else you invest.*)

Getting investment advice from an accountant

Some accountants are registered as independent financial advisers, for which they undertake extra training and pass exams. Usually they charge fees; they can earn commission but must make it clear how they work and get paid.

QUESTIONS TO ASK BEFORE GETTING INVESTMENT ADVICE FROM AN ACCOUNTANT

get the facts

- Are you registered as an independent financial adviser?

- What category of authorisation do you have? (*A low category allows them to give basic advice; the highest category means they can manage investment portfolios.*)
- Do you specialise in any particular areas of financial advice?
- Do you charge a fee or take commission?
- If you earn commission, will you refund this to me? (*Do not allow an accountant to charge a fee and keep commission.*)

Getting investment advice from a solicitor

A few solicitors belong to the Association of Solicitor Investment Managers (ASIM). They:

- take Law Society investment exams
- charge fees
- disclose the commission they earn
- refund commission to clients
- often specialise in managing portfolios
- are more suitable for wealthy people
- contribute to a compensation scheme protecting at least £1 million of your money
- can combine investment advice with estate planning
- have professional negligence insurance.

tip

> WARNING: **When solicitors' notepaper says: 'Authorised by the Law Society to do investment business', this does not mean that the solicitors are qualified to give investment advice. It means only that they can hold your money – perhaps the deposit for a house – in their clients account.**

QUESTIONS TO ASK BEFORE GETTING INVESTMENT ADVICE FROM A SOLICITOR

get the facts

- Are you authorised to give 'discrete advice'? (*This is what the Law Society calls full independent financial advice.*)

- Who will be looking after my investments?
- How experienced is this person?
- Are there any restrictions on where the manager can invest my money?
- What is the manager's investment performance for other clients?
- Will the investments be held in my name or in a nominee name? (*See p.97.*)
- Do you specialise in any particular areas of financial advice?

Discount brokers

Discount brokers do not give advice under any circumstances. They undertake nothing but execution-only business, when you tell them where you want to invest. Use a discount broker only if you know what you want to buy and when you will want to sell.

Discount brokers can save you money because they keep less of the commission paid by the investment companies and give you the balance. You can ask any independent financial adviser to share commission with you; some will, but discount brokers make a business from it.

ask Margaret

How can discount brokers sell investments more cheaply than financial advisers?

They sell only investments that pay commission, and they take less commission than other intermediaries. 'Intermediary' is a broad term for adviser, broker, market maker or middleman.

How much difference does this make?

Because less of your money has been taken in commission, more is left to be invested. For example, unit trusts usually pay 3 per cent commission, but discount brokers take only 1 per cent or 2 per cent; on with-profits policies, you can have up to 5 per cent refunded; and with annuities, guaranteed income bonds and endowments, expect to receive half the commission earned.

Can discount brokers earn a living on less commission?

They aim for bulk business, without frills, and often they earn just 0.5 per cent renewal commission each year.

Are discounts given only on commission?

As well as sharing commission, an intermediary can negotiate for the investment company to charge you less for particularly large investments. And product providers sometimes use part of their marketing budgets to cut the price for a special IFA promotion.

Are there any drawbacks to buying through a discount broker?

You get no advice on your investments, but your money is safe because you make cheques out directly to the investment company and not the broker.

What products do discount brokers sell?

Any investment that pays commission: life insurance, pensions, investment bonds, unit trusts and ISAs.

Could I get advice from an IFA and then, instead of buying through the IFA, buy more cheaply through a discount broker?

You could, and some people do. You could alternatively ask a financial adviser to share the commission with you.

Can I buy direct from a unit trust company and avoid paying commission?

You can usually buy direct, but it will not be any cheaper because the unit trust company will still deduct the 3 per cent fee from your investment – and then keep the money.

Where do I find a discount broker?

Look for advertisements in the national press.

QUESTIONS TO ASK DISCOUNT BROKERS

get the facts

- Do you give a discount on regular savings, or only on lump-sum investments? (*Not all accept regular-savings investments, and those that do are likely to give less discount.*)
- Are there any fees to pay? (*Some give a discount with one hand and take a fee with the other.*)
- Which companies' investments don't you sell? (*They won't deal with companies that pay no commission because there is nothing to discount.*)
- Will you send me the discount in cash or will it be reinvested? (*You should be given the choice, except with ISAs, where you must take cash.*)

3 Buying Investments

Understanding the basic products

Picking an investment is a tough decision. There are vast numbers to choose from, designed for many different needs. Choosing an inappropriate investment wastes as much money as buying a bad one. But it can be difficult to know exactly what you are getting: titles often tell you nothing and, worse, they can be misleading. Before you can begin to ask reasonable questions, you need to understand how the different investments work; then you can start to make sense of the answers and move towards making the right decisions.

Savings accounts

A savings account is the simplest form of saving: your money sits in a deposit account and earns interest. When you close the account, your capital (the sum of money you originally invested) is returned, with interest earned to date. Savings accounts and deposit accounts are the same thing.

ask Margaret

Who produces savings accounts?

- banks
- building societies
- insurance-company banks
- supermarkets and retailers
- foreign banks.

Where can I buy savings accounts?

At bank and building society branches; by telephone to banks and building societies; at some supermarkets and retailers; in response to advertisements; and through the Internet.

Which are better for savings accounts – banks, building societies or the new-style providers such as insurance companies and supermarket chains?

The new providers need to pay good rates to attract customers. They can afford to do so because they do not have expensive branch networks. Building societies try to pay better rates than banks to demonstrate the advantages of staying as mutual organisations.

tip

> **With all bank and building society savings accounts, apart from those paying a fixed rate of interest, you have a 14-day cooling off period. You can change your mind, switch to a different account, or ask for your money back with interest.**

QUESTIONS TO ASK BEFORE OPENING A SAVINGS ACCOUNT

Questions on interest rates

get the facts

- What rate of interest does the account pay? (*Financial institutions quote interest rates gross, before tax is paid.*)
- If the balance in my account falls to a level where it stops earning interest,

will you write and tell me? (*Probably not, unless this involves changing the original terms, in which case the bank must give you 30 days' notice and let you close the account or switch to another.*)

- Does the rate of interest depend on how much I invest?
- In accounts where the interest rate is higher for larger deposits, do the better rates apply to the whole balance in the account or only to the amount in the higher band?
- Does the account pay simple interest or compound interest? (*You nearly always earn compound interest, which is more valuable, but there are exceptions.*)
- Will the rate of interest change over the time I keep the account? (*Usually the rate moves up and down over the years, but some accounts pay a fixed rate of interest.*)
- Will the interest rate change whenever bank base rates change?
- How can I find out when interest rates change?
- Are there restrictions on how much the rate can change?
- If I find you have launched another account paying a better rate of interest, can I switch immediately without penalty? (*You will probably have to wait out the notice period.*)

tip

> **If you are checking the interest rates in a branch of a bank or building society, ask if they have postal savings accounts as well; these might not be promoted in the branch but usually pay more.**

- How frequently is interest paid? (*This can be annually, half-yearly, monthly or only when the account is closed. The more frequently interest is paid, the more you earn, although the interest rate is likely to be lower to compensate.*)

Questions on deposits

get the facts

- When I pay in a cheque, how soon does it start to earn interest?
- Do I have to deposit a minimum amount to open the account?
- Do I have to keep a minimum in the account at all times?
- What happens if my balance falls below the minimum required? (*You might earn no interest at all – at best a tiny amount – or the account might be closed.*)
- Do I have to keep the account open for a set period of time?
- Can I add to the account whenever I want? (*Usually you can, but not always.*)

- Can I add to it by depositing money at a branch? (*Some postal and telephone-based accounts accept money only by mail.*)
- Is there a telephone number to call if I have queries? (*Some telephone-based accounts operate 24 hours a day.*)
- If the account is called a one- or two-year bond, what happens at the end of the period?
- Can you change the terms of the account after I've opened it? (*It is sometimes possible – for instance, a raising of the minimum amount you must keep the account.*)
- Can I save in euros? (Several UK banks have euro accounts, paying interest at the rate paid to savers in Euroland – the countries that are using the single European currency.)
- Will you tell me about any new accounts you launch?

tip

> **Banks and building societies must send you, at least once a year:**
>
> - **a summary of all their savings products and the current interest rates**
> - **names of accounts that are no longer sold**
> - **names of the newspapers where they publish interest rate changes**
> - **telephone helpline numbers and any Internet site**
> - **the different interest rates applied to your account during the year**

tip

> **When rates change, banks and building societies must either advise you within 30 days by letter, e-mail, or other personal notice, or they must advise you within three working days by prominent notice in branches, by the newspapers they usually use, and on their telephone helplines and websites.**

tip

> **When comparing rates, make sure you check the exact name of your savings account, because banks and building societies sometimes produce new accounts with similar-sounding names but paying different rates of interest.**

Questions on withdrawals

get the facts

- Is there a limit to the number of withdrawals I can make?
- Is there a minimum amount I have to withdraw at a time?
- When do I stop earning interest on money that I withdraw?
- Is there any penalty for making withdrawals?

- How are withdrawals paid? (*It can be cash – over the counter or through an ATM – a cheque or sometimes only by electronic payment to a nominated bank account.*)
- Will I get a cash card with this account?
- Is there a charge for making withdrawals from a different bank's cash machine?
- Can I ask for a payment to be made direct to somebody else?
- Can I withdraw money whenever I want? (*Some accounts allow only one or two withdrawals a year. Fixed-term accounts usually allow none.*)
- If the account limits the number of withdrawals I can make, what happens if I exceed this number? (*You will probably be charged, but the account could be closed.*)
- Will I get a bonus if I make no withdrawals over a certain period? (*A few accounts pay loyalty bonuses.*)
- Can I get my money out with instant access – and how exactly do you define 'instant access'.
- Is there a charge for withdrawals if my balance falls below a certain amount?
- With a notice account, can I get my money out any quicker in an emergency?
- How much will emergency withdrawals from a notice account cost? (*Usually, you lose a certain amount of interest.*)

Fixed-rate savings accounts

get the facts

- What is the minimum I have to invest in the account?
- What is the rate of interest?
- How long is my money tied up? (*You can choose one, three or six months or, more usually, from one to five years.*)
- Will I earn more for tying my money up longer? (*Not necessarily, so check the rates before committing your money. The interest paid reflects the bank's view on long-term interest rates, and these might be falling.*)
- Is interest paid annually or only on maturity?
- Does the fixed-term start on the day I invest, or on some later date?
- If it is later, will I earn interest on my money in the meantime?

QUESTIONS TO ASK BEFORE OPENING A CHILD'S SAVINGS ACCOUNT

get the facts

- How old, or young, must a child be to open this type of account?

- Can the child withdraw money by itself?
- Can I stop the child withdrawing money?
- At what age is the child considered old enough to sign its own name?
- Will the staff ensure that the child doesn't take out too much money?
- What is the minimum investment?
- How much interest is paid?
- What perks come with the account?
- What will you offer when the child is too old to keep the account?

SPECIAL ASPECTS OF BUILDING SOCIETY SAVINGS ACCOUNTS

get the facts

- With this account, do I have the right to vote at annual and extraordinary general meetings? (*This is important if you want a vote if, perhaps, the building society proposes converting to a bank or is being taken over.*)
- Is the account a share account or a deposit account? (*This is a technical difference, but only share account holders receive hand-outs if the building society converts to a bank or is taken over.*)

tip

> **When checking with branch staff whether it is a share or a deposit account, get the answer in writing because branch staff sometimes make mistakes; with a letter you can prove you were given wrong information.**

BANKS' CODE OF PRACTICE FOR ADVERTISING SAVINGS ACCOUNTS

Banks operate a voluntary Code of Practice when advertising savings accounts.

- Every advertisement quoting a rate of interest must include an Annual Effective Rate (AER). This is a notional rate of interest showing what the interest rate would be if it were paid and compounded once a year. This makes comparing accounts easier.
- Advertisements must show the minimum deposit required to achieve the stated return. (*'Return' is a broad term for any interest and profit you might make from an investment.*)
- If the advertised return includes the value of the original deposit,

this must be explained in the main part of the advertisement.
- Savings products that advertise an introductory bonus must make the terms clear.
- Withdrawal and transfer details must be clearly shown.
- Accounts cannot be called 'instant access' if you have to accept withdrawals by cheque.

THE TAX POSITION ON SAVINGS ACCOUNTS

- Income tax is payable on the interest you receive from all savings accounts, unless the money is inside an ISA or TESSA.
- Banks and building societies deduct tax before paying interest, unless you have completed form R85 to claim interest gross.
- Non-taxpayers can have the interest paid gross by completing form R85 available from bank and building society branches.
- Non-taxpayers can reclaim any tax unnecessarily deducted.
- Lower- and basic-rate taxpayers have no more tax to pay.
- Higher-rate taxpayers must pay additional tax through their year-end tax return.
- There is no capital gains tax on bank and building society savings accounts.

National Savings

ask Margaret

Who provides National Savings products?

The government.

Where can I buy these products?

At post offices, direct from National Savings by post, by responding to National Savings' advertisements, and through independent financial advisers. (Contact details for National Savings are given in the Appendix.)

Why should I buy National Savings products?

For safety. You won't ever lose money because they are guaranteed by the government.

Do they pay good rates of interest?

That varies, depending on how urgently the government wants your money. Always compare National Savings rates with bank and building society rates before you invest.

tip

> WARNING: **Many National Savings products tie up your money for five years; if you need to get it out any sooner, you will not get the full rate of interest – and you might not get any interest at all. Matured National Savings certificates earn a rotten rate of interest; cash them in or switch them into a better paying account – with National Savings or with another institution.**

THE TAX POSITION

Some National Savings products are free of all tax:

- National Savings certificates
- Children's Bonds
- Individual Savings Accounts (ISAs)
- Ordinary accounts on the first £70 of interest
- Premium Bond winnings.

Income tax has to be paid on all other National Savings products. All products, apart from First Option Bonds, pay interest gross. No capital gains tax is payable on National Savings products.

Unit trusts

ask Margaret

What is a unit trust?

A unit trust is a portfolio of investments, worth millions of pounds, bought with money invested by hundreds – sometimes thousands – of small investors. The portfolio is divided into units and each investor holds a number of units.

What is a unit worth?

It is the value of the fund on any day, divided by the total number of units in issue. As the value of the portfolio changes, units become worth more, or less. It is called an 'open-ended' investment because the fund manager creates and redeems units, according to investor demand.

tip

> **'Fund' is a broad term for a pot of money such as a unit trust, an open-ended investment company (oeic – see later section in this chapter) or a pension. A 'fund of funds' is a unit trust that invests in other unit trusts.**

Who provides unit trusts?

- unit trust groups
- insurance companies
- stockbrokers
- banks
- large building societies
- stockbrokers
- retailers that sell financial services.

Where can I buy unit trusts?

- through independent financial advisers
- from company salespeople
- direct from unit trust groups
- direct from insurance companies
- direct from banks
- from large building societies
- through some retailers, by phone or post
- from stockbrokers
- by responding to advertisements
- through the Internet.

Who advises on which unit trust to buy?

Independent financial advisers, stockbrokers, and tied advisers who can advise only on one company's range.

For small investors, what is the advantage of unit trusts over buying individual shares?

Your money is amalgamated with money from all the other savers in the same fund so that, with a large amount, the fund manager can buy shares in dozens, or hundreds, of different companies – not only in the UK but around the world. This spreads your money more widely. Unit trusts are a 'collective' or 'pooled' investment, because your money is combined with that from many other investors.

How much money do I need to invest in unit trusts?

Most funds set a minimum of £500 or £1,000 for lump-sum investments. You can start saving regularly with £20 a month, although the minimum is more usually £30 to £50. Indeed saving regularly is a good way to overcome the problem of deciding when is the best time to invest. If the units rise in value, your investment is worth more; if they fall, your monthly contribution buys more units.

What does my money buy in a unit trust?

You decide how much you want to invest and buy a number of units to that value.

tip

> **If you are investing a substantial amount, ask for a discount on the price you pay for the units; these can be readily available from the unit trust providers. Ask your IFA to negotiate on your behalf, or ask the unit trust group directly.**

How much does it cost to invest in unit trusts?

You pay an initial, or buying, charge, which is usually between 3.5 per cent and 5.5 per cent of the amount you invest. Some funds, as a marketing ploy, make no initial charge. Every year after that, there is a charge of around 1.5 per cent of the value of your investment at the time. When the value of your investment rises, you pay more – and vice versa.

How do I pay the buying charge?

Most unit trusts show two different prices on any one day: the buying price (the 'offer' price), and the selling price (the 'bid' price), which is lower. The gap between the two prices is called the 'spread' and can be 7 per cent; this includes the buying charge which, in turn, includes advisers' commission. Your investment has to grow by that 7 per cent just to get you back to where you started.

How do I pay the annual charge?

This is usually deducted from dividends before they are paid but, with some funds, it is deducted from the capital you have invested.

tip
> Increasingly, unit trust groups are quoting a single price for buying and selling and showing charges separately.

tip
> Unit trust performance tables that show 'offer to bid' figures are comparing the price you pay to buy with the price you get for selling at the later date. This is better than comparing offer-to-offer prices, because you cannot get the offer price when you sell. A bid-to-bid comparison shows the fund's real performance but not the return that investors would get.

tip
> Figures in unit trust performance tables include dividends paid over the period. You cannot make a straight comparison with a stock market index because an index does not include the value of dividends.

How much commission do IFAs earn from selling unit trusts?

Generally, 3 per cent when you invest and sometimes 0.5 per cent each year.

Who pays the commission?

The unit trust group writes the cheque, but the cost is taken from your investment.

If IFAs earn commission, is it cheaper to buy direct from the unit trust company?

It can be; but some unit trust groups deduct the amount of the commission anyway.

tip
> While charges are important, it is a false economy to pick a fund with low charges if the performance is poor. Some funds are simply more expensive to run than others. Funds investing in emerging markets are the most expensive, while tracker funds are cheapest.

How can I make money from a unit trust?

You earn income from dividends, which are usually paid twice a year and, if you sell the units for more than you paid, you make a profit or capital gain. Note that income is paid out only with 'distribution' or 'income' units. If you have 'accumulation' units, the income is instead reinvested in the fund and the unit price adjusted to reflect the higher value.

Are unit trusts risky?

There is the risk that the value of your investment will go down because the underlying portfolio of most unit trusts is invested in shares – and share prices fluctuate. The risk varies depending on which fund you buy. Some funds are comparatively safe, some are more risky, and others are very high risk indeed. And the risks are real: in a high-risk unit trust you can lose a large proportion of your investment.

tip

> WARNING: **The best performer in any year is probably a highly specialised fund, which is the most risky. You are likely to do better over a period of time with an investment that produces steady, good results. Don't take much notice of performance tables produced by companies showing themselves at the top of the list. Tables produced by independent research companies, often published in newspapers and magazines, are more reliable.**

How can I tell how much risk I am taking?

The larger the companies within the portfolio, and the more broadly spread they are worldwide, the safer it is.

How can I be sure I am not taking more risk than I want?

You can telephone or write to the unit trust fund manager to discuss it – most have a customer services desk – or talk to a financial adviser.

What about the risk of the unit trust manager running off with my money?

That cannot happen because all the investments are held by trustees outside the unit trust group. And, if you did lose money because the management group went into liquidation, you can claim compensation through the Investors Compensation Scheme (see p.29).

Who are the trustees?

Large, established banks.

How can I tell where a unit trust invests?

Usually by the name of the fund; and they are all listed according to their category. If you are not sure, ask an adviser or the unit trust company itself. The manager's report lists every investment held in the portfolio.

How long can I keep a unit trust once I've bought it?

You can sell whenever you want, although you should plan on holding a unit trust for at least five years to give the investment time to grow and show a profit.

How quickly can I get my money back when I sell?

It usually takes around a week.

Can I change my mind after I've signed the application form?

You have a 7 and sometimes 14-day cooling off period.

How do I sell unit trusts?

Contact the person you bought them through, or send written instructions to the unit trust group direct.

tip

> Many unit trust groups run a share exchange scheme. They charge a low price, or sometimes have a free offer, to sell shares you already own and with the money buy units in one of their unit trusts. They take only shares quoted on the London Stock Exchange, and some accept only shares in the largest 100 companies.

What effect is the euro having on unit trusts?

Several new unit trusts were launched investing in Euroland countries. There is no currency risk when buying and selling shares in the various Euroland countries. If the UK adopts the euro, UK investors will have currency stability as well.

INDEX-TRACKER UNIT TRUSTS

ask Margaret

What do tracker funds track?

The return from a tracker fund aims to match the performance of shares within a chosen index, such as the FTSE100 or the All-Share index, or the index for stock markets in Europe, America or the Far East. This is in contrast to managed funds, where a fund manager decides which investments to buy and sell. The results from a tracker fund are not identical to the figures quoted for an index because charges are deducted before the tracker's returns are paid out.

Do tracker funds produce a better return than managed funds?

Sometimes they do, to the shame of fund managers who are paid to beat the index, but not always.

What is the argument for investing in tracker funds?

Your investment will always be in line with the index, when it goes up and also when it comes down. And there is the argument of cheapness: no manager is being paid to decide where to invest the money.

What is the argument against tracker funds?

Your investment cannot perform better than the index it tracks and, theoretically at least, managers of active funds should be able to beat the index because they are buying the shares they believe will perform particularly well.

If two funds both track the FTSE100 index, is the result exactly the same?

No, for two reasons. The funds can impose different charges; and they can track an index in different ways. Managers rarely buy every share in the index, but instead buy a representative sample that the manager believes will produce the same return as the entire index.

CORPORATE BOND FUNDS

ask Margaret

What are corporate bonds?

Corporate bonds are loans issued by companies, for a set number of years, and on which they pay a fixed rate of interest. They are similar to gilts but gilts, issued by the government, are safer.

What are corporate bond funds?

Corporate bond funds are unit trusts whose portfolios contain corporate bonds, sometimes including preference shares, gilts and cash.

How are corporate bond funds different from other unit trusts?

Corporate bond funds aim to pay higher income. Other unit trusts' portfolios comprise mainly ordinary shares.

tip

> WARNING: **Corporate bond funds that pay the highest interest involve the greatest risk because they invest in corporate bonds issued by risky companies, including those with the highest-risk called 'junk' bonds. And some funds, to maintain high income, take money from your capital to pay interest.**

QUESTIONS TO ASK AN ADVISER OR UNIT TRUST SALES-PERSON BEFORE BUYING UNIT TRUSTS

get the facts

- Where geographically can the fund invest?
- Where is the fund investing at the moment?
- Can the fund change its investment criteria without my knowing?
- Does the unit trust concentrate on providing income, or capital growth, or is it balanced between the two?
- What is the fund's performance record compared with others in the same sector for the past five years? (*You want a fund with a consistently good performance rather than being top of the charts one year and near the bottom the next.*)
- How risky is the fund?
- What is the minimum I can invest in this fund?
- Is there a regular-savings scheme and, if so, what is the minimum monthly investment?
- What does it cost to buy into this fund?
- How much do I pay in charges each year?
- Are there any charges when I sell?
- What are the maximum charges the fund could impose without getting unitholders' permission?
- Will you give a discount for a large investment?
- Is there a discount on the buying charge if I sell this fund and buy another one from the same manager? (*Often there is.*)
- What is the size of the fund? (*You should prefer funds with at least £15 million in them and no more than £50 million.*)
- Can I put this unit trust in an ISA? (*Almost certainly 'yes'.*)
- Is there a share-exchange scheme?

THE TAX POSITION

- Income tax is payable on dividends.
- Tax is deducted by the unit trust manager before the dividends are paid.
- Lower and basic-rate taxpayers have no more tax to pay.
- Higher-rate taxpayers must pay additional tax through their year-end tax return.
- Non-taxpayers cannot reclaim the tax credit.
- Income tax is not payable on dividends from unit trusts inside

ISAs and PEPs until 2004, at which time it becomes payable.
- Interest earned on corporate bonds in ISAs and PEPs continues to be tax-free even after 2004.
- Capital gains tax is payable on profits from selling unit trusts, unless they are inside ISAs or PEPs.

Open-ended investment companies (oeics)

Open-ended investment companies (oeics, pronounced 'oiks') are a cross between unit trusts and investment trusts. Investors buy shares in the investment, although oeics are open-ended funds like unit trusts and so the number of shares available changes according to demand. Oeics quote one single buying and selling price, with charges shown separately. Oeics can be umbrella funds, which means one fund can offer a number of sub-funds (like the spokes of the umbrella) investing in different sectors, perhaps UK shares or US shares or corporate bonds, and allowing investors to switch around without the cost of buying a new investment.

ask Margaret

Are oeics shares listed on the London Stock Exchange?

They can be. Or they might be listed on some other stock exchange – perhaps Dublin or Luxembourg.

Who provides oeics?

Unit trust groups, insurance companies and European investment companies can all provide oeics. Many managers are converting their established unit trusts to oeics. In time, they may all convert.

Where can I buy oeics?

Through unit trust or insurance company sales representatives, through independent financial advisers, or through stockbrokers.

Who advises on which oeic to buy?

Independent financial advisers, tied advisers (but only on one company's range) and stockbrokers.

How safe is my money in an oeic?

As safe as it is with unit trusts and investment trusts. The value of your investment can fall but, if you lose money because someone who sells or manages the oeic goes bankrupt, you can claim through the Investors Compensation Scheme (see p.29).

Can I put an oeic in an ISA?

Yes.

QUESTIONS TO ASK BEFORE BUYING AN OEIC

get the facts

- Which stock market are the shares listed on?
- How many sub-funds does the oeic include?
- What are the sub-funds?

QUESTIONS TO ASK IF YOUR UNIT TRUST IS CONVERTING TO AN OEIC

get the facts

- Will the investment criteria change?
- What will the charges be?
- What are the benefits of switching?
- Will I have the choice of extra funds in which to invest?
- Is there any way in which I might lose out?

THE TAX POSITION FOR OEICS

The tax position for oeics is the same as for unit trusts.

Investment trusts

Investment trusts are in fact not trusts at all; they are companies with shareholders. They are called trusts because, when they first appeared a hundred years ago or so, they were in trust form. This structure didn't actually last long, but the name has stuck.

ask Margaret

What are investment trusts?

They are limited companies quoted on the London Stock Exchange. Each investment trust is a separate company, and every time a new investment trust is launched, a new company is created.

How are investment trusts different from other companies?

Most companies manufacture goods or provide a service of some kind. Investment trusts use their shareholders' money to buy shares in other companies around the world and manage these portfolios.

Who provides investment trusts?

Investment trust groups.

Where can I buy into investment trusts?

- direct from investment trust groups
- through stockbrokers
- through execution-only stockbrokers by phone
- through independent financial advisers
- through the Internet.

Who advises on which investment trust to buy?

Stockbrokers and specialist independent financial advisers.

How do I invest in investment trusts?

You buy shares, just as you do in any other UK company, either when they are launched or, after that, through the stock market. Many investment trust management groups have set up savings schemes so shareholders can buy shares directly, instead of using an outside stockbroker. This is cheaper, particularly for small deals.

Why should I buy shares in an investment trust rather than, say, one of the large FTSE100 companies?

It depends what you want from an investment. Buying shares in one company is risky because your returns depend on the success of that one company. An investment trust is also only one company, but it runs a portfolio that invests in – perhaps hundreds – of other companies, and this spreads your risk more widely.

How much money do I need to buy investment trusts?

For a lump sum investment, around £1,000 through a stockbroker but sometimes less through a savings scheme. Most savings schemes take regular monthly payments as well as lump-sum investments, from about £25 a month.

What is the difference between investment trusts and unit trusts?

In many ways they are similar. Both are collective or pooled investments; and with both, investors with a modest amount of money can invest across a wide range of companies worldwide. The main difference is their structure: investment trusts are companies with a fixed number of shares; unit trusts are trusts and the number of units in issue changes according to demand.

How much are the charges to buy investment trust shares?

If you buy when the shares are first issued, there are no charges. If you buy later, in effect buying second-hand shares, you pay stockbroker's commission and stamp duty.

Do I have the usual shareholder rights?

You do if you buy through a stockbroker. But, if you buy through the investment trust's savings scheme, your shares are held in a nominee account, where generally you lose the right to receive annual reports, attend annual meetings and vote. Some savings schemes, though, do include shareholders' rights. For more on nominee accounts, see p.97.

tip

> **If you hold investment trust shares in a nominee account, through a savings scheme, PEP or ISA, you have the protection of the Financial Services Act and access to the Investors Compensation Scheme. You don't if your name is on the share register.**

How do I go about selling investment trust shares?

You can sell by the same route as you bought: through a stockbroker or savings scheme.

How do I make money out of investment trusts?

You are likely to receive dividends, which provide income, and if the share price goes up, you can sell the shares for more than you paid and make a profit or capital gain.

tip
> Investment trusts' value differs from unit trusts: a unit trust unit is always worth the value of its portfolio divided by the number of units; an investment trust's share price can be lower than the value of its portfolio divided by the number of shares, if market forces drive down the price. At these times, investment trust shares are said to be 'trading at a discount'.

How frequently are dividends paid?

That depends on the investment trust. Usually it is twice a year, but it can be monthly or quarterly. Some investment trusts concentrate on producing capital growth and pay no dividends.

Could I sell the shares for less than I paid?

Absolutely. Like any shares, prices move up and down all the time.

What makes an investment trust's share price go up?

Partly it is the manager's ability to increase the value of the portfolio, but shareholders' sentiment also has an effect. Sometimes investment trusts are unfashionable, few shareholders want to buy the shares, and so the price falls.

Are investment trust shares always good value if you buy at a discount?

Not necessarily. Buying at a discount means you pay less for the shares than the portfolio is worth – but the discount could widen even more.

tip
> Some investment trust companies buy back their shares, hoping to reduce the discount and improve the net asset value (NAV) of the portfolio. Shareholders can sell or not, as they choose.

Can share prices rise above the portfolio value?

Yes, in which case they are 'trading at a premium'.

INVESTMENT TRUST SHARE STRUCTURE

There are different classes of share, and you need to understand which you are buying. Most investment trust companies issue ordinary shares, where an investor is entitled to a share of the profits through dividends. Some, called split capital investment trusts, issue more than one type of share; they are set up to last for a fixed number of years and then wound up.

ask Margaret

How do split capital investment trusts work?

The simplest have income shares and capital shares within one portfolio. Investors choose which they want to buy. All the dividends earned by the portfolio go to the income shares and benefit only income shareholders. All the capital growth from the portfolio goes to the capital shares, benefiting only capital shareholders.

What are the other types of investment trust shares?

There are zero-dividend preference shares or 'zeros'. The 'zero' means the shares pay no income; instead, they concentrate on capital growth, and this makes them attractive to higher-rate taxpayers.

What is the difference between zeros and capital shares?

Zeros are safer because, if the company went bankrupt, zero-holders would be paid before other shareholders. With zeros, you know from the start how much capital will be repaid. The return on capital shares depends on how much the assets increase in value.

What are investment trust warrants?

Often, when investment trust shares are issued, the company includes free warrants to make the package more attractive to potential investors. Warrants give you the right to buy shares in the company at a future date at a pre-set price. You don't have to buy them if you don't want to.

tip

> WARNING: **If you own warrants, don't forget about them or ignore them. They can be worth money.**

How do I know when it is worth converting warrants?

Warrants are worth converting when the cost to convert plus the price you paid for the warrant (if anything) is less than the share price at the time and, as far as you can tell, for the future.

INVESTING IN INVESTMENT TRUSTS

ask Margaret

Who decides what goes into an investment trust's portfolio?

Investment trust managers, who are individuals within companies that specialise in fund management. They are employed by the investment trust board of directors to manage the portfolio.

Can the managers buy and sell what they like?

Up to a point. The investment trust's articles of association set down the main parameters, which always include quoted shares. Some investment trusts invest broadly throughout the world; others specialise in particular geographical areas.

Does anyone keep an eye on the managers to make sure they are doing what they are meant to be doing?

Yes. Each company has a separate and independent board of directors, who are responsible to shareholders. The directors negotiate how much the managers get paid and can fire them if appropriate.

Do these directors really stand up for shareholders?

Some years back you could have accused them of being inactive, but today the rules – and the penalties for breaking those rules – are much stricter.

Can I put my investment trust shares into an ISA?

Yes, all investment trusts can be put in ISAs – unlike PEPs, which are more restrictive.

Can I buy investment trusts through an IFA?

You can, although many independent financial advisers are ill informed about investment trusts.

Do advisers earn commission from recommending investment trusts?

Some management groups pay commission on their savings schemes and ISAs – up to 3 per cent of the amount invested and sometimes 0.5 per cent a year on ISAs as well.

How risky are investment trusts?

They are linked to share prices, which makes them riskier than bank savings accounts. But there is a wide choice of investment trusts, from high to low risk.

Can I tell how risky the shares are?

The more widely spread the portfolio, the safer the investment. Investment trusts investing in only one part, or one sector, of the world are far riskier; those investing in only one country are riskier still.

Who regulates investment trusts?

Investment trusts must comply with the Companies Act and Stock Exchange regulations.

Once I've bought investment trust shares, do I have to keep them for a certain length of time before I can sell them?

No. You could sell them the next day – although this would be foolish because the share price is most unlikely to have risen enough to offset the buying and selling costs, so you will lose money.

Do investment trusts carry on for ever?

Some carry on indefinitely, but split capital investment trusts are set up to last only a fixed period. Sometimes investment trusts are taken over by other investment trusts; sometimes the shareholders (more likely institutional shareholders than private individuals) vote to wind up a company that is trading at a discount so that they can sell their shares for more than the current market price.

QUESTIONS TO ASK AN INVESTMENT TRUST COMPANY OR AN ADVISER BEFORE BUYING INVESTMENT TRUSTS

get the facts

- Where geographically can the fund manager invest?
- Where is the fund investing at the moment?
- Can the fund change its investment criteria without my knowing?
- Is there a savings scheme attached to this investment trust?
- How much does it cost to buy and sell shares through the savings scheme?
- What is the discount at present?
- What is the highest and lowest the discount has been in the past three years, and when was that? (*This indicates whether the share price is volatile, and whether it is worsening.*)
- How high are borrowings at present, compared with historic levels? (*The more a company borrows, the greater the risk for shareholders.*)
- Does the investment trust concentrate on providing income, or capital growth, or is it balanced between the two?
- Are dividends paid quarterly or half-yearly?
- What is the company's dividend record? (*If you want income, look for steady or gradually rising dividends.*)
- Is there a share exchange scheme? (*See p.70. Investment trust share-exchange schemes work in the same way as unit trust swap schemes.*)

THE TAX POSITION WITH INVESTMENT TRUSTS

- Income tax is payable on dividends.
- Tax is deducted by the investment trust manager before the dividends are paid.
- Lower- and basic-rate taxpayers have no more tax to pay.
- Higher-rate taxpayers must pay additional tax through their year-end tax return.
- Non-taxpayers cannot reclaim the tax credit.
- No income tax is payable on dividends from investment trusts inside ISAs or PEPs until 2004, but it will be payable from then on.
- Capital gains tax is payable on profits from selling investment trusts, unless they are inside an ISA or PEP.
- The tax position is the same whether investment trust shares are bought through the stock market or through a savings scheme.

Individual Savings Accounts (ISAs)

ask Margaret

What are ISAs?

ISAs are the successor to PEPs and TESSAs. They have a structure that turns taxable investments, such as cash, shares and unit trusts, into tax-free investments.

Who provides ISAs?

ISA managers, who must be authorised by the Inland Revenue:

- unit trust groups
- insurance companies
- investment trust managers
- stockbrokers
- banks
- large building societies
- large friendly societies
- retailers and supermarkets that sell financial services
- National Savings (cash ISAs only).

Where can I buy ISAs?

- through independent financial advisers
- direct from insurance companies and large friendly societies
- direct from unit trust groups and investment trust managers
- at bank branches
- at large building societies
- from stockbrokers
- by phone from some retailers and supermarkets
- by responding to advertisements
- from National Savings
- through the Internet.

Who advises on which ISA to buy?

Independent financial advisers, stockbrokers, and tied advisers (but only on one company's range).

What sort of investments can I put in an ISA?

The investments allowed fall into three categories: stocks and shares (which includes shares, unit trusts, investment trusts, oeics, gilts with at least five years to run, and corporate bonds); cash (covering bank and building society savings accounts, National Savings cash-ISAs, and cash unit trusts); and life insurance (including own-life policies that provide both protection and investment – unit linked or with-profits.

Do all ISAs provide all three?

No. There are two different types of ISA. A 'maxi-ISA' can include all three elements and must accept shares or unit trusts, but it might or might not – and you can buy just one mini-ISA, or one for each element, and you can buy them from three different ISA managers.

Can I buy one maxi-ISA and one mini-ISA in the same year?

No. You can buy one maxi-ISA for shares, cash and life insurance; or up to three different mini-ISAs. And note that if you choose a maxi-ISA because it pays good interest on cash, you have to use the same manager for unit trusts, whatever its investment record.

Does every ISA manager sell the full range?

No. Within maxi-ISAs, many providers have chosen to omit life insurance –

even some life insurance companies. With mini-ISAs, a fund manager can choose to sell only one, or two, or all three elements.

How much money can I invest in an ISA?

There are limits to the amount you can invest in any one year. In 1999/2000, the total is £7,000, all of which can be invested in shares, unit trusts or investment trusts; and of that total, up to £3,000 can be in cash, and up to £1,000 in life insurance premiums. In subsequent tax years, the total is £5,000, with a maximum of £1,000 in cash and £1,000 in life insurance premiums.

Mini-ISAs have the same limits each year and, because the cash and life insurance amounts are deducted from the total, it means that in any one year you are limited to investing £3,000 in shares, instead of £7,000 or £5,000 in a maxi-ISA.

tip

> WARNING: **Once you buy a mini-ISA, you cannot then start a maxi-ISA in the same year. This limits to £3,000 the amount you can invest in shares, unit trusts or investment trusts in that year.**

What sort of unit trusts can I put in an ISA?

Any UK authorised unit trust investing in shares and bonds, including some that are not allowed for PEPs.

Can I put shares from only one company into an ISA?

Yes.

Can I put building society windfall shares into an ISA?

Not without selling them first and using the cash to buy them back through the ISA, which could give rise to a capital gain. This is different from the PEP rules.

tip

> **Only shares from an employee share scheme can go straight into an ISA without first being sold.**

Can I put any National Savings product into an ISA?

No, only the National Savings product especially designed for ISAs.

Is the life insurance element worth having?

This is questionable. As the premiums are restricted to £1,000 a year, it might not provide as much life cover as you need.

Do I have to hold the ISA for a minimum period?

No. Your investments inside an ISA are tax-free whenever you sell them. But, once you cancel the ISA itself, you cannot buy another until the next financial year.

Might ISAs be scrapped after a few years, like PEPs?

ISAs are unlikely to last for ever, although the government has said that they will be available for at least ten years and reviewed in 2006. If they were abolished, at worst it would mean you had to pay tax on the investments inside. And, like PEPs, you might be able to avoid tax on any you had already bought.

Can anyone buy an ISA?

Anyone who is a UK taxpayer and over 18.

Is there a minimum I have to put in an ISA?

Each ISA provider sets its own minimum investment; some comply with the CAT standard – namely 'fair **C**harges, easy **A**ccess, and decent **T**erms' (see the section later within this ISA section).

Can I have ISAs with more than one manager?

You can buy mini-ISAs from three different managers, but you cannot have a different manager for the same element. This means that you can't put some unit trusts with one manager and more with another.

Can I make withdrawals from an ISA?

Yes, and it will not affect the tax relief. But if you invest, say, the maximum in an ISA, and withdraw half, you cannot invest any more in that year because you have already used up your limit.

tip

> It is safest not to wait till the last moment to buy an ISA, because advisers and providers are always rushed at the end of the tax year. And, if April 5 falls at a weekend or at Easter, this reduces the time even more.

QUESTIONS TO ASK BEFORE BUYING AN ISA

get the facts

- Is this a mini-ISA or a maxi-ISA?
- Do you offer all three elements of a maxi-ISA?
- What rate of interest do you pay on cash?
- What do I get with the life insurance?
- Does it meet CAT standards? (see immediately below)
- What are the charges?

CAT STANDARDS FOR ISAs

Some ISA providers sell ISAs that meet CAT standards: fair Charges, easy Access, and decent Terms. These are boundaries set down by the government to produce straightforward, reasonably-priced ISA investments.

- *For the ISA share element*: the annual charge must be no more than 1 per cent of net asset value; no other charges should apply; the shares must be quoted with a single unit price for buying and selling; the minimum investment must not exceed a £500 lump sum or £50 a month; and marketing literature must explain the risks involved.
- *For the ISA life insurance element*: the annual charge must be no more than 3 per cent of the value of the fund each year; no other charges are allowed; the minimum premium must not exceed a £250 lump sum or £25 a month; surrender values must reflect the value of the assets; and, after three years the surrender values must at least return the premiums paid.
- *For the ISA cash element*: there must be no one-off, annual or withdrawal charges allowed; the minimum investment must be no more than £10; cash withdrawals must be made available within seven days; interest rates can be no less than 2 per cent below base rate; and there must be no limits on the number of withdrawals allowed in a year.

ask Margaret

How will I know if an ISA meets the CAT standards?
It must say in the literature.

Does the government guarantee CAT-standard ISAs?

Absolutely not. Nor does it give them a seal of approval.

Are CAT-standard ISAs better than non-CAT-standard ones?

They are probably cheaper and simpler, but providers do not spend a great deal on marketing or giving advice. They are investments for people who have only a small amount to invest.

Should I avoid non-CAT-standard ISAs?

Not at all.

Do all ISA managers sell CAT-standard ISAs?

No. Each company takes a marketing decision about whether it wants this business.

THE TAX POSITION WITH ISAs

- There is no capital gains tax to pay.
- There is no tax to pay on the proceeds from the life insurance element; and the insurer pays no tax on income or gains on the investments behind the policies.
- There is no income tax to pay on interest or, until 2004, dividends from ISAs.
- Dividends on UK shares include a tax credit of 10 per cent, and the ISA manager can reclaim this credit – but only until April 1994.
- Dividends on foreign shares include no tax credit, and so in these cases no tax can be reclaimed.

Personal Equity Plans (PEPs)

ask Margaret   **What are Personal Equity Plans (PEPs)?**

A scheme making investments such as shares and unit trusts tax-free; they are the forerunner of ISAs.

Can I still buy PEPs?

No. PEPs stopped when ISAs arrived.

Do I have to transfer my existing PEPs to an ISA?

No. You can keep your existing PEPs, but you cannot add to them. Existing PEP investments are to remain tax-free until 2004, at which time tax becomes payable on dividends.

Can I change the investments inside a PEP?

You can switch the investments inside the PEP and you can transfer to a different PEP provider.

Is there any point in keeping PEPs going?

Absolutely. PEPs have the same tax advantages as ISAs, and your investments within a PEP should continue to grow.

If I cash in part of a PEP, can I later reinvest the same amount of money in the PEP?

No.

What is the tax position with PEPs?

The tax position with PEPs is the same as for ISAs, described above.

Tax Exempt Special Savings Accounts (TESSAs)

Like PEPs, TESSAs still exist but they are being phased out.

ask Margaret

Can I put my TESSA in an ISA?

There is no point until the TESSA matures because you can keep existing TESSAs for their full five years of life tax-free.

What happens to TESSAs on the fifth anniversary?

When a TESSA matures, you can invest the capital, up to £9,000, in an ISA in one go without affecting that year's ISA cash limit. Money from a matured

TESSA can go into the cash component of a Maxi-ISA, a cash Mini-ISA, or a TESSA-only ISA. You cannot transfer any interest from a TESSA directly to an ISA, although you can use the money to invest in an ISA subject to the annual limits.

What is the tax position with TESSAs?

There is no income tax to pay on interest from a TESSA, provided you keep the capital intact for five years. There is no capital gains tax charged on TESSAs.

Guaranteed equity bonds

ask Margaret

Who provides guaranteed equity bonds?

Banks, large building societies and insurance companies.

Where can I buy guaranteed equity bonds?

Direct from a bank, building society or insurance company that sells them, or through an independent financial adviser.

How do guaranteed equity bonds work?

You invest a lump sum for a fixed period. Your money is invested not in shares but in 'futures' and 'options' so that the provider is certain it can pay out on the maturity date. Futures and options are contacts to buy and sell shares in the future.

What is 'guaranteed' about a guaranteed equity bond?

The original capital invested is returned, whatever happens to share prices – but only on one set future date (often the fifth anniversary). If the stock market has gone up by that date, you also get a proportion of the rise in share prices. For this reason, guaranteed equity bonds are sometimes called 'guaranteed stock market bonds'.

Is this guarantee worth having?

If the stock market does well, you could earn more than you would have done in a savings account, but less than from a stock market investment without guarantee because you get only a proportion of the stock market rise – perhaps half – and you do not earn any dividends. That is the price you pay for the guarantee that keeps your capital safe. If the market does badly, you will not lose your original capital, but you will have done worse than in a savings account because you will have earned no income.

tip

> WARNING: **The more of your money that is guaranteed, the more the guarantee costs you. Note also that some investments are called 'capital protected' or 'secure': the return is almost guaranteed but not quite. However, your money is not tied up for five years.**

Are guaranteed equity bonds worth buying?

Only if you are an extremely nervous investor, yet want to benefit from the stock market.

Is my money really safe?

Yes. Products can call themselves 'guaranteed' only if they are totally certain of fulfilling their promise. And they are usually structured as single-premium policies, so an investor has the protection of the Policyholders Protection Scheme.

How do guaranteed equity bonds differ from tracker funds?

With trackers, the value of your investment goes up and down as the stock market index fluctuates; with guaranteed equity bonds, your investment will not fall below the amount guaranteed, which might be your original investment or could be less. You can lose more with a tracker fund, but you might gain more because guaranteed equity bonds do not give you all the increase in share prices or dividends.

tip

> WARNING: **Do not confuse guaranteed equity bonds with guaranteed income or growth bonds, for which see p.119.**

QUESTIONS TO ASK BEFORE INVESTING IN A GUARANTEED EQUITY BOND

get the facts

- What is the minimum I have to invest?
- How long is the term during which my money is tied up?
- When does the term start?
- What happens to money I invest before that date? (*You should earn interest or get a bonus on it.*)

- In an emergency, can I get my money out earlier? (*Almost certainly not, because guaranteed equity bonds are structured to meet the guarantee on one particular day. If you can get your money out, the penalties will be high.*)
- What are the charges? (*They are usually built into the return you are promised.*)
- Which stock market index do you follow?
- What percentage of the share index rise will I get on maturity?
- Exactly what is guaranteed?
- Is there a ceiling on the amount I get from share price rises? (*Often the bonds pay all the growth in share prices but only up to a limit –often 60 per cent. If share prices rose by 50 per cent, you would get it all, but if they rose by 80 per cent, you would get only the 60 per cent ceiling.*)
- Are the share price rises paid on 100 per cent of my original investment or less?
- How do you treat share price rises in the final months? (*It is safer if they are averaged over a number of months, in case share prices crash just before the bond matures.*)
- Does the bond lock in stock market increases along the way? (*This gives added protection against a stock market collapse later in the term.*)

THE TAX POSITION WITH GUARANTEED EQUITY BONDS

- Income tax is payable.
- The return is paid after basic-rate tax has been deducted.
- Non-taxpayers cannot reclaim the tax credit.
- There is no capital gains tax payable, even though the returns reflect share price rises.

Offshore investments

Offshore investments are financial products sold by a company based in a country that has a more benign tax regime than your home country, such as Dublin, Luxembourg, the Isle of Man, Jersey, Guernsey or Bermuda.

Who provides offshore investments?

Offshore investments are provided by investment companies, insurance companies, foreign investment companies, unit trust groups, banks and some building societies.

Where can I buy offshore investments?

You can buy them through specialist independent financial advisers, from a bank or building society's offshore branch, or direct from the providers.

What sort of financial products are sold offshore?

Almost anything you can buy onshore can also be bought offshore, including open-ended investment companies (oeics), mutual funds similar to unit trusts, insurance products, pensions, and bank or building society savings accounts. Offshore funds can be 'roll up' funds, where all the return is paid as income and only paid when you cash it in, or 'distributor' funds, where income is paid out regularly.

Are offshore investments tax-free?

Absolutely not, even though some salespeople might try to suggest it. As a UK domiciled taxpayer, you have to pay income tax and capital gains tax on your investments, wherever they are in the world.

tip

> **If you are not a permanent UK resident and are not sure whether you are 'domiciled' for tax purposes, ask the Inland Revenue.**

How will the Inland Revenue find out about any offshore investments I buy?

When you fill out your tax return.

What if I omit to mention the offshore investments?

It is a criminal offence to lie on a tax return.

Can I avoid paying tax on an offshore investment if I travel to the offshore island and spend the money over there?

No. The UK tax is still due.

Will my estate have to pay inheritance tax on money held offshore when I die?

If you are a UK taxpayer, inheritance tax is calculated on your assets wherever in the world they are situated.

tip

> WARNING: **Getting probate for an offshore account is difficult and expensive. You have to pay fees, often have to obtain probate locally, and then, if the executor can't turn up in person, use a local lawyer, which is expensive. Simple trusts can overcome this (see p. 25).**

What is the point in offshore investments, then?

For most UK taxpayers, not a lot − except that often the funds themselves pay little tax. Interest and dividends are paid without tax deducted, which gives some scope for financial gain, although you need to offset any advantage with the charges, which can be high, and the risk that sterling loses value against the currency of the offshore account. The tax advantages are that: you have more time to pay your tax bill due on the investments; if the tax falls due after you have switched from being a high-rate to a basic-rate taxpayer, you need pay only at the lower rate; and non-taxpayers are paid in full, whereas they can no longer reclaim the tax credit on dividends earned onshore.

Are there advantages for people who are not UK taxpayers?

Possibly. If you are working in the UK for a few years, and paying UK tax for that time, leaving your investments offshore keeps them away from the UK taxman. It does not mean you will avoid tax in your own home country; that depends on the local laws. If you are a British subject, working abroad for a number of years and not currently subject to UK tax, you might be able to avoid tax during that time.

tip

> **While you are not paying UK tax, you cannot contribute to a UK pension plan with tax relief, but you can save towards your retirement in an offshore pension savings scheme.**

Is my money safe offshore?

Offshore investments linked to shares can go down in value, as they can onshore. But protection against a company going bankrupt or someone stealing your money depends on which offshore country you use. In Jersey, Guernsey, the Isle of Man and Bermuda, you are as well protected as you are here, although only the Isle of Man has a compensation scheme.

Do I get Swiss-style secrecy from these accounts?

You do unless the drug squad or taxman are after you.

Can anyone open offshore accounts?

Some are restricted to non-UK taxpayers.

Who produces the bank and building society offshore accounts?

Names you would recognise from the high street, as well as foreign banks.

Are the bank and building society offshore accounts the same as the ones at home?

Very similar, although the interest rates differ. Within any given bank or building society, the offshore rates are likely to be better than it pays onshore.

Can I save in a foreign currency?

Several banks have US dollar accounts, and a few accounts include a multi-currency cheque book.

Shares

When you buy a share, you own a small slice of the company you are investing in. You are therefore entitled to a share of its profits, which is paid out in the form of a dividend from time to time. 'Shares' and 'equities' mean the same thing.

ask Margaret **Where can I buy or sell shares?**

Through stockbrokers (usually by telephone), through banks (in branches or by telephone), through a few building societies, direct from the company whose shares you are buying, when shares are newly issued, or through the Internet.

Who can advise on which shares to buy and sell?

Stockbrokers, in person or on the telephone. To choose a stockbroker, see the section on getting advice from a stockbroker in Chapter 2.

Why are shares sometimes called 'stocks and shares'?

Stocks are different from shares; they are fixed-interest securities, such as 'gilts' (see next section). However, many people, including Americans, use the word 'stock' to mean shares; and, indeed, we talk of stock markets, stockbrokers, and The Stock Exchange. (A stock market is where people buy and sell shares on behalf of investors: in London, they used to meet on the trading floor of The Stock Exchange, but today they stay in their own offices and communicate through computers.)

How rich do I need to be to invest in shares?

Not rich at all. You may have bought a few hundred pounds-worth of privatisation shares during the 1980s or 1990s, or received a small number of shares when your building society converted to a bank, or inherited some shares; all these investments make you a shareholder. But, if you are thinking of becoming an active share-dealer, you should have several thousand pounds to spare; you need to understand that shares are a risky investment, and that you could lose some of this money – or all of it if you choose badly.

Is it possible to invest in shares without losing money?

Certainly, but when you buy shares you have to accept that your investment will at times go down in value as well as up. Picture a graph showing how share prices over a long period have moved: this never goes up in a straight line. Share prices continually move up a bit and down a bit.

Why, then, do people invest in shares?

Investors hope that, by holding the shares long enough, they can sell them for more than they paid (allowing for buying and selling costs and inflation). In addition, while you are holding the shares you usually receive periodic dividends, which provide income.

How long is my money tied up in shares?

You could buy and sell on the same day if you wanted, although you are unlikely to make money that way. It depends upon what sort of investor you want to be. For instance, you can buy shares to put away and forget about for years, in which case you should invest in companies with a solid, long-term record. In contrast, if you are a speculator, you can jump in and out, looking for companies whose share price you think is about to rise, but you need to keep a close eye on the stock market and be prepared to act quickly.

How much are the charges to buy shares?

The one set expense is stamp duty, which is 0.5 per cent of the amount you invest – and so you do not pay stamp duty when you sell shares, only when you buy. The other outlay is stockbroker's commission, which varies enormously and also depends on how much advice you want from your stockbroker.

I've got a few shares from when the building society converted to a bank. How can I sell them?

Contact the bank by phone or letter, or visit the branch and ask if they have a special dealing service for shareholders. Or you could try one of the many cut-price share-dealing services around.

Can I give the shares I own to my children without selling them?

You can give shares to anyone by completing a stock transfer form. Some shareholder-friendly companies print these on the back of the share certificates. Otherwise, your stockbroker might provide one, or you can buy them from specialist stationers. Send the stock transfer form to the company's registrars (the name and address is printed in the annual report and on share certificates), who will substitute the new name for yours on the register of shareholders.

How much does it cost to transfer shares?

There are no charges.

Can I do the same kind of transfer for shares held in a nominee account?

Yes, but you have to ask the stockbroker, as legal owner, to complete the transfer form, and you will probably have to pay a fee.

I've inherited some odd parcels of shares which will cost me more to sell than they are worth. What can I do?

If the companies are still trading and their shares are still quoted on the London Stock Exchange, you can exchange the shares for investments in unit trusts or investment trusts. Ask a few trusts if they have a share-exchange scheme (see p.70). Or you can donate them to charity through ShareGift, whose address is given in the Appendix.

Is it worth buying shares for the sake of the shareholder perks?

It depends how much you value the perks – which are usually discounts on holidays, restaurant meals, hotel stays, or retailers' vouchers. The shares could be a good investment in their own right but, if not, it is better to invest in shares you believe will be profitable and pay the full price for the services.

Are 'penny shares' worth buying?

These shares, so-called because each share costs from a few pence up to around £1 to buy, are highly risky. They are not bargains simply because they cost a small amount: a share costing 5p can, for instance, easily fall to 1p or less. Invest in penny shares only if you are a gambler by nature.

Can I buy European shares?

Yes, although only a few stockbrokers provide a full European service.

Can I buy other foreign shares?

You can, but it is unrealistically expensive for small investors to buy shares not quoted on the London Stock Exchange.

How can I keep track of the value of my shares after I've bought them?

Check the share price in a newspaper and read the financial pages and financial magazines for any news story about the company or its shares.

How can I tell whether my shares are doing as well as others?

You can compare your shares with their relevant index and check whether their performance is in line with the average. For example, if your company is in the 'retail' sector, compare the share price movements with changes in the retail index. These are published every day in newspapers' financial pages.

How can I find out more about becoming a shareholder?

Contact ProShare, an organisation that encourages share ownership. It also supports investment clubs, which are groups of amateur investors who meet regularly to talk about shares and pool their money to invest collectively. Also contact the London Stock Exchange for their leaflet. Both addresses are given in the Appendix.

tip

> **Remember that you may already have an interest in stock market investments without realising it: your pension contributions and life insurance premiums are largely invested in shares.**

Do I always get a share certificate when I buy shares?

Increasingly, since the introduction of Crest, shares are held in your stock-broker's nominee account, so you do not receive a certificate.

What is Crest?

Crest is electronic share settlement, which shortens the time between agreeing to buy shares and paying for them. ('Settlement' is paying for shares you buy, or delivering the share certificate when you sell.) Crest transactions are carried out, and the information is stored, by computer. This means that paper share certificates are not necessary and, if you don't want to hold share certificates, you can keep your shares in a nominee company.

What is a nominee company?

A nominee company is an account set up by a stockbroker to hold clients' shares. The nominee company is the legal owner of the shares you buy. Although you remain the beneficial owner of the shares, you have no auto-matic right to vote in company meetings, to receive annual reports, or to attend and speak at annual meetings.

Is there any way I can keep my legal rights as a shareholder?

You can become a sponsored member of Crest through your stockbroker. You pay an annual fee to Crest, and possibly to your stockbroker as well. It is suitable only for shareholders who buy and sell frequently.

Can I choose whether to hold my shares by certificate or in a nominee account?

Yes, although you have to find a stockbroker who offers the service you want. Many provide the choice, but some deal only through nominees and a few have no nominee service.

Which is best: certificates or nominee accounts?

It comes down to personal choice. If you deal regularly in shares, nominee accounts or sponsored membership of Crest will save you time; and, although you have to pay a fee, some stockbrokers charge less when you deal. You have no share certificates to keep safe and, when you sell, you do not have to worry about delivering the certificate within the required five days for settlement. On the other hand, if you deal in shares rarely, certificates cost nothing to hold and you keep your full shareholder rights.

tip

> **All ISA and PEP investments are held in nominee accounts. Some investment trusts, and banks that used to be building societies, grant full shareholder rights, including the right to vote, to their shareholders with shares in nominee accounts.**

How much is the fee for nominee accounts?

You might pay nothing, or you may be charged an annual fee. If the annual fee is low, be careful that you are not paying high commission instead. In addition, you might be charged if you want to attend annual meetings, for collecting dividends on your behalf or for receiving a copy of company annual reports (although you can get round this by writing directly to the company yourself; you do not have to be a shareholder to request copies of annual reports).

What proof of ownership do I get when I buy shares and put them in a nominee account?

You will receive a contract note.

With nominee accounts, how do the companies in which I have invested know to whom to pay dividends?

It depends how the nominee accounts are organised. If they are pooled, everyone's shares sit in one account and your holding is identified in a separate record held by your stockbroker. Other nominee accounts designate the shareholdings with each client's name, and this may appear on the company's register.

Is my money safe in a nominee account?

Yes. It is a regulated activity, and so anyone offering nominee services must be authorised under the Financial Services Act. Your money must be ring-fenced from the nominee company's other business interests.

What if the whole group goes bankrupt?

You can claim on the Investors Compensation Scheme (see p.29).

I bought some shares mainly because they give holiday discounts as a shareholder perk. Will I still get these perks if I put the shares in a nominee account?

Some companies will not extend perks to investors in nominee accounts, but a few do. Check if yours is one and, if so, confirm to the company in which you have invested that you qualify for the perks, because it will be unlikely to have your name on the shareholder register.

Can I do anything to keep the perks from companies that don't pass them on?
Become a sponsored member of Crest. In that way, your name is still on the register and the perks come straight through to you.

Is it worth becoming a sponsored member of Crest just for the perks?
No. It is not.

tip

> **Many shares are traded through the Stock Exchange Electronic Trading System (SETS). Investors' orders to buy shares are electronically matched with orders to sell, and it is called an 'order-driven' system. Under the old system, a 'quote-driven' system which is still used for smaller shares, brokers quote both buying and selling prices for investors who want to deal and then find someone to buy or sell the shares.**

THE TAX POSITION WITH SHARES

- Income tax is payable on dividends, and that tax is deducted by the company before dividends are paid.
- Basic-rate taxpayers have no more tax to pay.
- Higher-rate taxpayers pay additional tax through their year-end tax return.
- Non-taxpayers cannot reclaim the tax credit.
- Capital gains tax is payable on profits when shares are sold.
- If you give shares away, note the share price on the day, published in the following day's newspapers, because the gift counts as a disposal for capital gains tax purposes.

tip

> WARNING: **Never ever take any notice of an unsolicited phone call urging you to buy a particular share.**

Gilts

Gilts are government debt. The government has three ways of raising money: by imposing taxes, by selling National Savings, and by borrowing.

When the government needs to borrow, it asks institutions and private investors to lend it money. In return for the loan, the government promises to pay a fixed rate of interest twice a year and to return the money in full on a set date a number of years in the future. These loans are British Government stock, also called 'gilt-edged' stock or 'gilts'. When you buy gilts, you are lending money to the government.

ask Margaret

How are gilts different from shares?

Shares are your stake in a company that you invest in; their value fluctuates with the company's performance and with investor demand. Gilts are debt and are guaranteed to be repaid in full on a certain date.

Are all gilts the same?

No. They can be:

- short-dated gilts, which mature within the next five years
- medium-dated gilts, which mature in something between 5 and 15 years' time
- long-dated gilts, which mature after 15 years
- undated gilts, which have no maturity date
- index-linked gilts, where capital growth and income are both linked to inflation.

Who provides gilts?

The government.

Who advises on which gilts to buy?

Stockbrokers and some IFAs.

Where can I buy gilts?

From the Bank of England when they are first issued, through stockbrokers, and at post offices through the Bank of England gilts' register.

How do I buy and sell gilts, and how much are they?

You can buy gilts when they are first issued, in units of £100, and hold them to maturity, when you will get £100 back from the government for each unit. But you do not have to keep them that long. You can sell them at any time through the stock market, when you might get £100 or you might get more, or less. If you buy through the stock market, you might pay a little more, or a bit less, than the £100 face value.

What happens at the end of the period?

The original £100 invested for each unit is returned, or 'redeemed', by the government at the same value – apart from index-linked gilts, where the amount you get back will have been increased above £100 in line with inflation.

How can I tell what rate of interest a gilt pays?

There is a nominal rate of interest, the 'coupon', which forms part of the gilt's title. But the 'yield' is a more accurate guide, and there are two ways of measuring this. The 'running' yield (also called the 'current' or 'interest' yield) is the return on investment as a percentage of the gilt's current price. The 'redemption' yield or 'yield to maturity' is the return you are likely to get on your investment each year, from the day you buy the gilt and assuming you hold it to maturity. As the price of a gilt goes down, the yield goes up – and vice versa.

Are gilts a safe investment?

Extremely safe, because the government guarantees both the rate of interest and to return £100 per unit on maturity. Between issue and maturity, you take the risk that you could sell the gilt for less than you paid.

How can I tell which gilt is best to buy?

You could ask a stockbroker but, if you want to make your own decision, it depends how long you want to keep the investment, whether you want income or growth, and what rate of tax you pay.

If you want high annual interest and are not worried about capital gains or losses, look for the highest running yield you can find for the length of time you want to invest. If you want to make a profit, go for a low-coupon gilt, trading at below £100, and take your profit through capital gains.

How can I check on gilt prices?

They are published each day in many newspapers' financial sections.

THE TAX POSITION WITH GILTS

- Income tax is payable on the interest received from a gilt.
- Interest is paid gross, although you can ask for it to be paid net. If you bought gilts before April 1998 through a stockbroker, interest was automatically paid net and you are still receiving it net unless you asked for it to be paid gross.
- Higher-rate taxpayers pay additional tax through their year-end tax return.
- No capital gains tax is payable, even when the gilt is sold for more than it cost.

4 Buying Investments

Life insurance as an investment

There is no logical reason to combine life insurance with investment. It started when policyholders enjoyed tax relief on the premiums; the habit stuck, and investment–insurance policies became unnecessarily complex. This murkiness was often used to disguise high charges and poor terms.

Insurance companies now have to disclose their charges, but you still need to know which questions to ask to make sure you are buying at a reasonable price an investment product you want.

For information about life insurance purely for protection, see Chapter 10.

ask Margaret **Who sells life insurance?**

Life insurance companies and friendly societies sell life insurance.

Where can I buy life insurance?

- direct from insurance companies or friendly societies, by phone or post

- through company salespeople
- from independent financial advisers
- by responding to mailshots
- by responding to newspaper advertisements
- through the Internet.

Who advises on which policy to buy?

Independent financial advisers, and company representatives from within their own company's range.

How do I pay for my life insurance?

You can buy life insurance by paying regular premiums to endowment or whole-life policies, or with one lump sum of money for single-premium policies (often called 'investment bonds').

How are life insurance premiums invested?

The money is invested in one of two ways, depending on the type of policy you buy: in a with-profits fund, which is a large, widespread, international fund; or in unit-linked funds, which are many separate funds, each one specialising in different parts of the world. You can choose which fund or funds you want.

Whatever type of life insurance policy or bond you buy, your money is invested in the stock market. Whenever you read that stock markets have gone up, or down, this ultimately changes the value of your insurance policy. Stock market movements affect unit-linked policies more than with-profits policies, where the returns are smoothed out over a number of years.

tip

> **Insurance policies 'mature' when they pay out, whether this is because they have reached the end of the agreed term or because the person whose life is insured has died.**

If life insurance pays up when I die, what is the point of using it for investment?

Some life insurance policies pay out only on death. Other types pay out after a set number of years, when, hopefully, you will still be alive.

How does life insurance differ from other forms of investment?

Insurance policies designed for investment always include at least a small amount of life insurance. If you die while investing, your estate gets more than you paid in premiums.

How much is paid out if I die prematurely?

That depends on which type of policy you buy, and how your premiums were divided between protection and investment. For with-profit endowment policies, typically used with mortgages, there is a guaranteed sum plus bonuses. Unit-linked endowment policies pay the amount by which the policy has grown, or the guaranteed sum if that is greater. Single-premium policies repay the value of the investment at the time, and often 1 per cent extra.

Do premiums go up as I get older?

With endowment policies, the premiums remain constant once you start a policy; premiums for whole-life policies can go up. However, the older you are when you start the policy, the more expensive the premiums will be.

Does my state of health affect the premiums for life insurance investments?

Your state of health and your age affect the terms you are offered.

Do I have to take a medical when I buy life insurance?

It is unlikely, unless you are buying a huge amount.

If I have an inherited illness, can I still buy insurance?

Insurance companies abide by a code of practice that dictates how they must treat genetic tests. See the final section in Chapter 10 for further details.

Can I change my mind after I've signed an application form for a life insurance policy?

You have 14 days in which to cancel, starting from the date you receive the cooling off notice from the insurance company.

Will I get all my money back if I pull out of the policy within 14 days?

With an endowment policy, you will get back the premiums you have paid so far. With a lump-sum policy, you might not get back as much as you paid if its value has fallen meanwhile.

What happens if I can't afford to keep paying the premiums?

Do not rush into making a decision. If you are suffering a short-term blip in your cash flow, check whether your policy has a waiver-of-premium clause that allows you to miss premiums for a few months without breaking the contract. Otherwise, see the section entitled 'Your options if you cannot afford to keep paying premiums or need the cash', (p.111).

> **tip**
>
> **When comparing quotations for life insurance policies, make sure you are looking at exactly the same type of policy, and also that the policies being compared run for the same number of years.**

Life insurance and tax

For 'qualifying policies', which are regular-premium policies that last for at least ten years or three-quarters of the original term, there is no tax on the proceeds, whether the policy matures at its set time or earlier because the policyholder dies.

For 'non-qualifying policies', which are usually single-premium policies, there is no capital gains tax and no income tax for basic-rate taxpayers, although higher-rate taxpayers might have to pay more when they cash in their policy. You can withdraw 5 per cent of your original investment in a single premium policy tax-free each year for 20 years.

> **tip**
>
> **There is no tax relief on life insurance premiums, unless you bought the policy before April 1984. But you can get tax relief if you buy term insurance as part of your personal pension.**

Endowment policies

Endowment policies pay a guaranteed minimum amount of money (the sum assured) plus bonuses, either on a set future date or when the person insured dies (if sooner).

Are endowment policies a good investment?

They can be, provided that you buy one for the right purpose. They are a long-term investment and so, if you fail to keep the policy going for its full term, it can be a poor investment.

How risky are endowment policies?

With-profit endowment policies are safer than unit-linked endowment policies (see p.109) because the insurer's actuary plans for the long term and tries to keep bonuses about the same each year, rather than reflecting what is happening on the stock market at that moment. The returns from unit-linked policies are more volatile, although you can choose whether you want a comparatively safe or a riskier fund.

tip

> **Actuaries are professionals who assess long-term financial risks. They set the premiums for life insurance and pensions.**

How long do endowment policies last?

You must hold an endowment policy for at least ten years to qualify for tax advantages, but beyond that the period of insurance can be as long or as short as you choose. Often, policies are bought over 25 years to match the term of a mortgage.

tip

> WARNING: **Beware of any salesperson who says you must surrender one endowment policy and buy another when you move house. Cashing in a policy gives you a poor return but gives the salesperson good commission. Instead, you should keep the existing policy (which is not tied to your home) and top it up with another if necessary.**

Are the charges the same for both types of endowment policy?

An insurance company's costs are much the same for all endowment policies, but they are recouped in different ways. The costs of with-profits policies are reclaimed by reducing the bonuses that would otherwise be paid; the costs of unitised policies are deducted from premiums and from the value of the money in the fund.

WITH-PROFITS ENDOWMENT POLICIES

'With-profits' means that a policy earns a share of the insurance company's profits from a large, well spread, investment fund. The money is mainly put into shares worldwide, but it also goes into gilts, bonds and sometimes commercial property.

ask Margaret

How do with-profits endowment policies work?

You pay regular premiums for a set number of years; at the end of the period, or when you die if sooner, the policy pays out. There are three elements to the return: a guaranteed amount of money, called the 'sum assured', that was known from the start; annual bonuses that have been added to the policy each year; and, usually, a final, or terminal, bonus that is paid only when the policy matures.

How much will the bonuses be?

You will not know before you buy the policy how much the bonuses are going to be. Annual bonuses are declared at the beginning of each year, as a percentage of the amount guaranteed by the policy. Terminal bonuses are declared each year but apply only to the policies maturing in the coming 12 months.

Do bonuses always stay the same?

No. Historically, when the stock market did well for a long time, insurance companies paid slightly higher bonuses each year; but, in recent years when the market has slowed down, companies have had to reduce bonus rates.

tip

> **WARNING: With such a long-term investment, you want to be confident that the insurance company will pay good levels of bonus and still be around to pay you at maturity. You should choose a financially strong insurance company; ask a financial adviser which are the best.**

How does the size of a terminal bonus compare with an annual bonus?

This varies from company to company. Some pay comparatively small annual bonuses and pay as much again in the final bonus; others pay larger annual bonuses.

Which is preferable, annual or terminal bonuses?

Annual bonuses have the advantage that, once they have been added to your policy, you know you will get the money. You won't know the size of the terminal bonus until the time arrives.

tip

> **The trend nowadays is for insurance companies to hold back on the annual bonuses and pay more in the terminal bonus. This is safer for the insurance companies but riskier for policyholders, because up to half the total payout can hang on stock market performance in the policy's last few years.**

Is there any risk that an endowment policy might not pay bonuses in any year?

It is theoretically possible, because there are no rules to say they must pay bonuses. But in practice a company that missed an annual bonus would already be in a dire financial state and have attracted the attention of the regulator.

Am I guaranteed to get what the insurance company promises?

You are guaranteed the sum assured, and the annual bonuses as they are added; these are paid in full on death or at the end of the term. If you die before the end of the term, you might get a reduced terminal bonus.

Can I be sure that a with-profits endowment policy will pay off my mortgage?

All mortgage endowment policies guarantee to pay off the loan if you die while still paying the mortgage. Most will produce enough if you survive until the loan is due to be repaid, but some low-cost endowment mortgages might not produce enough. See also Chapter 6 on Mortgages.

UNIT-LINKED ENDOWMENT POLICIES

Unit-linked policies serve the same purpose as with-profits policies but the premiums are invested differently. Instead of going into the large with-profits fund, your money goes into one, or several, unit-linked funds investing in specific parts of the world; you choose which you want. As the funds are more narrowly invested than a with-profits fund, unit-linked policies are riskier – although the better-performing ones can produce higher returns.

UNITISED WITH-PROFITS ENDOWMENT POLICIES

Confusingly, many insurance companies have replaced their traditional with-profits policies with unitised with-profits policies. These combine elements from both with-profits policies and unit-linked policies. The policies earn bonuses, but the amount paid on maturity is not guaranteed; bonuses are reinvested each year but in the form of additional units.

tip

> **Endowment policies are a comparatively expensive form of life insurance.**

QUESTIONS TO ASK A SALESPERSON OR ADVISER BEFORE BUYING AN ENDOWMENT POLICY

get the facts

- How much has the insurance company paid in bonuses in each of the past ten years?
- How does this compare with other companies? (*The gap between the best and worst performers is considerable so you must make comparisons or ask a financial adviser for recommendations.*)
- Is the company financially strong? (*Financial advisers can obtain performance tables showing the company's comparative strength.*)
- If I buy direct from the company, without taking advice, will the company still deduct the salesperson's commission?
- How much will I get if I cash in the policy early?
- How much terminal bonus will I get if I die early?

QUESTIONS YOU HAVE TO ANSWER FOR YOURSELF BEFORE BUYING ENDOWMENT LIFE INSURANCE

ask yourself

- Which gender are you?
- How old are you?
- Do you smoke? (*Premiums are often higher if you do.*)
- What is your state of health?
- What is your occupation? (*A dangerous occupation can make premiums more expensive.*)
- Do you want a with-profits or unit-linked policy?
- What is your purpose for investing in this type of product? (*You need to be able to answer this so that your adviser can check that you are buying the right type of policy.*)

YOUR OPTIONS IF YOU CAN'T AFFORD TO KEEP PAYING PREMIUMS OR NEED THE CASH

You can cash the policy in, which is known as 'surrendering' the policy. This is the worst option because most of the selling costs are deducted in the first few years; if you surrender when the policy has been running only a couple of years, you could get nothing and, even after a few years, you might get back less than you have paid in premiums. You also then have no life insurance.

You can have the policy made 'paid-up'. This means that you pay no more premiums but leave the money where it is. The investment should continue to grow, but the insurance company deducts the cost of premiums for life insurance from your investment. This could use up all the money you have invested, in which case when the policy comes to an end, you have no investment and no life insurance.

You can borrow money from the insurance company against the policy. You can borrow only if the policy has been going for several years and the insurance company agrees, and you should note that you cannot borrow against a policy that you are using to repay your mortgage. Interest rates that the insurance companies charge, change slowly, and sometimes they are competitive but at other times not. If you borrow against the policy, you can repay the loan at any time or use the proceeds when the policy matures.

You can sell the policy to another investor, provided that you have a with-profits policy. You should get more than you would by surrendering. You can get information through a financial adviser and sell through a specialist broker or auctioneer. See the questions on p.112 on investing in traded endowment policies.

Questions to ask the insurance company if you can no longer afford the premiums

get the facts

- How much is the surrender value?
- What would the policy be worth if I have it made paid-up?
- What are the likely future charges if I have the policy made paid-up?
- Can I borrow against this policy?
- If so, how much can I borrow?
- What is the rate of interest and when did the interest rate last change?

Traded endowment policies

Traded endowment policies are provided by people who want to sell endowment policies that they previously bought and that they would otherwise surrender (for less money) to the insurance company. Traded endowment policies are also called 'second-hand endowment policies'.

ask Margaret

Where can I buy traded endowment policies?

You can buy traded endowment policies through a specialist auctioneer or specialist brokers known as 'market makers'.

As the original policyholders no longer want to continue with them, is there something wrong with these policies?

No. Sometimes policyholders simply cannot afford to keep paying the premiums, or they urgently need the cash; they hope to get more money from selling the policies to other people as an investment than from surrendering them to the insurance companies. The market for second-hand policies deals only in with-profit endowment, and sometimes whole-life, policies sold by reputable insurance companies.

How do traded endowment policies work?

As the investor, you pay a lump sum to buy the policy second-hand and then start paying the remaining premiums until the policy matures.

When does the policy mature?

Either when the original person insured dies or the endowment policy completes its set number of years.

How will I know if the first policyholder dies?

That person should have nominated two people to inform the insurance company.

Will the insurance company pay up if the person had died some years earlier and I didn't find out?

Yes. You will get the value of the policy at the time the person died, plus interest on the money between then and the date you claimed. Any premiums you paid since the person died will be returned with interest.

If I bought a policy, and the original policyholder was murdered, would I be a suspect?

Assuming you didn't do it, no.

Will a second-hand policy pay out if I die?

No. Your life has nothing to do with it.

What happens if I die before the policy matures?

When you die owning a traded endowment, the policy forms part of your estate. Its current surrender value is added to your estate, unless you had it written in trust (see p.123). You can bequeath it to a beneficiary, or your executors can sell it on again in the second-hand market.

What sort of life insurance policy can I buy in the second-hand market?

Only with-profits endowment or whole-life policies that have run for at least eight years with a minimum surrender value of about £2,000.

How much are second-hand policies likely to cost?

From around £2,000 to tens of thousands of pounds. The cost will be more than the surrender value plus the policyholder's cost of selling; otherwise there is no point in the policyholder selling.

How will I know how much is reasonable to pay?

You want the purchase price plus remaining premiums to total less than you will receive on maturity. A specialist auctioneer can give you guidance. Brokers issue regular sales lists showing the policies they have for sale, including the purchase price. IFAs can also advise on an appropriate amount, but they will probably get their information from a specialist in the business.

How can I tell how much I will get on maturity?

You can't, and that is where risk comes in. You know you will get bonuses that have already been declared, but future bonuses are unknown and might not be so good.

Do I have to pay tax when I receive the proceeds of the second-hand policy?

Yes. Unlike original policyholders, you are subject to capital gains tax on the profit you make, assuming it is a qualifying policy (as most second-hand policies are). With non-qualifying policies, higher-rate taxpayers may have to pay income tax.

Can I lose money from buying a traded endowment policy?
Yes. If bonus rates fall, you could find that the price you paid, plus the ongoing premiums, is more than the amount you eventually receive.

Where can I complain if that happens?
Like any investment, you have no grounds for complaint if its value falls. That is the risk you take when you purchase it.

What protection do I have if anything else goes wrong?
The business itself is not regulated under the Financial Services Act but, to deal with the public, brokers must be regulated.

QUESTIONS TO ASK A BROKER BEFORE BUYING A SECOND-HAND ENDOWMENT POLICY

get the facts

- Is the policy with a secure, well known life insurance company?
- What is the insurance company's record for paying bonuses in the past?
- What is the outlook for bonuses from this company?
- Who owns the insurance company?
- What are the charges for buying this policy? (*Usually these are built in to the price you pay.*)
- Do the charges included in the price also include the legal fees?
- Are you, as a financial adviser, regulated under the Financial Services Act? (*Brokers have to be to deal with the public.*)

Whole-life insurance policies

Whole-life insurance policies pay out when you die, whenever that is; they can be with-profit or unit-linked.

ask Margaret

Do I have to keep paying premiums for the rest of my life?
This varies with insurers. Some policies let you stop contributing, yet keep the policy going, when you reach 70, 80 or 85.

A 'whole life' is a long time, and my circumstances will almost certainly

change. Am I really committed to keep paying for years?

You are. But some companies sell flexible whole-life policies that allow you to make changes: you can insure for a larger, or smaller, sum and the premiums are adjusted accordingly.

How expensive is whole-life insurance?

Whole-life insurance is more expensive than term insurance but cheaper than endowments. 'Flexible' whole-life insurance is cheaper still: policyholders choose how much of their premiums go towards investment and how much to protection; the premiums start low but they can be increased after a few years.

tip

> WARNING: **Protection is more expensive as you get older and insurers pay the extra by taking money from the investment side. If you chose maximum protection under a flexible whole-life policy, there is unlikely to be enough built up in the investment side of the policy and after, say, ten years you will have to pay sharply higher premiums.**

Will the premiums go up if I become ill?

No, and this is the advantage of whole-life insurance. Premiums can rise when you are older but not because of your state of health.

What is the purpose of a whole-life policy, then?

Mostly people buy whole-life policies to pay their inheritance tax bill, so that beneficiaries can inherit the estate with tax paid; or they can use the proceeds to pay for funeral expenses. Do not buy whole-life insurance to repay a mortgage.

QUESTIONS TO ASK A SALESPERSON BEFORE BUYING WHOLE-LIFE INSURANCE

get the facts

- Is this a flexible whole-life policy?
- If so, exactly what is flexible about it?
- How much are the premiums?
- Will the premiums rise at any point? (*If the salesperson says premiums can rise, interpret this as saying that they will rise.*)
- How much will the policy pay out?
- How much will I get if I cash in the policy after ten years?
- Does there come a time when I can stop paying premiums?

Single-premium insurance bonds

Single-premium insurance bonds are whole-life insurance policies that you buy with a one-off lump-sum payment. They can be with-profits or unit-linked. They come under various names:

- with-profit bonds
- unit-linked bonds
- guaranteed growth bonds
- guaranteed income bonds.

ask Margaret

Who provides single-premium insurance bonds?

Single-premium insurance bonds are provided by insurance companies, foreign insurance companies and friendly societies. They can be bought through insurance company salespeople or independent financial advisers.

How long do single-premium policies last?

For as long as you want to keep them. There are no restrictions on the minimum or maximum term, but the longer you keep them the more money they are likely to earn you.

What return do I get from single-premium insurance bonds?

With-profits bonds earn bonuses, which are paid out when you cash in the policy; unit-linked bonds pay whatever your units are worth when you cash them in. Guaranteed bonds work differently (see p.119).

tip

> **Before buying a single-premium insurance bond, compare it with an ISA, which is more flexible.**

As a single-premium insurance bond is a life insurance policy, what is paid out when I die?

Usually 101 per cent of the value at that time.

Can I make withdrawals without cashing in the whole policy?

The tax rules allow you to take, every year without paying tax, up to 5 per cent of the amount you originally invested. This is cumulative and so, if you took nothing for ten years, you could then withdraw 50 per cent without paying tax.

Do I have to pay tax later?

Only if you are a higher-rate taxpayer when you cash in the policy.

tip

> **WARNING: The proceeds from cashing in a single-premium policy count as income. If you receive the age-related tax allowance, this income could mean you pay more tax.**
>
> **Also, be careful about how much you withdraw. Although you are allowed to take out 5 per cent each year without paying tax, if the policy earns less than 5 per cent that year, you will be cashing in some of your capital.**

WITH-PROFITS BONDS

ask Margaret

What is the difference between a with-profits endowment policy and a with-profits bond?

With both, your premiums are invested in the insurance company's with-profits fund and earn annual, and sometimes terminal, bonuses. With-profits endowment policies pay out on a set date, at least 10 years ahead and maybe 25 years. With-profits bonds can be held for any length of time, with no minimum, although you get poor value if you cash them in too early.

tip

> **WARNING: Salespeople have been warned by their regulator not to compare with-profits bonds with building society savings accounts. With-profits bonds can pay higher income than savings accounts, but the value of the capital fluctuates, which does not happen in building society accounts.**

What are the charges for with-profit bonds?

- an initial charge, which varies from nothing to 5 per cent
- possibly an annual charge
- possibly an early-surrender penalty during the first five years that the investment is held, amounting to around 5 per cent in the first year and reducing to 1 per cent in the fifth
- possibly a 'market-value adjustment' (MVA), which entitles insurance companies to reduce the value of annual bonuses already declared. It is rarely applied and insurers do so only if the stock market is depressed and large numbers of policyholders want to cancel at the same time. Insurers argue that this protects the value of investments

for customers who hold on to their policies. Usually, insurance companies agree not to apply the MVA on certain anniversaries.

tip

> Some insurance companies say they invest, say, 103 per cent of your contribution (the allocation rate) – in other words, they invest more than you hand over. Not surprisingly, there is a snag. They might charge an initial fee of 5 per cent of your money: so you give them 5 per cent and they give you 3 per cent back.

Questions to ask a salesperson or adviser before buying a with-profits bond

get the facts

- What proportion of the bonus is paid with the terminal bonus?
- Is there an early surrender penalty?
- Could a market value adjustment be applied?
- Has a market value adjustment ever been applied?
- Are you confident this is a financially secure insurance company?
- How much will I get if I have to cash in the bond early?
- What is this company's bonus record for with-profits bonds?

UNIT-LINKED BONDS

Unit-linked bonds are similar to with-profits bonds, but premiums are invested in one or more chosen unit-linked funds rather than in the with-profits fund.

ask Margaret

How can I decide which unit-linked fund is best?
You will not know at the outset which fund will perform best. You can take guidance from a financial adviser or look for recommendations in newspaper and magazine articles.

Do I have to stick with the first fund I choose?
No. You can switch around from time to time.

GUARANTEED INCOME BONDS

Guaranteed income bonds are investments that pay a guaranteed rate of interest for a set number of years.

ask Margaret

What happens at the end of the set period of years?

You are guaranteed to get back the money you originally invested or, with some bonds, a proportion of the money you originally invested plus interest.

How is the interest paid?

Interest is paid net of tax – and non-taxpayers cannot claim it back.

Do higher-rate taxpayers pay additional income tax?

Yes, but only when they cash in the policy and only if they are higher-rate payers in that particular tax year.

Is there capital gains tax to pay?

No. All returns on this type of investment are treated as income.

Who sells guaranteed income bonds?

Insurance companies, but usually newer and sometimes foreign companies because they have tax advantages that enable them to pay higher rates than traditional insurers.

Do guaranteed income bonds pay high rates of interest?

Not necessarily. There might be times when their rates are good and, when rates are falling, you can lock in to a good rate of interest for a period. Mostly you have the security of knowing how much you will earn for a few years ahead.

If I buy from a new insurance company, or a foreign one, how safe is my money?

Totally safe: your investment is protected by the Policyholders Protection Scheme (see p.29).

Will I earn more for keeping my money tied up longer?

Not necessarily; it depends on the insurance company's view of long-term interest rates, which could be coming down.

How much will the bond pay out if I die while investing?
Probably 101 per cent of the premium you paid.

What are the charges for buying this type of investment?
They are built into the interest you earn, and so there is nothing more to pay.

GUARANTEED GROWTH BONDS

Guaranteed growth bonds are similar to guaranteed income bonds: they pay out interest and there is no capital growth involved. No interest is paid out until the bond matures, and that interest is subject to income tax only, paid net, with non-taxpayers unable to reclaim the tax paid.

Questions to ask a salesperson or adviser before buying guaranteed income or growth bonds

get the facts

- What is the minimum amount I must invest?
- How long is my money tied up for? (*You can choose between one and ten years, although few companies offer the whole range of years.*)
- What is the rate of interest?
- Is the interest higher if I invest for longer, or less, time?
- Is interest paid annually or monthly?

tip

> WARNING: **Do not confuse guaranteed income and growth bonds with guaranteed equity bonds (for which, see p.88 in Chapter 3).**

DISTRIBUTION BONDS

Distribution bonds are a comparatively safe investment, where your money is invested in shares, gilts, property and cash, and provide capital growth and good income. All income earned from the investments in the portfolio is kept separate from capital and paid out to investors. Investors can withdraw income, paid monthly if they choose, knowing that this will not eat into their capital.

ask Margaret

Where does life insurance come in?

Distribution bonds are single-premium life insurance policies, although the insurance is minimal. In each tax year you can withdraw up to 5 per cent of the amount you invest without paying tax at that point, (see p.116).

If the bond earns more than 5 per cent, can I still withdraw only 5 per cent?

You can withdraw however much the fund earns but, if this is more than 5 per cent, higher-rate taxpayers have to pay tax on the balance in that year's tax return.

Is there any option about taking income from a distribution bond?

You can reinvest the income but, if this is your plan, you might do better with a different type of investment because distribution bonds aim for high income; the portfolio is invested conservatively so the potential for capital growth is moderate.

Questions to ask a salesperson or adviser before buying a distribution bond

get the facts

- How much income does this distribution bond pay? (*The highest income is not necessarily best, because higher income involves more risk. Compare several bonds to get an idea of the going rates.*)
- What are the management charges? (*There might be a buying charge, an annual fee and occasionally a penalty for cancelling the policy within five years.*)
- What is the past performance of the bond?
- Where is the portfolio invested? (*The more that there is in shares, the higher the risk.*)

Friendly society policies

Friendly societies' products include one that only they are allowed to sell – a special tax-exempt policy that is tax-free. It is a savings policy – either with-profits or unit-linked – and has a small amount of life insurance protection.

How does this tax-exempt policy differ from ordinary life insurance, where there is no tax on the proceeds either?

The friendly society itself pays no tax, and so more of your money is used for investing.

Is the tax-exempt policy worth buying?

It is a close decision. The investment is tax-free, but you can invest only a few hundred pounds each year and each person can hold only one policy at a time. The charges are high for running such small accounts.

Can I buy the special friendly society policy for children?

You can buy them for as many children as you like, in the child's name, although they can hold only one each.

Are friendly societies' products safe investments?

They are as safe as any insurance-linked investment. Your money is invested in shares, bonds and gilts.

How long is my money tied up?

For at least ten years to qualify for the tax-free status. If you need to cash in the policy early, you could get back less than you paid in premiums.

Can I change my mind once I have signed the application form?

Yes, during the 'cooling off' period. You have 14 days from receiving the cancellation notice from the friendly society in which you can pull out.

QUESTIONS TO ASK BEFORE BUYING FRIENDLY SOCIETY LIFE INSURANCE

get the facts

- Is this a tax-free policy?
- What are the charges that apply?
- What are the penalties if I can't afford to keep the policy going?
- How much are the policies that are maturing now paying out?

Minimising inheritance tax on life insurance proceeds

It is possible to minimise inheritance tax by getting your life insurance policies 'written in trust'. This is a simple procedure.

ask Margaret

What does getting a policy 'written in trust' mean?

You tell the insurance company whom you want to receive the proceeds when you die.

Why should I get a life insurance policy written in trust?

Without a trust, when you die the money from your life insurance policy goes into your estate and, if your estate is large enough, there is inheritance tax to pay. In contrast, with a trust the money goes directly to your beneficiaries. They get it faster because they do not have to wait for probate to be granted and, as the proceeds do not go into your estate, you reduce any inheritance tax due.

How can I get my life insurance policies written in trust?

Ask your insurance company for a form. You nominate the beneficiaries, sign the form and return it.

Do I have to do this when I buy the policy, or can I do it later if I didn't realise it was an option when I bought the policy?

You can do it at any time, but clearly it is better to do it as soon as possible.

How much does it cost to get a policy written in trust?

Nothing.

Can I change my mind about whom I want to have the money after I've written a policy in trust?

Yes, you just need to fill out a replacement form.

Can all life insurance policies be written in trust?

All except those you have used as security for a debt. So you cannot write in trust a policy connected with a mortgage.

5 Pensions

Questions to ask when planning for retirement

A pension is your largest and most important investment; on retirement it should be worth more money than most people have tied up in a house. To afford a retirement income of £12,000 a year from a pension, you need to have saved roughly £200,000 – and that is spare money, aside from the value of your home.

The precise figures depend on the prospects for the economy, your age, gender and the type of pension you want. That sounds complicated enough, but it is only one aspect of a subject that everyone finds confusing.

As a result, many people put off making decisions about pensions – and the pensions mis-selling scandal has given them another excuse. But you will regret doing nothing about providing for your retirement, or even delaying starting a pension, because the message from the government is clear: everyone has to provide for themselves. You cannot rely on the state for a retirement income, and few workers have a job for life to provide a pension.

Pensions became a popular issue only when it was discovered, after his death, that Robert Maxwell had pilfered his employees' funds. The Maxwell fiasco uncovered great gaps in pension fund protection; he was not the first employer to embezzle the company pension fund, and yet few people had noticed that there was no compensation when workers lost out. That has now changed, and the scene is still shifting as the government continues to reform pension provision – with the overall aim of pushing people into buying their own pensions.

Your pension can come from three different sources: the state pension, a company pension, and a personal pension.

Your contributions towards company pensions and personal pensions are invested in the stock market to make money to pay out when you retire. Every time you hear that the stock market has crashed – or boomed – it affects your pension. So never think you have no interest in what happens on the stock market. The largest investment you possess depends on it.

The state pension

ask Margaret

What do I get from a state pension?
You get a basic pension, based on your National Insurance contributions during your working life, and possibly a state earnings-related pension, also called 'additional pension', if you contributed to SERPS. Some people get a minuscule amount from the disbanded graduated pension scheme. Everyone gets a derisory extra amount once they turn 80.

tip

> **SERPS is being replaced by a new additional pension, being phased in from 2002 at the earliest.**

How many National Insurance contributions do I have to make to earn the basic state pension?
For the full basic state pension, you must pay, or be credited with, National Insurance contributions for a whole year covering 90 per cent of your working life.

How long is a 'working life'?

For men, 49 years and, for women, 44 years at present. This rises to 49 for women when the state retirement ages are equalised in 2020. So, given the 90 per cent rule, men need to contribute for at least 44 years and women, at present, for 39 years but rising to 44 years.

tip

> **At present, the official retirement age is 60 for women and 65 for men, but the rules are changing. Later retirement for women is being phased in from 2010 and first affects women born after April 5 1950. Women born after March 6 1955 will have to wait until they are 65 for a state pension.**

How much basic state pension will I get if I make fewer National Insurance contributions than the maximum?

The pension is scaled down. The minimum paid is one-quarter of the basic state pension for men with 11 years' contributions and, at present, women with ten years'. The rules are different for people born before July 5 1932; check with your local Benefits Agency if you fall in that category.

If I haven't made enough National Insurance contributions through my life, can I make them up later to qualify for a full state pension?

First check whether you are entitled to credits for any of those periods. If not, you may be able to pay voluntary contributions for some years.

What happens if I can't pay National Insurance contributions because I'm unemployed?

If you are claiming benefits, you get National Insurance credits, which count towards the state pension.

Do I get the same state pension if I'm self-employed?

You will get the basic state pension, assuming you've paid the right number of National Insurance contributions. But you won't get any additional pension, unless you contributed during previous employment.

What happens during the years I spend looking after my children, and parents?

You may receive Home Responsibilities Protection, which protects your right to a basic state pension. And a married woman can claim a basic state pension on her husband's contribution record, although she cannot claim this until her husband is taking his state pension which, if he delays it, means waiting until he is older than 65. (See also the section on Divorce on p.153.)

Do I have to take the state pension at the official retirement age?

You can delay it for up to five years and, for each year that you wait, your pension rises by about 7.5 per cent. However, this sounds more attractive than it is. If, for example, you put off the pension for one year, you need to receive the higher pension for around 13 years to get back the money forgone in that one year.

tip

> Twenty years ago, the basic state pension equalled 20 per cent of average earnings; today it is 15 per cent; by 2030, when today's 30-year-olds retire, it will be worth around 9 per cent or, in today's terms, about £30 a week.

How do I claim the state pension?

The DSS should contact you about four months before you reach the official retirement age. If you don't hear anything, ask your local Social Security office for claim form BR1.

What is SERPS?

It is a top-up to the basic state pension for employees, based on earnings.

How is the new additional pension different from SERPS?

It is designed to give more to the lower-paid and middle earners, and to carers and the long-term disabled with broken work records. But it will pay a flat-rate pension, whereas with SERPS the pension is earnings-related.

How do I know if I'm in SERPS?

Unless you belong to a contracted-out company pension scheme or have taken out an 'appropriate personal pension', and if you pay full-rate National Insurance contributions, you will automatically be in SERPS. People outside SERPS get a rebate on their National Insurance contributions. Ask your pensions department at work.

What is the National Insurance rebate?

When you are contracted out, and therefore not paying into SERPS, you and your employer pay lower National Insurance contributions. If you want to put the money saved into a personal pension, you can take it as a rebate. However, be warned that rebate-only personal pensions are small, and they will not produce nearly enough money to live on in retirement.

Can I stay in SERPS if my employer has contracted out?

You could, by leaving the company scheme, but the benefits are not worth it.

Should I contract out of SERPS or stay in?

It depends on your age and how much you earn. Broadly, younger and middle-aged people probably do better to contract out and take out a personal pension, while older people and low-paid workers are better in SERPS. Take financial advice before acting.

If I come out of SERPS while I'm young, can I go back in again when I'm older?

You can, but as the rebates are higher for older people you might as well stay out of SERPS. Check your individual circumstance at the time with a financial adviser or the insurance company providing your personal pension.

Can I claim the state pension if I retire abroad?

Yes, but in some countries, including Canada and Australia, the pension never rises because you are not allowed to get the annual increases.

tip

> **You can pick up leaflets about the state pension at your local Social Security office. Start with leaflet RM1,** *Retirement***, which is a guide to benefits for people who are retiring or have already retired.**

Company pensions

There are two different types of company pension available: the 'final salary' scheme, and the 'money purchase' scheme.

In a final salary scheme, your employer guarantees the amount of pension you will receive, regardless of how much money you paid in and how the pension fund investments have performed. It is also called a 'defined benefit' pension. In a money purchase scheme, the value of your pension depends on how much you and your employer have contributed and how well the investments in your pension fund have grown. It is also known as 'defined contribution' and is the way that most new company pensions are set up.

ask Margaret

Who provides company pensions?

Company pensions are provided by insurance companies and investment firms.

Where can I find out about company pensions?

You can find out about them at your workplace. Ask the trustees of the pension scheme or, if you cannot find them, the human resources department.

Which company pension scheme should I choose?

In many jobs, you have no choice but to accept the type of scheme your employer uses. If your employer offers a choice, an important element – and perhaps the deciding factor – is whether the employer contributes the same amount to both. If that is not the case, pick the scheme that gets the bigger contribution from the employer.

tip

> **Occupational pension and company pension mean the same.**

How does a final salary scheme work?

When you retire, instead of your employer paying your wages, the pension scheme pays you a pension each month, but less than you were earning before.

How much smaller than my salary is the pension likely to be?

You will get one-sixtieth, or one-eightieth depending on the scheme rules, of the salary you earned just before you retired, multiplied by the number of years you belonged to the scheme.

What is the maximum company pension I can earn?

Inland Revenue limits on tax relief mean that you can retire on no more than two-thirds of your salary. Usually you need to belong to the scheme for 40 years to achieve this (on the sixtieths basis); if you had an exceptionally generous employer, it is possible to earn a two-thirds pension after 20 years.

What is the advantage of a company pension?

Your employer might pay for life insurance and, assuming you stay with the same employer, you will almost certainly end up with a bigger pension because the employer pays the administration charges and contributes to your pension, perhaps paying in more than you do. If it is a final salary scheme, the employer guarantees your pension.

Can I be forced to join my employer's company scheme?

No.

Can I start in the company scheme and then switch to a personal pension?

Yes. Employers cannot prevent your leaving the company scheme, but they will probably stop contributing to your pension even though they could continue paying.

I'm starting a new job that provides a company pension but I'm already contributing to a personal pension. What should I do?

You are not allowed to contribute to both a company pension and a personal pension at the same time for the same job, and so you have to choose one or the other.

What happens to my pension if my employer is taken over?

The new owner might keep your pension fund running separately, or it might amalgamate it into its own scheme.

tip

WARNING: **Keep a close watch on the trustees if your company is being taken over; it will take ages to sort out, but you want to make sure they handle the negotiations in your very best interests. The Occupational Pensions Advisory Service (OPAS, whose address is given in the Appendix to this book) has a useful booklet on this subject.**

What happens to my pension if my employer goes out of business?

If your employer ceases trading, the company pension scheme has to be wound up. It might tick over with the existing members until the last one has died, or it can pass the fund over to an insurance company to run.

tip

WARNING: **Sometimes, when companies get into financial difficulties, the directors stop forwarding employees' National Insurance contributions to the DSS, even though this is illegal. If it happens, your National Insurance record is protected – but it is better to avoid the problem in the first place. If you suspect your company is in trouble, make sure that the trustees are watching closely what is happening.**

How can I tell if a company pension scheme is any good?

Look at the benefits and, crucially, ask how much your employer pays into the scheme from its own resources. To retire on a pension that maintains your standard of living, you and your employer between you need to contribute between 17 per cent and 19 per cent of your salary throughout your working life. Often employers contribute only 5 per cent.

Do I have any choice about how much I pay into a company pension?

Quite often, no. The pension fund rules set down the percentage of salary that everyone pays, although perhaps not with group personal pensions. If you want to pay in more, see Additional Voluntary Contributions (AVCs), on pp.134–6.

What if I can't afford to pay as much as the scheme says I should?

It is worth making the effort because of the advantages over a personal pension: if you contribute just a small amount to a personal pension, the charges are disproportionately expensive and you will almost certainly lose your employer's contribution. If you are tempted to leave a company pension scheme to save money, you might forego a widows' or widowers' pension. You should not cut back on a widows' pension if you want your partner to have an income after you die.

Once I've retired, what increases will I get to my pension?

By law, income from a company pension must rise each year by the rate of inflation, but only up to a maximum of 5 per cent. Employers can voluntarily pay more, but this is unlikely – apart from public service pensions which are totally index-linked.

tip | **You can use AVCs to buy an annuity that provides higher increases than your main pension. See the questions on annuities on p.144.**

Can I keep my pension with an ex-employer after I've left the company?

Yes. When you eventually claim your pension, it should rise each year by the rate of inflation up to a maximum of 5 per cent on at least some of your contributions.

If I resign, after contributing to a company pension, will I get my money back?

You can claim the money back only if you have been in the scheme for less than two years. Otherwise, you can leave it with your ex-employer or transfer the money to another pension scheme.

Do I have to take the company pension immediately I retire?

Your employer can insist on it.

If I retire abroad, will I still get my pension paid ?

Yes, and you will get all the increases due to you. But it will arrive in sterling, and so you will have to pay to convert it to the local currency, which is expensive.

If I die before I have a chance to draw my pension, what happens to the money?

It depends on the scheme rules, but usually a lump sum and a pension are paid to your spouse; or to your children as long as they are financially dependent.

Who gets the money if I have no dependants?

You can leave a note with the trustees nominating who you want to receive it, but the trustees are not obliged to comply with your wishes.

Can I ask for the money to go to a new partner if I am still married but no longer living with my spouse?

The trustees might refuse, particularly if you still have dependent children. You can explain your reason for cutting them out of your pension in the instructions you leave with the trustees.

Who are 'the trustees'?

The trustees are the group of people – who can include the employer, employees, retired employees or an outsider with specialist pension knowledge – who are responsible for making sure the pension scheme is properly run, in the beneficiaries' interests, and that the person investing the pension money is doing a good job.

What information do I get about my company pension scheme?

A copy of the rules, statements at least once a year showing how much you have contributed and what it is worth, the accounts, and a trustees' report. These may appear tedious documents, but they are important and you should make the effort to read them. If there is anything you cannot understand, ask the trustees to explain.

What can I do if I'm not happy about the way the company pension scheme is being run?

Cross-question the trustees; even stand for election as a trustee yourself.

What can I do if my employer doesn't provide a company pension?

Check whether your union has an industry-wide scheme; or buy a personal pension.

QUESTIONS TO ASK THE TRUSTEES ABOUT A COMPANY PENSION

get the facts

- Can I join the company pension scheme? (*Employers cannot discriminate against any members of staff on grounds of gender or race. But they can refuse to allow into the pension scheme part-timers, workers under a certain age, and workers who have not yet been with the company for a minimum period of time.*)

tip

> **If part-timers are not allowed into the pension scheme but most are the same gender (women working in a supermarket, or men working on a computer helpline, for example), you could claim that refusing to allow them to join the company pension scheme amounts to sex discrimination.**

- Does the employer provide life insurance?
- Does the firm run an Additional Voluntary Contributions scheme? (*All employers must offer one.*)
- If I leave the company and keep my pension there, are there ongoing charges to pay? (*If you leave a company, also make sure the pension scheme trustees always have your current address.*)

Questions about a final salary pension scheme

get the facts

- How much will I contribute to the pension? (*Around 5 per cent of your salary is usual.*)
- How much will the employer pay in?
- At what age may I retire? (*The company's retirement age must be the same for men and women, but it will not necessarily be the same as the state retirement age.*)
- Is the pension paid based on overtime and bonuses as well as basic salary? (*It can be but this is unusual.*)
- Will I get a lump sum at retirement? (*Almost certainly yes – and it will be tax-free.*)

- Will my family get anything if I die before retiring? (*They should get 'death in service' benefit, around four times your salary as a lump sum, plus a pension.*)
- What is the trustees' attitude to giving a pension to my partner when I die if we are not married? (*Unmarried partners have no right to share your pension, but the trustees can allow it.*)
- Will I be paid a full pension if I have to retire early through ill health? (*Some schemes provide an 'ill health pension', so that you can get as large a pension as if you had continued with the company up to retirement age.*)

Questions about group money purchase schemes

get the facts

- Who invests the pension fund money? (*It should be an investment management company with a good record.*)
- Who pays the charges for managing the fund? (*It should be the employer.*)
- Is there a penalty if I transfer my pension fund to another employer? (*There usually is.*)

tip

> **As a member of a company pension scheme, you have a right to information about the scheme, and within a certain period of time. Exercise that right. Frightening as it sounds, ask to see the triennial actuarial valuation, which shows how the pension scheme is shaping up. If the scheme is in deficit, and your employer is struggling, it could be a signal to leave the scheme. If you want help understanding it, contact OPAS (address in the Appendix); it makes no charge.**

Additional Voluntary Contributions (AVCs) and Free-standing Additional Voluntary Contributions (FSAVCs)

AVCs are a supplementary pension, through an insurance company, which your employer must make available if the staff request it. You can choose whether or not to subscribe. AVCs have the same tax relief as pension contributions.

AVCs are sold by insurance companies, unit trust groups, investment trust groups, banks and friendly societies.

Where can I buy AVCs?

AVCs are provided by your employer. FSAVCs can be bought direct from the providers listed above, as well as through financial advisers.

Who buys AVCs?

The people in company pension schemes who want to pay more into their pension than the main company scheme allows. You do not need an AVC if your employer provides a group personal pension because you can choose to pay higher contributions anyway.

Is my money locked up, as with my main pension?

Yes. You have to use the proceeds from an AVC to buy an annuity, but you do not have to activate it at the same time as your main pension.

tip

> **This is a recent change to the previous rules and a great help to people forced into early retirement who want to keep some pension fund growing.**

Is there a ceiling to the amount I can contribute to AVCs?

Your AVCs and main pension contributions together must not exceed the maximum percentage of salary the Inland Revenue allows you to contribute.

Do I have to use the AVC provider that my employer has set up?

No. You can choose to go elsewhere, in which case you make FSAVCs instead, which work in exactly the same way.

Which is better: AVCs or FSAVCs?

AVCs have the advantage that your employer usually pays the charges for administering them. FSAVCs give you more choice about who manages your money and where it is invested; and you can maintain an FSAVC when you move jobs.

Where do I find out about AVCs?

Ask the company pension trustees.

Where can I find out about FSAVCs?

Contact an insurance company or financial adviser.

Personal pensions

With personal pensions you invest in a pension fund while you are working and then, when you retire, you use the money to buy an annuity. The amount of pension you end up with depends on how much you have contributed, how well the investments have performed, and how much has been deducted in charges.

The annuity provides an income for the rest of your life. You can choose to take up to a quarter of your pension fund as a tax-free lump sum, but, if you spend that money, you have less left to buy an annuity and therefore have a smaller retirement income. If you need all the income, it is still worth taking the tax-free lump sum: you can use it to buy another annuity.

ask Margaret

Who provides personal pensions?

Personal pensions are provided by insurance companies, banks, large building societies, unit trust companies, investment trust groups, and friendly societies.

Where can I buy a personal pension?

- through independent financial advisers
- through specialist advisers
- direct from insurance companies, usually in person but sometimes by phone
- direct from investment companies, usually in person but sometimes by phone
- direct from banks and building societies
- from retailers, including some supermarkets, that have financial services subsidiaries.

How much should I invest in a personal pension?

Having a personal pension is not the same as having enough money to live on in retirement. If you have no more that a contracted-out personal pension using your SERPS rebate, you certainly have nowhere near enough. If you start a pension in your early thirties, you need to put in around 10 per cent of your salary. If you delay starting until you are 40, you should think of contributing 20 per cent.

Are there limits to the amount I can pay in to a personal pension?

The Inland Revenue puts a ceiling on the tax relief you can get, which in effect restricts the amount you can contribute. The regulations allow you to contribute more to a personal pension as you grow older.

What happens if I inadvertently contribute too much to a pension?

The Revenue finds out eventually and instructs the pension to return the excess. You might be taxed on it as well.

If ever you have pension contributions returned, make sure the insurance company adds interest at the rate you would have earned if you had put the money in a long-term savings account. Some offer interest but try to pay only the rate you would get in an instant access account – that is not enough.

How safe is money in a personal pension?

Aside from investment risk, pensions are far better regulated than they used to be, and so are the people who sell them. You can claim on the Investors Compensation Scheme if you lose money through theft or company collapse. See p.29.

What happens once I agree to buy a pension?

The salesperson must send you a written 'reason why' letter explaining the reasons for the particular recommendation; and he or she must also send you a 'key features' document, which is produced by the insurance company and details the important points of the particular pension you are buying, including the amount of commission the adviser earns.

Can I change my mind after buying a personal pension?

If you sign the contract in someone's office, you cannot pull out. But if you sign in your own home, you have ten days to cancel the contract without penalty. After that, you are completely committed and in no circumstances can you get back money you have invested in a pension, until you retire.

I'm never certain exactly how much I earn until the end of the year. Can I make pension contributions once a year?

Yes. You can make regular once-a-year contributions or a one-off contribution.

tip

> Sales representatives earn more commission from selling regular-contribution pensions than single-premium ones, which makes the policies more expensive. Ask for a 'single-premium contract', not an annual or regular-premium policy.

I already have an old personal pension from the 1970s. Is it the same as the newer variety?

This is a retirement annuity contract or 'Section 226' policy. These were superseded by personal pensions in 1988, which are similar – although you are likely to get a higher tax-free lump sum from one of the old plans.

If I die first, will my spouse get a pension?

Only if you paid for this option when you bought the annuity.

If we're not married, will the pension go to my partner when I die?

It can, but you need to let the insurance company know whom you want to receive the money. Your partner does not have to be financially dependent on you and can be a same-sex partner.

If I die before I retire, what happens to my pension fund?

Your estate should receive the contributions you have paid plus interest, but it depends on the terms of the contract.

Can I ask for my children to get my pension?

You can, for as long as they are under 18 or still financially dependent.

tip

> Make sure you have the pension policy written in trust. Then, if you die young, your pension fund goes immediately to your beneficiary; otherwise, it first passes through your estate and can add to your inheritance tax bill. See p.123, on writing life insurance policies in trust, for more detail.

Apart from my contributions, are there any other costs to me of paying into a personal pension?

Charges are around 5 per cent of the amount you pay in, plus a monthly plan fee, plus between 1 per cent and 2 per cent of the value of your pension each year for an annual management charge.

What do all those charges pay for?

They pay for the insurance companies' costs for managing and investing pensions, and paying commission to the salesperson.

Do all pensions cost the same?

No. But insurance companies now have to make their charges transparent and, as a result, some companies – particularly the newer pension providers – are producing simple, straightforward pensions for lower charges.

Where will I find cheaper pension providers?

Ask a financial adviser or look out for advertisements.

Can I contribute to more than one pension at a time?

You can have several personal pensions, provided that your total contributions are within the Inland Revenue limits. You are not allowed to contribute to a company pension and a personal pension at the same time, unless you have two jobs with a different pension for each.

What happens if I have a personal pension and then join a company scheme?

You must stop contributing to the personal pension.

Can I transfer a personal pension into a company pension?

Only if the company pension rules allow, or you can leave it invested where it is.

tip | **If there is any possibility that you might not be able to afford to keep making regular payments until you retire, make sure you pick a pension that allows flexibility. Some penalise you for missing payments.**

Do I have to activate my personal pension when I retire?

No, assuming you have enough money from other sources to live on. Both men and women can choose to take a personal pension at any time between the ages of 50 and 75. Similarly, you can start your pension before you stop work.

You state your preferred retirement age on the personal pension application form: choose the earliest age you might retire. You can always take the pension later than you said, and meanwhile keep contributing. But if you choose to go earlier, some pension plans penalise you. The later your stated retirement age, the more the salesperson earns.

tip

> **If you have bought several personal pensions, or had the pension divided into separate policies, you can activate part of your pension and leave the rest to grow. See the section on 'retiring gradually' on p.152.**

I don't have a job but I want to plan for my retirement. What can I do?

Without a job that pays money, you cannot contribute to a pension. But that does not stop you investing for your retirement in other ways, such as with ISAs or by buying a property to provide rental income. Tax relief makes pensions attractive but, in fact, they have some drawbacks: your money is locked away until you retire; and the pension income ceases when you or your widow die. If your retirement income were to come from other types of investment, the savings would still be there to pass to your beneficiaries.

I work bringing up the children and my husband pays me housekeeping money. Can I use any of this for a pension?

No. Housework doesn't count as work as far as pension contributions are concerned.

I'm retiring in a couple of years' time. Have I left it too late to start a pension?

There is not a great deal of time for investment growth on any contributions, but you can take advantage of the tax relief for this year and the past seven years if you can afford to put that much into a pension.

Do I have to stick with a pension that turned out to be a bad investment?

No. You can transfer it to a new pension provider, although there will be new set-up costs to pay. The company you are leaving translates the amount you have invested into a surrender value (a single monetary figure), from which they deduct their charges, including future charges you were due to pay. If you believe the transfer value is too mean, tell the insurance company how you feel and ask for it to be recalculated; sometimes they will agree. Beware: if you start an inflexible personal pension and stop it within a few years, you cannot get your money back and the high up-front charges make the policy worthless. You can waste a lot of money.

What happens if I can't afford to keep paying the premiums on a personal pension?

It depends on the terms of your policy. The more flexible ones allow you to miss payments.

What if I can't pay the premiums because I've become ill?

With many policies, you can buy 'waiver of premium' benefit, where the insurance company effectively pays the premiums for you, if necessary until you retire. But you have to choose this option when you buy the policy.

tip

> **Before buying waiver of premium benefit, check closely whether the insurer will meet the premiums if you are unable to continue with your usual occupation, or only if you are incapable of doing any work at any occupation, which is harsher.**

When I'm drawing my pension, will it go up each year?

Unlike company pensions, there is no statutory protection against rising prices, apart from any pension you bought with a SERPS rebate.

Does that mean my pension never rises?

It can; when you buy the annuity, you choose whether you want one that increases or not. See the section on annuities, p.144.

If I retire abroad, will I still get my pension paid?

Yes, but the payment is in sterling and the cost of converting to the local currency is expensive. If you can afford the longer time span between payments, so as to minimise foreign exchange costs ask the insurance company if you can have the pension paid once a year rather than monthly.

Where are my pension contributions invested?

It depends on the pension you have chosen. Generally your money will have gone into shares, but the pension fund can include gilts, property and cash.

Am I stuck with the investment choice I first make?

It depends which type of pension you bought, but often you can switch from one fund to another.

Which type of investment is best for my pension contributions?

It depends how much risk you want to take. As you get closer to retirement, you should take less risk. Indeed, many pensions automatically transfer your investments into safer funds as you get nearer retirement.

Do any pensions invest ethically?
Some; ask a financial adviser which they are.

tip

> **You can use part of your pension contribution allowance to buy term insurance, with tax relief on the premiums. Normally there is no tax relief on life insurance contributions.**

QUESTIONS TO ASK A SALESPERSON OR ADVISER WHEN CHOOSING A PERSONAL PENSION

get the facts

- Must I pay regular premiums, or can I make one-off contributions?
- Can I change the premiums I pay, upwards or downwards?
- How much money is taken in charges?
- Are there any penalty charges if I retire earlier than I expected?
- Can I retire later than planned?
- Can I stop paying contributions for a while without penalty?
- What are the charges if I stop paying contributions? (*These charges can be significant, even if the policy is described as 'flexible'. They are deducted from the value of your pension, possibly until all the money in your pension has been used up.*)
- What are the penalties if I miss contributions?
- What are the penalties if I transfer to another policy?
- If I can't work through illness or redundancy, will the policy pay the premiums for me?
- Are there any charges for switching investments within this pension?
- When I retire, can I buy the annuity from a different insurance company? (*You can, through an open-market option; and you might get a better annuity rate from a different company.*)
- How much would my family get if I died before retiring?
- Why are you recommending this particular pension? (*The adviser has to give you this information in writing before you commit yourself.*)
- How much commission will you earn?
- Is there another pension I could buy for equal benefits that pays you less commission?
- Will you share the commission with me?

Questions for a unit-linked pension

- Where is my money invested?
- Can I choose where my money is invested?
- Can I switch between funds?
- How much does it cost to switch between funds?
- Is there a limit to the number of times I can switch between funds?
- How many free switches am I allowed each year? (*Usually one.*)
- Do you have a free telephone helpline?

Future government plans for pensions

STAKEHOLDER PENSIONS

Stakeholder pensions are a new variety of pension that the government is planning, due from April 2001 (at the earliest). These pensions are targeted at employed people although, once you start contributing to a stakeholder pension, you can continue for a time after losing your job or starting a maternity break.

ask Margaret

What are stakeholder pensions?

A simple, low-cost pension intended to encourage more people to buy their own pensions, rather than relying on the state through the additional pension which is replacing SERPS.

Does that make them a state pension or a private pension?

Stakeholder pensions are private pensions. The government's involvement is to force employers and pension providers to offer reasonably priced, flexible pensions by imposing limits on charges.

Does that mean they are inferior to personal pensions?

No one yet knows, but there is no reason to think they will be.

Who will provide stakeholder pensions?

Certainly some insurance companies will provide them, and maybe also some trades unions or trade associations.

Who will be able to buy a stakeholder pension?

Anyone in employment, when they start contributing at least.

What will stakeholder pensions be like?

They could be just a unit trust or investment trust with pension tax relief or an Individual Savings Account (ISA). Contributors will get financial encouragement to opt out of the additional state pension.

Do I have to buy a stakeholder pension?

It will not be compulsory.

How safe is money in a stakeholder pension?

Such pensions will be more tightly regulated than personal pensions have been before.

LIFELONG INDIVIDUAL SAVINGS ACCOUNTS (LISAs)

LISAs, which will almost certainly be called something different when they come into effect, arise from a government plan to run another pension alongside stakeholder pensions, company pensions, AVCs and personal pensions. Contributors are expected to be allowed to put money in unit trusts, investment trusts and oeics, but with the same tax advantage as pension contributions.

Annuities

Unless you are in a final salary scheme, on retirement, you use the money you have saved in a pension to buy an annuity, and this pays your retirement income for the rest of your life.

tip

> **WARNING: On the day you buy an annuity, your retirement income is fixed. If annuity rates are low at that time, you are stuck with a low rate for ever. Once you buy an annuity, you have spent that money and will not get it back. It is important to choose the best annuity for your needs. Once the annuity starts paying, you cannot change the terms.**

ask Margaret

Who provides annuities?

Insurance companies.

Where can I buy an annuity?

An annuity can be purchased direct from insurance companies, through specialist advisers, and from independent financial advisers.

Must an annuity be provided by the same insurance company to which I was making pension contributions?

It can be or, through the open-market option, you can buy from a different insurance company. It is essential that you compare annuity rates on offer from a number of insurance companies, to see which offers the best deal.

tip

> **Annuity quotes are held only for a short time and so, if rates are moving down, when you get a quotation, you need to decide quickly. Make sure everyone involved acts fast as well.**

tip

> **You might find that a pension company takes months to send your pension fund money through to the insurance company handling your annuity. This happens all too often. Do not sit back and wait: keep nagging everyone involved. And if you end up with a worse annuity rate because of the delay, demand compensation. If the various parties cannot agree who was responsible, contact the Pensions Ombudsman, whose address is given in the Appendix.**

How can I tell which annuity is best?

Compared with most investment decisions, it is easy to spot the best annuity for you. Just pick the one offering the highest annuity rate because, once you have bought an annuity, the insurance company guarantees to pay that amount for the rest of your life. You also want a company with good and speedy administration; an IFA should steer you clear of the poor providers.

What is an annuity rate?

An annuity rate is the return you get on your money through the annuity, like a rate of interest.

Why do some insurers offer better annuity rates than others?

Sometimes companies do not want to take on any annuity business and so they offer poor rates in the hope that customers will go elsewhere. This is another reason why it is important to get independent advice before buying an annuity.

What affects the amount I'll get from an annuity?

There are several factors: first, your age, because insurance companies base their calculations on how many years they reckon they will have to pay you; second, your gender, because statistically women live longer than men, and so companies give women worse annuity rates; third, gilt yields. Because insurance companies guarantee to pay the agreed annuity rate for the rest of your life, they cannot take chances when investing the money, which means that they largely buy long-term gilts – a safe investment – to provide the income that they have to pay you.

What makes annuity rates go up and down?

Annuity rates fluctuate as gilt yields improve or worsen. For more information on gilts, see p.100 in Chapter 3.

tip

> WARNING: **Annuity rates are likely to be dragged down in future years because the population is living longer. To set annuity rates, insurance companies use official figures that show how long you are likely to live at any given age, known as mortality rates. And people are living longer.**

Does my state of health make a difference?

It can if you are seriously ill or you smoke. Some insurers in fact give better rates to people who are expected to live less than their full lifespan. Ask for an 'impaired life' annuity.

Are all annuities the same?

There are two main types and you have to take the one that matches your reason for buying.

When you retire, the annuity you buy with the money in your pension fund is called a compulsory purchase annuity (CPA). All the income from a

CPA is taxable – because you have already had tax relief on your pension contributions.

The other type of annuity is not linked to your pension fund and you can buy it at any time. It is called a purchased life annuity (PLA). Not all the income from a purchased life annuity is taxable; some of it is treated as a return of your capital.

Is it worth waiting a year or so after retiring before buying an annuity?

If you are older when you start an annuity, you have less time to live, so you get a better annuity rate. But, by delaying, you could still end up with a smaller pension: the value of your pension fund could fall while you are waiting and annuity rates could worsen. And, even if both improved, they are unlikely to do so well that they make up for the income you forgo by delaying.

Can I change my mind after I've bought an annuity?

No. Once you have signed the application form, you are committed.

What is the point in buying an annuity, where my money is gone for ever, when I could invest in a building society account and earn about the same?

Annuities guarantee to pay an agreed amount, perhaps increasing each year, for the rest of your life, however long that is. Every time interest rates in a building society account come down, your income falls. Because of inflation – even low inflation – the money in your building society account buys less after only a few years. Indeed, if inflation stayed level at 3 per cent a year, after 20 years your pension would be worth only half what it was at the start.

QUESTIONS TO ASK YOURSELF BEFORE BUYING AN ANNUITY

ask yourself

- Do I want my income to stay the same each year? (*This is a 'flat' annuity. A 'flat' annuity pays a higher pension than an increasing annuity to begin with. Later on, the increasing annuity catches up.*)
- Do I want my income to rise each year? (*If so, you will want an increasing, or escalating, annuity.*)
- If I buy an increasing annuity, how much do I want it to go up each year? (*You can choose 3 per cent, 5 per cent or the rate of inflation. Most people*

choose 3 per cent. An index-linked annuity is expensive when inflation is high. It is unnecessary if the forecasts for low UK inflation are correct.)

- Do I want a single life annuity that pays out only as long as I live?
- Do I want my spouse to continue receiving a pension after I die? (*If so, you will want a joint life annuity that pays until the second person dies.*)
- Do I want my spouse's pension to be the same as mine after I die, or less?
- If I die within a short time of retiring, do I want my annuity to continue being paid to my dependants for a few years? (*This is called a 'guaranteed period annuity'.*)
- Do I want to retire at state pension age?

tip

> **Every additional benefit you buy costs money, whether you take advantage of the benefit or not. This cost means that you start out on a lower income than you otherwise would.**

Getting advice on personal pensions and annuities

ask Margaret

Who gives advice on pensions?

- independent financial advisers
- specialist financial advisers
- tied advisers on the pensions sold by the company they work for
- a few accountants and solicitors
- actuaries.

Who gives advice on annuities?

Specialist financial advisers, actuaries, and company salespeople on their own products.

How do I find someone to advise me on pensions?

In the same way as you would look for someone to advise on investments generally (see Chapter 2 on getting advice), but make sure that you choose someone who specialises in retirement planning.

Will the same person give me advice on annuities?

Probably, but you might do better with a person who advises only on annuities.

Is it cheaper to buy from a company salesperson or from a financial adviser who earns commission?

For the identical pension, the costs are probably the same: charges are deducted from pensions sold through company salespeople as well. However, an IFA might agree to share some of the commission with you.

Can I ask for advice if I buy a pension over the telephone?

Only from company salespeople, not independent financial advisers. Some companies selling by telephone give advice, but you first have to answer a long questionnaire, which can be tiring over the telephone. Remember you will not be talking to an independent financial adviser but a company sales-person, who can sell only that insurer's pensions.

QUESTIONS TO ASK WHEN YOU ARE CHOOSING A PENSIONS ADVISER

get the facts

- Are you independent or tied?
- Do you specialise in pensions and annuities? (*You are best dealing with one that does.*)
- Have you taken specialist pension exams?
- Do you charge a fee or take commission?
- How much commission will you take?
- If I am investing a substantial amount, will you refund some of the commission you earn? (*Advisers should, as they are likely to earn a lot from your pension.*)
- Will you earn additional commission if I subsequently increase my contributions?
- What will you do for the commission you earn in future years?
- Might you recommend a pension from one of the high-street retailers now in the market? (*This is unlikely because they do not pay commission.*)

tip

> **If you are confused by any of the answers you receive to your questions, ask again. Advisers and salespeople are duty-bound to explain every detail in terms that you can understand. If the person is incapable of explaining things clearly, find another.**

tip

> **Advisers will ask you many questions for a 'fact find'; the regulations say they have to do this. If you do not want to answer the questions, the adviser cannot give you proper advice.**

Having enough money to live on when you retire

This subject is the nub of why you are taking any trouble at all in deciding how you will invest for the future.

ask Margaret

How can I find out how much pension I have coming?

You can get forecasts for all your pensions. For the state pension, you can get a forecast from the Department of Social Security; ask at your local Benefits Agency office for form BR19. For a company pension, you should ask the trustees where you stand for pension and for AVCs. For any personal pension that you have taken out, ask the insurance company providing the pension for a forecast; and do similarly for any FSAVCs.

For pensions from previous employment, write to the companies concerned. If some relate to employers who are no longer in business, or if you have no contact address, write to the Pension Schemes Registry, which holds records of thousands of pension schemes and can help trace entitlements due from years ago. The Registry's address is given in the Appendix, and the search facility is free.

How can I tell if my pension is going to be enough?

Work out a post-retirement budget. Use the value of your pension in today's terms and assess your outgoings on today's bills, guessing where you might spend more after you retire and where you could spend less. Include household bills, travel and entertaining, and the cost of enjoying hobbies and pastimes. Then compare your spending forecast with your estimated income to see if you can make ends meet.

What can I do if I find I'm unlikely to have enough?

If you think you have been realistic on the expenditure front, there is only one thing you can do: start saving immediately.

If you are likely to get less than the full state pension, ask if you can make up missing National Insurance contributions. If you are eligible for a company scheme but have not joined, investigate doing so. If you are in a company scheme, think about making Additional Voluntary Contributions. Otherwise, buy a personal pension or start another form of saving.

Retiring early

ask Margaret

Many people nowadays retire before the official retirement age.

Will my pension suffer if I retire early?

Yes, for four reasons. The fund will be smaller because you have paid in less money; there has been less time for it to grow; your pension fund will have to stretch over more years; and the pension fund might impose a financial penalty.

tip

> WARNING: **You can reckon to lose 0.5 per cent of income for every month you go early. So, for example, if you retired five years early, your pension would be 30 per cent less, for the rest of your life. If you also allow for five years' fewer contributions, your income will be 42 per cent lower than a colleague's who has worked until age 65.**

Will I get my state pension any sooner if I retire before the official retirement age?

No. Whatever your circumstances, men cannot claim the state pension before reaching age 65 and women at age 60, but there are changes coming to women's retirement age, as described on p.126.

Will I be penalised if I have to start my pension earlier than planned because illness or disability mean I can't work again?

With a company pension, your employer might help. With a personal pension, you can insure against this at the outset.

Are there any drawbacks to activating a personal pension at age 50?

Unless you have been pumping maximum contributions into your pension since your twenties, it is unlikely to provide enough money to live on. Statistically men who retire at 50, unless it is through ill health, live longer than those who work to 65. This makes annuity rates even worse.

Retiring gradually

There is a scheme called 'phased retirement', available on newer pension plans, where you convert your pension fund into around 1,000 separate policies. You can then activate them gradually over the years. The remaining pension stays in your control until you convert it, although there are drawbacks (see below) that you need to take seriously. Another option is 'income withdrawal' but there are drawbacks here as well.

ask Margaret

Do I have to take my pension immediately I retire?

You might have to with a company pension, particularly a final salary scheme, although you can leave an AVC to continue growing. With a personal pension or group personal pension, you can delay buying an annuity.

What are the drawbacks to phased retirement?

Phased retirement is more expensive and not worth the cost until you have at least £200,000 in your pension pool. You still have to activate all the pension by the time you reach 75.

Are there any other ways of gradually activating a pension?

There is 'income withdrawal' or 'income drawdown'. After you retire, you keep your pension invested but you are allowed to take income from it each year until you want to buy an annuity. But you need to understand the drawbacks:

- If you take out more income than the fund is earning, you eat into your capital.

- You cannot be sure what will happen to your investment while you are waiting before buying your annuity: if stock markets rise, it becomes worth more but, if they fall, you could have less money when you want to buy an annuity.
- This type of arrangement is suitable only if you have an enormous pension fund.
- You will have to pay an annual administration charge.

Pensions and divorce

The divorce courts must take company pensions and personal pensions into account, but pensions are difficult to value. The government wants to introduce 'pension splitting' or 'pension sharing' but it is taking a long time to find a way of making it work. On divorce the breadwinner's pension would be divided, giving a clean-break divorce and providing each spouse with his or her own pension (albeit small) on retirement.

Meanwhile, the other possibilities (each with drawbacks) for splitting pension benefits so you get a fair share are:

- To ask for a proportion of the tax-free lump sum paid on retirement to be ear-marked for you (although your spouse could delay retirement to be awkward; alternatively, your spouse might stop work to avoid continuing to pay into a pension).
- To get the pension fund valued at today's figure and ask for a cash payment of between one-third and half that amount (although your spouse might not be able to pay you such a substantial amount).
- To ask for a share of the pension payments when your spouse retires (although on your spouse's death, the pension payments would stop).

tip

> **On divorce, make sure that the pension fund is included in the assets being shared out. Legally, the pension must be taken into account, but solicitors often skirt round the issue because it is a complicated area.**

> **Make sure the insurance company handling the pension always has your current address.**

ask Margaret

I've been paying maintenance to my wife since we divorced and she has no plans to remarry. Will I have to continue paying her after I retire, when my income will drop substantially?

You will if that is what the court order says. You can go back to the court to try to get it changed.

Pensions and tax

Workers get tax relief on personal pension contributions. For every pound you put into a pension, you get back a percentage at the same rate as you pay income tax. If you are an employee, you pay the premiums net of basic rate income tax; your salary is adjusted accordingly through your PAYE tax code. If you are a higher-rate taxpayer, you reclaim the difference between the basic and higher rates through your tax return. You are still allowed the tax relief even if you earn too little to pay tax. Self-employed people claim their tax relief by paying contributions gross and reclaiming the tax relief through the tax return. On retirement you can take around 25 per cent of your accumulated pension fund as a tax-free lump sum.

All pension payments are subject to income tax, including the state pension. Income tax is charged on the dividends earned by shares in the pension fund portfolio.

6 Mortgages

The tables have been turned on mortgage providers. You can shop around, compare the offers and make demands. You no longer need to buy a mortgage for life: while staying in the same house, you can cancel one mortgage and start another. There are always home-loan deals on offer, and you can jump around to find the best.

But progress produces problems: the choice of mortgages is bewildering and picking the wrong one can be an expensive mistake because you face penalty charges if you cancel too quickly. No longer can you just ask for a mortgage. You have to decide what sort of mortgage you want, what type of repayment terms you prefer, and whether the perks are worth the penalty. You have to ask the right questions.

Questions about mortgages

Who provides mortgages?
- banks

- building societies
- insurance companies
- centralised lenders (companies that do nothing but provide mortgages)
- large friendly societies
- some retailers
- large estate agents.

Who advises on mortgages?

Intermediaries, who can be mortgage brokers or independent financial advisers, insurance company salespeople, estate agents, solicitors and accountants.

Where can I buy a mortgage?

You can obtain a mortgage direct from the providers listed above (in person or by telephone), or through financial advisers, mortgage brokers, estate agents or housebuilders, or through the Internet.

Which should I look for first: the house or the mortgage?

Do your market research for mortgages before you start house-hunting. You will have more time to think calmly about what is available. Once you have found a house, you will be under pressure to make an offer and too excited to think clearly.

How can I find out about all the different loans available?

You can use a broker or do your own research by talking to lenders, buying a specialist magazine, and scanning the Internet.

How do I choose between lenders?

One lender might offer a better rate of interest, another might offer you more money on your mortgage. Neither of these is a good enough reason on its own to make a decision. You need to compare the charges and restrictions as well.

Do I need to be an existing customer to ask for a mortgage?

No. But when you take a loan, some lenders insist that you open a current account to handle the mortgage payments.

Why do lenders give better terms to new borrowers than to long-standing ones?

To attract new business – although this attitude is changing. Lenders cannot take customers' loyalty for granted any more, and so some give incentives to existing borrowers as well.

tip

> If ever you see your lender advertising an attractive rate to new customers, ask if you can have it too. They might agree – or at least offer you an improvement on your current rate.

Can a lender force me to buy its own house insurance policy?

Yes, lenders are allowed to make it a condition of getting a mortgage, but usually they do this for special-rate deals rather than ordinary variable-rate loans. However, even when it is not compulsory, they have a panel of insurers they want you to use. Some mortgage providers allow you to buy from an insurer outside the list, but they then usually charge an administration fee (around £25) if you do.

tip

> Some lenders charge this administration fee every time you change insurer, and so you should calculate carefully to make sure the saving from a different insurance policy is worth while.

Can a lender force me to pay a penalty if I cancel a special-deal mortgage within its set period?

Yes, provided that this was made clear in writing at the outset.

Can I get mortgage offers from several lenders at the same time?

You should not take an application too far with numerous lenders because, before agreeing the loan, lenders always check your credit reference agency file. Each search is logged on your file as a mortgage application and, to the next lender, it appears that you have been repeatedly rejected, which makes you look like a bad risk.

Are there any drawbacks to getting a cashback with a mortgage?

A different mortgage deal without cashback could offer a lower rate of interest, in which case you have to decide which is more important, getting a large lump sum immediately or paying less each month. There is a penalty to pay if you redeem a cashback mortgage within a certain period of time.

tip

> **WARNING: Be clear about the difference between an immediate cashback when you start the mortgage and the promise of cashback in five years' time, where there is no certainty that you will get the money.**

Will I have to prove how much I earn?

Yes. The lender will want to see payslips.

How can I prove my income if I'm self-employed?

Lenders require three years' accounts.

Can I get a mortgage if I'm a contract worker?

Yes, provided your employer confirms that the contract will be renewed.

Can my partner and I get a joint mortgage if we're not married or we are of the same sex?

Yes. Lenders are interested only in your ability to repay.

Can four of us get a mortgage together?

Yes, but that is the maximum number because no more than four people can have their names on house property deeds (the legal document showing who owns the property).

If I have an endowment mortgage, where the loan is repaid when the insurance policy covering the mortgage matures, what happens if I want to move house?

There is no problem. You can switch the endowment to your new property, buying additional insurance if you are buying a more expensive home.

tip

> **WARNING: Be wary if any adviser suggests surrendering the original policy and buying a new larger one. It is unnecessary to cash in a life insurance policy: you get poor value while the adviser earns good commission.**

Will I have to cash in the endowment if I pay off the mortgage?

No. If you have enough money from another source, you can repay the mortgage loan and keep the endowment going as an investment to its full term.

I've had an endowment mortgage for many years, and it has already earned enough to pay off the loan. Is it worth cashing in the policy in these circumstances to repay the loan?

Almost certainly not, because you will miss out on future bonuses. If you feel strongly that you want to pay off the mortgage, discuss it with a financial adviser.

Can I be sure the endowment will produce enough to pay off the mortgage?

You could in the past, but not with newer low-start endowments. Low-start endowments taken out in the past few years, particularly those running for only ten years, might not produce large enough investment returns to meet your debt.

But doesn't the endowment guarantee to pay out a certain amount?

Yes, the sum assured is guaranteed. But with a low-cost endowment, the sum assured is less than the size of your mortgage; you rely on earning sufficient bonuses to make up the difference. But bonus rates have been falling, and there is the possibility of a shortfall.

tip

> WARNING: **A low-cost endowment guarantees to repay your mortgage if you die before the loan is due to be repaid, because it includes term insurance for this purpose. But it doesn't guarantee to repay the loan if you survive. You hope that the policy has earned enough bonuses to repay the mortgage, but that is not guaranteed.**

How will I know if my endowment is likely to fall short?

The insurance company should get in touch with you, but if you are worried you can always ask the insurer for an opinion.

What can I do if the insurance company says my endowment won't pay off the mortgage?

They are more likely to say 'might not' rather than 'won't' but, either way, you will have to produce extra money to repay the mortgage when it is due. You can increase the premiums for the endowment or start saving somewhere else.

The insurance company told me how much to invest in the first place, and so does it bear any responsibility for the shortfall?

The insurance company might have a moral duty, but they do not have any legal liability. At the start, insurers estimate how much you need to invest, based on their assumptions of how much the investment will grow. Many of today's endowments were calculated on forecasts that turned out to be over-optimistic. But it is still your problem.

How do the insurance companies set their premium levels for my mortgage?

Insurance companies set premiums at the level they think will be high enough to produce the payout needed to match the loan. But they can make only an estimate of future investment returns, and so there is an element of guesswork. If they believe returns will be high, they can charge lower premiums, which is obviously attractive to housebuyers. But lower premiums are not a bargain if you have to increase the amount you pay later because the endowment policy is showing a shortfall.

What can I do if the lender's valuer says the house is worth less than I am prepared to pay?

In that situation the lender won't give you the loan. You need to be subtle in any discussions on the subject, though: valuers do not want lenders to think they make mistakes. You can appeal against the valuation: provide additional information to support your argument that the home is worth more than they think. Or you can try a different lender; another valuer is likely to come to a different conclusion, although not necessarily in your favour.

Do I have to tell the lender if I intend building an extension or converting the loft?

Yes. You should get written agreement for any changes.

Will I have to pay for the lender's valuation if I don't go ahead with the mortgage?

Yes.

How can I avoid this if I'm thinking of buying one of, say, three houses?

Decide which one you want before getting to that stage.

Will the lender give me a copy of the valuer's report?

They are not obliged to but, as you have paid for the report, it is unfair if they won't. Most will, and it is always worth asking.

tip | **Some lenders provide a free valuation as part of the mortgage package.**

If I have paid for the lender's valuation, do I need a survey as well?

The lender is concerned only that, if you fail to keep up the payments, it can sell your house for at least as much as you are borrowing. Buyers need more detailed information about the condition of the property.

Is there any reason why I shouldn't use the same valuer to do a fuller survey at the same time?

This is how it is usually done. You can pay for a 'full structural survey' or a 'half-way' report and valuation known as a housebuyer's (or flatbuyer's) report.

What tax relief do I get on a mortgage?

There is tax relief on the interest payments, called Mortgage Interest Relief at Source (MIRAS), but only for buying your main home. It is a minimal amount allowed only on the first £30,000 you borrow, and the government is withdrawing MIRAS in April 2000.

How often is the interest on my mortgage calculated?

Many lenders recalculate once a year and so, if you repay some of the loan during the year, it is not taken into account until the end. Newer lenders recalculate daily.

tip

Do not pay off your mortgage with money that you might need for something else in a few years' time. It is cheaper to borrow through a home loan than through a personal loan.

How much does it cost to buy a house?

You face the following costs before you move in, although not all apply in every case:

- the deposit, perhaps 5 per cent of the agreed purchase price, but sometimes 10 per cent
- stamp duty – on properties worth more than a certain amount
- an arrangement fee to the lender
- two sets of solicitors' fees (work for you and the lender)
- valuer's fee
- surveyor's fee in addition to valuer's
- a mortgage indemnity guarantee (or mortgage indemnity premium), sometimes payable when you borrow a high proportion of the house price – often above 75 per cent – to insure the lender in case you fail

to keep up the mortgage payments
- Land Registry fee to register your ownership of the property
- your removal costs.

How much will all that come to?

Reckon on 5 per cent of the purchase price to cover your costs, plus another 5 per cent or 10 per cent for the deposit. Once you are in your new home, you need to find money for:

- furniture, carpets, curtains
- decorating
- contents insurance
- buildings insurance
- mortgage repayments
- life insurance premiums
- and all the other normal running costs of owning a property.

When I buy a mortgage, do I have the same protection from being given bad advice as when I buy investments?

No. Mortgages do not come under the Financial Services Act. The only regulation covering mortgages is the Mortgage Code. Complying with it is voluntary, but all the lenders with well known names have signed up to it. See the last section of this chapter for details of the code.

Do I have protection if I buy an endowment mortgage?

The endowment life insurance policy is covered by the Financial Services Act, but not the loan itself.

Can I get a mortgage to buy a property to rent out?

Some mortgages are designed specifically for this, and lenders take rental income into account when deciding how much you can borrow.

How can I get a mortgage at euro rates of interest?

A few lenders sell euro-mortgages, but you should consider one only if you are paid in euros; otherwise, you take a currency risk: if sterling loses value against the euro, you will have to pay more, in sterling, to meet the monthly payments. In any case, the interest rates are not very different from some special mortgage deals available in the UK.

Do I have to use all the money from a mortgage to buy a house, or can I use some of the money for other purposes?

That depends on the deal you do with the lender.

If I borrow £50,000 for 25 years, how much will it cost altogether?

Excluding fees, insurance, and tax relief, and assuming that interest rates stay level at 7 per cent, you will pay a total of £107,262.

Mortgage intermediaries

ask Margaret

Do I have to use a broker to find a mortgage?

No, not at all. Mortgage lenders are well used to dealing directly with customers.

Is there any point in using a broker?

They can help with the complicated choice of mortgages available. And they might be able to find you a home loan if your credit rating is poor or if you are trying to mortgage an unusual property.

If I buy through a broker, are my dealings afterwards with the mortgage broker or with the lender?

It could be either, depending on your relationship with the broker or adviser. But you can certainly talk directly to the lender about any queries on the mortgage.

Do brokers get paid for selling mortgages?

Some banks and building societies pay £100 or £150 for each loan taken out. Sometimes they pay only large intermediaries.

tip

> **If you are paying a fee to an intermediary for finding a mortgage, make sure that they refund to you any commission they earn.**

How does an intermediary find the best loan for me when there are so many choices?

Some pass your name over to a 'wholesaler' who deals between intermediaries and lenders. Others use computer programs to search the market.

> WARNING: **If you receive a mailshot from a company claiming to save money on your mortgage, be careful. They might reschedule your borrowing to cost less each month but they could well charge substantial fees for doing so. They tempt you with a cashback, returning the fee in five years' time, but there is no guarantee you will ever get this money.**
>
> **And be wary of brokers who offer to cut the cost of your mortgage, for a fee. Borrowers can reduce the amount of interest they pay on home loans by paying chunks off the mortgage, but talk to your lender if you want to do this. Don't pay someone else to do it for you.**

Questions to ask a lender or broker before taking a mortgage

get the facts

- Is there a fee for arranging this loan? (*You are unlikely to pay an arrangement fee for a standard mortgage, but you probably will for a special deal.*)
- How much will the mortgage cost in fees, insurance premiums and monthly repayments?
- What is the minimum amount you will let me borrow?
- What is the maximum I can have as a mortgage?
- What is the highest amount I can borrow as a percentage of the price of the house?
- Can I borrow 100 per cent of the house price? (*A few lenders from time to time lend over 100 per cent, but be careful about borrowing so much. It is likely to be expensive.*)
- What multiple of my salary can I borrow? (*Lenders use different criteria but it can be three-and-a-half times your salary.*)
- What multiple of my partner's salary can I add to that? (*Usually you can add one multiple of your partner's salary, or two-and-a-half times your joint salaries.*)
- Can I include bonuses and overtime payments in my salary figure? (*Usually not, which is safest, because bonuses and overtime might not always be paid.*)

- How quickly will you tell me that I can have the loan? (*Don't sit back and wait if the offer is slow in coming through. Find out who is causing the hold up – the lender or someone providing references – and keep chasing.*)
- Can I get outline approval before finding the house I want to buy?
- Is the interest rate variable, or at a discount or fixed rate?
- If it is a special rate, how does this compare with the variable rate?
- How long does the discount or fixed rate last?
- Is there a penalty charge if I pay off the mortgage, or repay some of it, during the discount or fixed-rate period? (*There will be a penalty, and the penalty period could last longer than the special rate you pay.*)
- How long is the penalty period?
- Is the penalty still imposed if we have a joint mortgage and one of us dies? (*Lenders have agreed not to impose penalties in this situation.*)
- What happens at the end of the discount period? (*You probably start paying the standard variable rate of interest.*)
- What happens at the end of the penalty period? (*You should be able to switch to another special rate loan, although you might not be able to do this more than twice with the same lender.*)
- When mortgage rates go up, can I keep paying the same amount each month or must I pay more? (*This depends on the individual lender but, in any case, you have such a choice only with repayment mortgages. If you do not increase your payments after rates have risen, you are effectively increasing the length of the loan. You cannot do this with an endowment mortgage because the package is geared to pay off the debt on a fixed date. With many mortgages, repayments are recalculated only once a year and then reflect interest rate changes from the previous year.*)
- What perks are you offering with this mortgage? (*It is always worth asking for any add-ons, even if they are not being publicised at the time. These can include:*

  - *paying your legal fees*
  - *paying for the valuation*
  - *giving a cashback*
  - *charging a discounted rate of interest*
  - *charging a fixed-rate for a set period*
  - *waiving a mortgage indemnity premium*
  - *giving free mortgage payment insurance (see loan protection insurance on p.259).*

- Will you fill out the application form for me? (*The lender should be willing to help you, but always read it through before you sign.*)

tip

> **When the offer comes through, check that it matches what you were expecting and that it is correct in every detail. Mistakes happen.**

- How frequently is interest calculated?
- Can I pay chunks off the mortgage from time to time?
- What is the minimum I can pay off the mortgage?
- Will any lump-sum repayments I make be deducted from my debt immediately?
- If I want to pay off some of my mortgage now, what will you do with the money I send? (*It might earn no interest until the lender's year end, in which case it would be better to put the lump-sum repayment into a savings account and pay it to the lender at the last moment.*)
- How can I make sure any money I send to pay off all or part of the mortgage is used immediately? (*Check with the lender before you send the cheque that it will accept the money as a loan repayment. Always enclose a letter explaining why you are sending this money – otherwise the lender might think you have sent the money to cover the next few months' payments in advance.*)
- What is the cost if I pay off the mortgage sooner than planned?
- If I pay off the whole mortgage, does interest stop immediately? (*Some lenders keep charging until the end of the month; others stop charging you interest on the day the loan is repaid.*)
- Will you give me financial advice? (*Only a few can give independent advice, which they do through an independent financial advice subsidiary.*)
- Will I have to pay for a mortgage indemnity guarantee (MIG)?
- Will I have to buy a mortgage indemnity guarantee again each time I take a new mortgage? (*You have to buy a new policy every time you buy a new house or remortgage with a different lender. You should not, though, if you stay put and borrow more from the same lender. Some lenders now waive MIGs.*)
- When I move, is the unused portion of the MIG premium refunded? (*Unlikely but you can ask for clemency if you move within a few months of starting the loan.*)
- How much of the endowment goes towards life insurance and how much to investment? (*About 5 per cent of your premiums is used to buy life insurance.*)
- Can I make repayments weekly or fortnightly instead of monthly? (*This might suit the way you are paid; banks are more likely to agree than building societies.*)

- Can I take a break in repayments when I have a baby? (*Mortgages allowing 'baby breaks' are becoming more common.*)
- Is there a charge for taking a repayment break?
- Do you have a free telephone helpline number for queries?
- What hours is the telephone helpline open? (*Helplines often operate into the evenings and on Saturdays and Sundays.*)
- Can I arrange everything over the telephone, or do I need to come in to your office?
- Can I contact you by e-mail?
- What happens to my mortgage payments if I'm made redundant? (*With home loans starting after September 1995, you get no Income Support for mortgage costs until you have been out of work for nine months.*)
- If I have difficulty repaying my mortgage, can I reduce the amount I send? (*Always talk through any problems with your lender before you find you can't pay. Always be co-operative, show you are willing to pay, and explain how you will make up the shortfall. See also loan protection insurance p. 259*)

tip | **You should tell the lender if you start working from home, take in lodgers, or rent out the house.**

Information you have to provide before getting a mortgage

- pay slips to prove your income
- references from your landlord if you are currently renting.
- references from your employer
- details of any existing loans
- proof that you have the money to put down as a deposit (if you have had to borrow the deposit from elsewhere, it could affect the decision to give you the mortgage)
- the address of your tax office and your tax code.

Getting a mortgage when you have a poor credit record

Getting a mortgage when you have a poor credit record is difficult.

ask Margaret

If my previous house has been repossessed by one lender, could I get a mortgage from a different one?
> The second lender will know all about it. The Council of Mortgage Lenders keeps a central register of everyone whose home has been repossessed, whether it was compulsory or you voluntarily handed back the keys.

How long does the Council of Mortgage Lenders keep this information?
> Six years.

Will I ever get a mortgage again if I've been repossessed?
> It depends how long ago it happened and how good your credit record has been since then. Once six years have passed, you can apply for a loan.

Is there anywhere else I can get a home loan if banks and building societies turn me down?
> Some companies specialise in lending to people who have been turned down by mainstream lenders. But you will pay a higher rate of interest than normal, and they will be less tolerant if you default.

Raising money from your home when you are retired

ask Margaret

The mortgage is paid off but we find it difficult making ends meet. How can we raise money from the house?
> You have three options for increasing your income: take in lodgers; sell all

or part of the house to someone who will let you continue living there under a home reversion scheme; or take out a new mortgage but pay no interest until you sell.

tip

> **You can earn several thousand pounds a year tax-free under the Rent-a-Room scheme by taking in a lodger. Ask at your local tax office for details.**

If I sold the house through a home reversion scheme, how can I be confident that the new owner won't throw me out?

You would have a watertight agreement.

How does the company purchasing my house make a profit?

It pays you only half – sometimes less – of the current value of the house and it benefits from any price rise, on the portion it owns, when you sell. Meanwhile, you still have to pay for repairs.

Do I have to sell the whole house?

You can, or you can sell just a portion of it.

Do I have to pay rent to the owners?

Only a nominal amount, say £1 a month. But check beforehand, because companies could charge more.

tip

> WARNING: **If you subsequently need to move, you will have little or no money from your old house with which to buy a new one.**

Will lenders give me a mortgage after I've retired?

Quite possibly, provided you can afford the repayments. But there are special loans for the elderly where you pay no interest during your lifetime called shared appreciation mortgages.

tip

> WARNING: **Do make a point of talking to your family before remortgaging your property, because there will be less for them to inherit.**

What are shared appreciation mortgages and how do they work?

With shared appreciation mortgages, you take a loan at a low fixed rate of interest (even at zero interest) and repay by giving the lender a proportion of the increase in house price when you sell.

tip

> **Shared appreciation mortgages are popular, but only a few banks sell them and they are available only when the banks have a tranche of money for the purpose. If you needed to move house, you would have less than its full value to spend on buying a new one because you would use much of the proceeds to repay the loan.**

What are 'home income plans' and how do they work?

You take out a mortgage and use the money to buy an annuity. This makes them feasible only for people aged over 70, but they lost any financial advantage when mortgage tax relief was withdrawn in the 1999 Budget.

Where can I find out more about using my home to raise money?

Talk to a financial adviser or mortgage broker, but do make sure they are experienced in this area. Write to Safe Home Income Plans (SHIP), whose address is given in the Appendix, for more information. This is a specialist field and not one where you can afford to make a mistake.

Different types of mortgages available

There are two main choices: repaying capital and interest as you go (a repayment mortgage) or paying just interest and making separate arrangements to accumulate enough money to repay the loan when it is due, by contributing to an endowment policy, pension or ISA (an interest-only and, most commonly, endowment mortgage).

REPAYMENT MORTGAGES

With repayment mortgages, each month you pay off some of the capital and some of the interest owing to the mortgage lender. In the early years, you repay mainly interest and only a little capital; the balance gradually switches until, at the end of the loan, you are repaying nearly all capital.

They are flexible, because you can switch around and extend the term as you want, and you know for certain that your mortgage will be paid off on the due date, but there is no life insurance unless you buy it separately. The lender may insist you buy life insurance as well, but this can be term insurance, which is cheaper than an endowment policy because it contains no investment element.

ENDOWMENT MORTGAGES

With an endowment mortgage, you pay only interest to the lender and separately pay life insurance premiums to an insurance company. The endowment policy repays the loan if you die prematurely, and it should also be enough to repay the loan at the end of the period.

Most endowment home loans sold now are 'low cost' mortgages. You buy a smaller amount of insurance than you need to repay the loan, in the hope that the investments will grow enough to make up the shortfall. Premiums are lower than for full endowment policies, although you might have to increase your premiums later to make sure the endowment policy produces enough to repay the loan. Low-cost mortgages include term insurance to ensure that the mortgage is repaid if you die.

tip **Endowment policies used to be assigned to the building society in exchange for the mortgage. Usually today they are not. With the lender's agreement, you need not use the proceeds of the policy to repay the loan, but instead can negotiate another mortgage and continue paying the interest due.**

For more details about endowment policies as an investment, see p.106 in Chapter 4.

FLEXIBLE MORTGAGES

These are becoming more widespread and are worth looking at because they can be adapted as your circumstances change during the life of the loan: there might be times when you can pay off more of the loan (for instance, you receive an inheritance or a large bonus) and others when you can afford less (if you lose your job or split with your partner). They can also allow for a maternity break.

Some of these mortgages are more flexible than others. With the most flexible mortgages, if you have paid in more than agreed, you earn tax-free interest and can make cash withdrawals; or borrow more without making a new application. They are sometimes called 'current account mortgages'.

However there is unlikely to be any cashback, or any discount on the interest rate, and some providers are only willing to lend up to 75 per cent of the house price.

PENSION MORTGAGES

With pension mortgages, you pay only interest to the lender and, separately, contributions to a personal pension scheme. When you retire, the lump sum you are allowed to take from your pension is used to repay the mortgage. Only self-employed people can do this.

Tax relief on your pension contributions gives a tax advantage to repaying a mortgage. But, when you retire, your pension will be smaller because some of your pension fund has been used to repay the loan.

INTEREST-ONLY MORTGAGES

With interest-only mortgages, you pay only interest to the lender; often it is left up to you how you find the money to repay the loan, although sometimes the lender insists on proof that you have something organised.

This is a flexible arrangement, suitable if your finances fluctuate and if you are confident of receiving, say, a large inheritance. But, if you fail to save to pay off the loan, you continue paying interest and never manage to buy the house, which is expensive.

ISA MORTGAGES

With this type of mortgage, you take an interest-only loan and save separately through an ISA to repay it.

tip

> WARNING: **If you want an endowment mortgage, make sure you buy an endowment life insurance policy and not a whole-life policy. Whole-life insurance policies pay out only when you die, not when the loan is due to be repaid.**

Interest rate choices

MORTGAGES WITH A VARIABLE RATE OF INTEREST

The interest goes up and down over the years as market rates move. Some lenders change borrowers' monthly repayments only once a year, adjusting up or down to account for any interest rate changes during the previous year. Others make adjustments each time the interest rate changes. You might get an initial interest-rate discount or cashback.

MORTGAGES WITH A FIXED RATE OF INTEREST

The rate of interest does not change for a set number of years (usually between one and five), so you can budget tightly for that period of time. You might have to buy the lender's house insurance and there is probably a penalty to pay if you cancel the loan early.

DISCOUNTED-RATE MORTGAGES

These are genuine money-off loans. You pay a lower rate of interest for, say, a year and then move on to the standard variable rate. Some mortgage providers let you choose when you want to take the discount – you may, for instance, prefer it in a few years' time when you start a family.

CAPPED MORTGAGES

With these, the rate of interest varies but, for the first few years, will never rise above a set figure.

COLLARED MORTGAGES

For these, the rate of interest varies but, for the first few years, will not fall below a set figure.

CAP-AND-COLLAR MORTGAGES

With these, the rate of interest varies but, for the first few years, there is both an upper and lower limit to how far the rate will move.

Mortgage jargon

Here are some of the abbreviations that lenders use:

- LTV = 'loan to value', which is the percentage of the house price that the lender allows you to borrow.
- MIG = 'mortgage indemnity guarantee', which is insurance you pay so that the lender is insured in case you default.
- MIPs = 'mortgage indemnity premiums' (sometimes called the 'high lending fee'), which are the premiums for the MIG.
- SVR = 'standard variable rate of interest', which is the ordinary mortgage rate that goes up or down whenever rates change.

The Mortgage Code

Adopting the Mortgage Code is voluntary, although all lenders who belong to the Council of Mortgage Lenders – and most do – have agreed to comply and also agreed to do business only through brokers and IFAs who have signed up to the Code.

They promise to:

- act fairly in all dealings with you
- give you information in plain language
- help you choose an appropriate mortgage unless you have already decided what you want
- help you understand the financial implications of the loan
- help you understand how your mortgage works
- correct errors and handle complaints speedily
- treat customers who have financial difficulties and arrears sympathetically and positively
- make sure their staff comply with the Code.

7 Obtaining Credit

Few people can get through life without borrowing money, and these days building a good credit record – and, more importantly, avoiding a bad one – is essential.

But, just as lenders are particular who they take on, customers too should choose lenders, and loans, with care. Chosen well, loans enable you to buy something you could not otherwise afford – your home is the obvious example. (For more on obtaining a mortgage, see Chapter 6.) However, picking the wrong loan, or the wrong lender, can make your financial situation worse, not better: you could spend several years repaying a loan and still owe more than when you started.

Whenever you borrow money, look for the loan that is appropriate to your need, and never borrow more than you are confident you can repay.

The basics of credit

ask Margaret

What counts as credit?

Any money that someone else gives you, to spend now, that you must pay back, usually plus interest. This includes:

- overdrafts
- personal loans
- credit cards
- hire purchase
- mortgages.

How easy is it to get credit?

Credit is readily available these days to anyone with a good credit record.

Can I get credit before I start working?

Students in university or college education can get bank accounts with overdrafts and credit cards. For young people leaving school, lenders looks at employment prospects and, if they are still living at home, their parents' credit record.

tip

> WARNING: **Be careful about making numerous applications for credit without going ahead. Each time you apply, the lender checks your credit reference agency file (see the later section in this chapter). This check is logged as a search, even if you pull out, but next time you apply for credit, the lender will see that multiple searches have been made but no credit taken. The lender could interpret this as showing that you are a bad risk.**

Is there a cooling off period after signing a loan agreement if I change my mind?

It depends where you signed the credit agreement. If the whole transaction takes place in a shop or the lender's branch, you are committed to the agreement as soon as both you and the lender (or the salesperson, as the lender's agent) have signed. If you sign first, you can still withdraw at any time before the lender has signed.

But if you discuss the deal face to face with a salesperson, anywhere, and then sign the agreement in your home or workplace, you can cancel the agreement within five days of receiving a copy of the agreement in the post. Note that telephone calls do not count as face to face meetings.

tip

> **WARNING: Always read a credit agreement carefully before signing, and take your time; do not rely on what the salesperson tells you.**

I've heard that credit companies should compensate me if anything goes wrong with something I've bought. Is that true?

This applies only to purchases costing between £100 and £30,000 each. It doesn't apply to personal loans, where you can spend the money on anything you want, nor to charge cards where you have to pay off the whole bill every month.

Lenders must reimburse you if you don't receive a purchase or service that you paid for on credit. For example, if you bought a holiday with your credit card but the tour operator collapsed, or a computer funded by a personal loan failed to turn up, you should receive compensation from the lender.

Most credit card companies have voluntarily extended this protection to purchases made abroad as well in the UK.

tip

> **Be prepared for a fight. Credit companies don't like having this responsibility and some don't pay up unless they are convinced you have lost out.**

tip

> **Some credit cards give you your money back if a purchase is damaged within the first three months. This is a perk that they add voluntarily and it doesn't reduce your rights under the Consumer Credit Act 1974.**

tip

> **WARNING: If you have already taken home goods you bought on credit that you then cancel, you must return the goods in an undamaged condition.**

tip

> **The item you buy and any loan to pay for it are separate: if something goes wrong with the goods, you must not stop repaying the debt.**

Credit cards

ask Margaret

Who issues credit cards?

- banks
- large building societies
- insurance-company banks
- foreign banks
- store groups and supermarkets
- many charities
- some football clubs.

Where can I get a credit card?

From your own bank or building society, at any other bank or building society, or through a charity or club with its own credit card.

tip

WARNING: **Never sign a credit card voucher without filling it in, however well you know the person who says they will do it for you.**

tip

Be cynical about credit cards advertising an extremely low rate of interest. These are likely to be teaser rates for the first year to encourage you to sign up. By all means take advantage of them, but keep alert to any increases coming along.

Can a shop charge me more if I want to pay on credit?

They are allowed to, although few shops do charge extra. You are more likely to face a premium when you have little option but to use that outlet, such as taxi cabs, tour operators or ticket agencies. The person you are paying by credit card must tell you about any surcharge before you sign the voucher. If a surcharge applies, you can avoid the charge by paying with a debit card instead.

How much extra can shops charge for paying by credit card?

Unless the credit card company writes a limit into its agreement, the shop can charge what it likes. Even when the credit card company has restricted the shop's charges, the retailer can get round this by calling the surcharge a 'handling fee', for which there are no restrictions.

tip

> **When booking a holiday or theatre tickets, check whether the company charges a booking fee once or for every person on the booking form. If it charges for everyone, this is expensive.**

Can shops set a minimum purchase price below which they won't accept credit cards?

Yes, whatever level the shop decides.

What should I do if I see a wrong payment on my credit card bill?

Contact the credit card company immediately and explain. They will suspend the amount in dispute, and interest charges, until they have investigated. If they agree with you, the payment will be cancelled; if not, you have to pay and argue your case with the retailer.

If I'm bad at managing credit cards, can I have my credit limit reduced?

Yes. Just ask.

How can I get my credit limit increased?

Again, just ask. Banks regularly increase limits for good customers, but you can anyway always request more. They might or might not agree to raise the limit.

Can I get cash on my credit card?

You can, but credit card companies charge an additional fee when you take cash: at least 1.5 per cent, with a minimum charge of £1.50.

What happens if I have a joint credit card account but the other person won't pay the bill?

Joint credit cards are different from joint personal loans where you are both equally liable. Joint credit cards are only ever in one person's name, with the other person named as an 'additional cardholder'. If the second-named person goes on a spending spree, the first has to pay; if the first refuses to settle the bill, the card company can't force the second-named to pay up, although they are likely to try.

tip

> **If your credit card payment always falls due a few days before you get paid, ask the card company to change the billing date until after your salary arrives.**

Why does a shopkeeper sometimes, but not always, telephone for authorisation when I present a credit card?

Each store has a 'floor limit', which is the amount below which they can accept credit card payments without phoning for authorisation. Floor limits are never disclosed to customers and are changed from time to time to stop fraudsters finding out how much they are. Sometimes floor limits are temporarily reduced to zero, and then every credit card purchase has to be checked.

If my credit card is stolen and misused, will I have to pay the losses?

If someone uses your card before you have had a chance to tell the card issuer, you are responsible for the first £50 that is stolen, although card issuers don't normally make you pay it. Once you have reported the loss, the card issuer accepts liability unless it suspects you of fraud.

tip

> **You can register all your plastic cards under a card protection scheme so that, if they are lost or stolen, you phone one number and they are cancelled immediately. If only one card is stolen, you can say which one you want stopped. But if you have joint credit cards, both are cancelled if one is lost.**

How do charity credit cards work?

The charity signs up with a credit card company and receives a donation from the card company when you take out the card and another based on the amount you spend with it. Such credit cards are also called 'affinity cards'.

Is it safe to use my credit card number to shop through the Internet?

You need to be careful, for if anyone dishonest got hold of your card number they could use it to make purchases. Deal only with reputable companies; if you can't use a secure browser, fax your application instead, or order through the Internet but post a cheque.

tip

> **When shopping on the Internet, be careful about giving your credit card details. Internet security is improving fast, and so check the latest position with your server – there are plenty of links giving up-to-date information.**

Can anyone put through payments on my credit card without my signature?

They can, if they have your credit card number. It is called a 'cardholder not present' transaction, which enables you to pay for goods over the telephone. This is a convenient way to shop, but it does mean you must be careful about giving out your credit card number.

How should I choose a credit card?

If you pay off the whole bill every month, pick a card with no annual fee; it won't matter to you if the interest rate is high. Otherwise choose a card with a lower rate of interest.

How can I minimise credit card interest payments if I don't repay the bill in full?

Do your shopping just before your statement is due, so that the purchases don't show up until the following month's statement. Secondly, pay whatever you can afford as soon as the bill arrives, to lower the daily average you owe and therefore the amount of interest to pay. Don't leave even the smallest amount unpaid; you will be charged interest unless you repay the bill in full.

Is there any advantage in having a 'gold card'?

'Gold card' is a vague term applied to credit cards and charge cards. Some people think it shows the world that they are wealthy, but it is not difficult to get gold cards these days. Broadly, you might get a larger credit limit and more perks, but the annual fee costs more.

Who is involved in a credit card transaction?

There are five participants:

- you, the cardholder
- the outlet where you are buying (shop, petrol station, hotel, restaurant)
- the bank that issues your card
- the bank that handles the transaction for the outlet
- the international network (Visa or Mastercard) that enables you to use the card abroad.

tip

Visa or Mastercard are international organisations that credit card companies join so that customers can use one plastic card to pay for goods and services around the world.

QUESTIONS TO ASK WHEN COMPARING CREDIT CARDS

get the facts

- What, if anything, is the annual fee charged?
- What is the APR for purchases? (*APR is the Annual Percentage Rate and a more accurate figure for comparing than the flat rate of interest.*)
- What is the APR for cash? (*This will be higher than the APR for purchases.*)
- Are there are charges in the small print? (*Card companies can charge extra if your payment is late or if you exceed your credit limit.*)
- How and when will the interest rate change? (*A few credit cards move their interest rates with bank base rates, but most change rates only when they feel competitive pressure to do so.*)
- What is the minimum charge for withdrawing cash?
- How quickly must the bill be paid after I receive it? (*Many card companies say they give up to 56 days' interest-free credit. But you can get 56 days' free credit only on purchases debited to your account on day one.*)
- From what date do you start charging interest? (*This may be the date you bought the goods, the date the item was charged to your account, or the date on the statement. A few cards charge interest even when you pay the bill promptly and in full.*)
- Will I get bonus points for using the card? (*Bonus points can build up to gifts, product or service discounts, or free air flights.*)

tip

> **Bonus points aren't necessarily an advantage: the interest rate might be higher than on other cards; and you might never take advantage of the rewards anyway.**

- Will you send emergency cash if I lose the card while I am abroad?
- Is there an emergency telephone number, where someone speaks English, that I can call from overseas?
- Is there a free or low-cost telephone helpline for UK calls; what hours does it operate?
- Does the card include legal expenses insurance? (*see p.243 for more on legal expenses insurance.*)
- Do you provide a list of approved tradespeople if I need repairs done?
- Do you have credit cards linked to charities?
- How much cash can I withdraw each day?
- Can I transfer the money I owe on my existing credit card to this new one? (*Such is the competition among credit cards, that many take on your debt, sometimes charging particularly low interest.*)
- With this credit card, can I get a personal loan at a special rate?

- Do you allow a credit 'holiday' so that I can miss a month's payment in an emergency? (*The break is only on your repayment; you continue paying interest on the outstanding balance.*)

Store cards

Large store groups issue these cards to encourage you to shop in their branches. They never charge an annual fee, but the cards can be used only within the issuing store group or chain of shops.

There are two types of store card. One is similar to a credit card, where you have a credit limit and each month choose how much of your spending to repay. With the other, you choose how much you want to pay in each month and can then borrow, often, 24 times that amount. Store cards entitle cardholders to discounts or to specially arranged shopping events.

QUESTIONS TO ASK WHEN CHOOSING A STORE CARD

get the facts

- How much interest do I pay on transactions? (*The rates will vary and are often more expensive than bank credit cards. Some stores charge less if you pay by direct debit.*)
- What date is interest charged from? (*It is usually the date you bought the goods, but can be the statement date.*)

tip

> **Stores sometimes offer a discount on the goods being bought if you take out their store card on the spot. If you are buying something expensive, perhaps furniture, it could be worth taking the card for one purchase alone.**

Charge cards

Charge cards impose no maximum on the amount you can spend, but you have to repay the whole bill each month, however high. This is therefore not credit.

Personal loans

Personal loans can be used for anything legal, but not for business purposes.

ask Margaret

Who provides personal loans?

- banks
- large building societies
- insurance-company banks
- finance companies
- foreign banks
- some retailers and supermarkets
- motoring organisations.

How can I decide if I need a personal loan or a credit card?
They are designed for different types of borrowing. Personal loans are for larger borrowing, say a minimum of £500 or £1,000, over a longer period – at least 12 months – at an interest rate that is usually fixed. You know from the start how much the interest and repayments will be for the life of the loan. Credit cards are for short-term borrowing.

Which is cheaper, personal loans or credit cards?
There is more variation in interest rates between different lenders than between the two types of loan. Existing bank customers sometimes pay lower interest for personal loans than others; if your repayment record is good, ask for a preferential rate.

tip

> Some personal loans are tied to a particular large purchase – a car or furniture – but there is nothing special about the loans. Compare the APR with other forms of credit to see whether there is a better deal by another means.

How long can I take a personal loan for?

You can choose, but between one and five years is common.

tip

> WARNING: **Monthly repayments are cheaper if you spread the loan over a longer period but do not take a personal loan for longer than you know you will need. If you repay the loan early, you could still pay part of the interest and charges for the period after you have repaid the loan.**

Is 'interest-free credit' as good as it sounds?

It should be, but see the warning tip below. If you sign any deal described as 'interest-free' and find you have been misled, complain to the credit company and, if you have no satisfaction, to your local trading standards department at the local council offices.

Before taking an interest-free loan, compare the cash price of the goods because you might be able to buy cheaper elsewhere; some retailers push up the cost before they offer interest-free credit.

tip

> WARNING: **Beware of interest-free credit deals where you pay a substantially higher amount as the final month's payment. If you are not able to afford that last payment, you are likely to have to pay heavy interest charges on it.**
>
> **Be careful with loans offering a 'repayment free' period. You could still be charged interest for those months, but you just don't start paying until later. Compare the total amount that the loans cost.**

QUESTIONS TO ASK A LENDER BEFORE TAKING A PERSONAL LOAN

get the facts

- How long can I borrow for? (*The longer you borrow for, the lower the monthly repayments but the more it will cost overall.*)
- How much is the APR on the loan?
- Is the rate of interest fixed for the life of the loan, or will it vary? (*It is usually fixed.*)

- Are there any other fees or charges? (*The APR should include everything, but loan repayment insurance, for example, may be optional and therefore extra. See p.259 for questions to ask about loan repayment insurance.*)
- Is there a broker's fee to pay?
- How much will my monthly repayments be?
- For how many months will I repay?
- If I repay the loan early, what are the penalties? (*Don't be fooled if the loan company says that there is an 'early settlement rebate': see 'Repaying a loan early' below.*)
- If I miss a payment, what happens?
- Can I see these answers in a written quotation? (*You are entitled to this and it is useful to read it in your own time.*)

QUESTIONS ON CREDIT APPLICATION FORMS

ask yourself

- name and address
- previous address
- telephone number
- date of birth
- employment details
- income and outgoings
- how much you want to borrow
- for how many years you want to borrow
- whether or not you want loan protection insurance. (*This is usually optional. See p.259.*)

Hire purchase

Hire purchase (HP) is different from other forms of credit because the goods do not become your property until you have paid all the instalments. If you fall behind with your payments, the lender can take back the goods without returning any of your money. You have more rights once you have paid one-third of the total due because then the shop cannot take the goods back without a court order. These conditions mean that it is illegal to sell anything you are buying on HP until it is fully paid for.

You can obtain HP through hire purchase companies (typically for buying cars) and retailers, although they are more likely to offer loans or store cards.

ask Margaret

Is there a cooling off period for HP agreements in case I change my mind?
It is the same as for personal loans (see p.177).

How long can I borrow for?
You choose how many months or years you want to take to pay.

Can I pay off the loan early?
You can settle up at any time, and keep the goods, but you will still be charged something for interest and costs for the full length of the loan. See 'Repaying a loan early' (p.194).

tip

> WARNING: **HP is often pushed by shop salespeople who earn commission from each deal, but it can be expensive.**

Secured personal loans

With a secured personal loan your home is used as security. Therefore if you default on repaying the loan, your home can be repossessed. Do not enter into a secured personal loan without long and serious thought.

Credit reference agencies

Credit reference agencies are companies that keep files on people's credit history for lenders to look at when assessing credit applications.

Will credit reference agencies have a file on me?

Almost certainly.

What do they put in the files?

Publicly available information: electoral roll details, county court judgements (CCJs), Scottish Decrees, bankruptcy notices and voluntary bankruptcy arrangements. And information from lenders about your credit repayment record – good and bad.

What if I don't want information passed to a credit reference agency?

There is nothing you can do to stop it.

How can I find out what is on my credit reference agency file?

Write to the credit reference agencies (there are two in the UK), send a £2 search fee to each, and ask for a copy of your entry on their files. The addresses of the credit reference agencies are given in the Appendix.

tip

> Some details on credit reference files are easy to understand, such as county court judgements. But there are also lines of numbers indicating how up-to-date your credit repayments are. There is a number for every month: 0 means you are up-to-date; 1 means your payment is one month overdue, and so on.

What can I do if I find a mistake on my file?

Write to the agency asking for the entry to be removed completely, if it is totally wrong, or for it to be amended if a detail is incorrect. If the agency refuses, you can ask for your point of view, up to 200 words, to be added to your file. Then, whenever a lender enquires about you, it sees your comments as well as the agency's information.

What if the file shows an accurate bad credit record?

In your amendment, show mitigating circumstances, such as losing your job through redundancy or illness, and emphasise your attempts to repay any debts.

Can credit reference agencies refuse even to add a note to my file?

Only if they regard your note as incorrect, defamatory, frivolous or scandalous. In that case, they will ask the Office of Fair Trading for a ruling. They must tell you they are doing this. As a last resort, you too can ask the Office of Fair Trading to intervene.

I've heard of people being turned down for credit because of someone else's bad credit record. How can this happen?

Your file can include information about other members of your family if you live at the same address and have the same surname. Lenders believe that, if one person in the family has a bad debt record, the others are more likely to default. And sometimes they just make mistakes.

Whose information can they keep on my file?

Only people who live at the same address, have the same surname and whom the agency can reasonably assume are closely related to you.

If one member of the family is bad at repaying loans, will everyone be turned down for credit?

It is possible, but you can ask the credit reference agency for a notice of disassociation. As long as you have no joint accounts, write saying that you want to be disassociated from the relative with a bad credit record. Next time you apply for credit, that name will not be included in the information shown to the lender.

How long are county court judgements kept on my file?

For six years, even if you paid off the judgement.

What if I couldn't be blamed for the debt – for instance when I just didn't have the money because I'd lost my job?

The information stays because it is a matter of fact, but you can write a note explaining the circumstances, which should be included in your file.

Can anyone ask to look at my credit reference file?

No. Only lenders who contribute information; and the police, Customs & Excise and the Inland Revenue if they are about to prosecute you.

How can I tell if a lender has used a credit reference agency to assess me?

They nearly always do. If your application is accepted, there is no problem. But if you are turned down, and an agency was used, the lender must disclose this fact, tell you which agency it was, and explain how you can get a copy of your file.

Does the credit reference agency tell the lender to turn me down?

No. The agencies just provide the information, without comment. The lender decides how to interpret it.

Credit scoring

Every answer you provide on a credit application form earns a number of points. If your total exceeds a certain figure, you get the loan; if your total score falls short, you don't.

ask Margaret

How many points do I need to get credit?

You won't know. Each lender has its own schedule and sets its own cut-off point; and the scorecard is likely to be different for young applicants.

If one lender turns me down, will another accept me?

Quite possibly.

What scores highly in credit scoring?

Anything that shows you are a reliable person, can afford the credit, and will repay:

- working for the same employer for years
- living a long time in the same property
- having held the same bank account for a long time
- being middle-aged
- having existing, regularly repaid, credit
- having a mortgage
- having a home telephone.

What counts against me for credit scoring?

Anything that shows you might not be reliable:

- being self-employed
- renting and frequently moving home
- no home telephone number
- a poor credit repayment record
- having no bank account, or having held one for less than a year
- being young.

Will a lender tell me if it has used credit scoring?

If you ask, it should. But you can assume that nearly all do – and for mortgages and cheque accounts as well as straightforward loans.

Can I appeal if I am refused a loan because I failed the credit scoring?

Yes. Talk to the company calmly, however angry you feel, and try to provide additional information they had not taken into account to show that you really can afford to repay the loan.

tip

> Some lenders also use 'behaviour scoring', which tracks your spending and repaying pattern. If you usually repay promptly, but then forget a few times, the lender will be more lenient with you.

Getting credit if you have a poor credit record

Bad credit risks come in different degrees. At the mildest, being consistently late with monthly payments indicates that the person is having difficulty making ends meet rather than being merely forgetful; some lenders ignore this while others regard it as cause for concern.

Failing to repay a debt altogether is more serious, particularly if it leads to a county court judgement and – worse – if the county court judgement is not paid in full within one month. Having a house repossessed shows someone to be an even worse credit risk. If a person has been declared bankrupt, that person is simply not allowed to borrow money until the bankruptcy is discharged.

ask Margaret

Sometimes my credit card payment is late because I just forget how fast time goes by. Would that count against me?

Not if this was the sum total of your mistakes.

tip

> You can arrange for your credit card bill to be paid, or part-paid, automatically by your bank to avoid missing the deadline.

With a poor credit record, is it worth even applying for credit?

It depends how bad your record is, how much you want to borrow, and the attitude of the lender. Some lenders are stricter than others.

If one lender turns me down, could I try somewhere else?

Certainly. Different lenders use different criteria, and some specialise in lending to people with poor credit records – although they usually charge higher rates of interest because of the extra risk.

Is it worth going to a lender that advertises loans for people with CCJs?

Avoid them. The interest rates are high and they are not the sort of outfits that react sympathetically if you have problems repaying.

tip

> WARNING: **Do not deceive yourself into thinking that, if you have debt problems, taking out a new loan will help. If you cannot meet the repayments on a loan you already have, you certainly will not be able to afford an additional loan.**

Will a lender tell me why I've been turned down for credit?

The lender is unlikely to give the exact reason, in case this helps you reconstruct your application next time to disguise the problem area. But there is growing pressure on lenders to be more forthcoming. They must tell you if they have used a credit reference agency to check up on you.

If I move without leaving a forwarding address, how can my creditors catch up with me?

Lenders contribute to a Gone Away Information Network (GAIN), which logs the names of customers who default on loans and disappear, or pretend to have moved house by returning letters marked 'Gone Away'.

Would a lender know if I used my correct name and address but, say, exaggerated my income on the application form?

They might check with your employer. Whenever lenders discover that someone has tried to obtain credit fraudulently, they report this to the Credit Industry Fraud Avoidance System (Cifas); and the next time you apply for credit, your credit reference agency file will show you as untrustworthy.

tip

> WARNING: **Some credit brokers make extravagant promises about getting loans for people with bad credit records: be wary about them. They will charge a fee and probably ask for it up front. If you still don't get a loan, they are allowed by law to keep no more that £5 of the fee; however, if you have a problem getting the balance returned, your only recourse is the county court.**

> **'Credit repair' companies claim they can change the information held on your credit reference agency file. They cannot, but they charge a lot of money and should be avoided at all costs.**

Repaying a loan early

ask Margaret

I wanted to pay off a loan early but the lenders charged me so much that I decided to keep the loan going. Can they do this?

Yes. This often applies with the type of loan you take out for a fixed period of time, such as borrowing for two years to buy a sofa. In contrast, when you pay off a credit card debt, you simply pay the whole amount outstanding and that is the end of it.

Why can lenders charge more on some loans?

The Consumer Credit Act allows it. When you take out a loan for a set period, the lender calculates how much you will pay for interest and charges, and spreads the cost over the life of the loan. If you were to repay early, the lender would lose money so the law allows them to recoup much of their costs, according to a set formula.

tip

> **The lender may mention an 'early settlement rebate'. This does not mean that you get a discount for paying early; the rebate applies only to the total amount in charges and interest that you would have paid if you kept the loan going for its full term.**

The Lenders' Code of Practice

All responsible lenders agree to:

- behave with integrity
- provide staff training
- comply with all relevant legislation

- use plain English
- promptly provide customers with information about their accounts
- explain to customers their rights and obligations
- provide the name of a senior official if a consumer believes that he or she has been unreasonably refused credit
- keep their advertising fair and reasonable and not misleading
- not put pressure on consumers to take out a loan that they may have difficulty repaying
- take particular care with applications from young people
- keep customers' information confidential
- respond sympathetically to borrowers who have repayment problems
- deal promptly with complaints and at a senior level.

Actions to take before obtaining credit

- Get a written quotation before completing an application form. This avoids problems caused by multiple credit searches that can make you appear a bad risk.
- Take the quotation home to read.
- Check how much you have to pay each month and for how many months.
- Compare several credit deals.
- Check particularly whether the loan is secured (when your home could be at risk) or unsecured.
- Check whether you can cancel the agreement at any time.
- If there is anything you do not understand, ask.
- If any salesperson puts pressure on you to sign, don't.
- If you have any hesitation, ask to read the terms and conditions in your own good time.
- Consider whether you want to buy loan repayment insurance. (See p.259.)

8 Bank Accounts

You can bank at the supermarket, over the telephone and through the Internet these days. New-style banks, such as retailers and insurance companies, make banking more accessible and provide many more accounts to choose from.

Most people already have at least one bank account and so the new banks need to offer better interest rates to attract attention. But they do not provide full-scale banking and some are simply savings accounts. To get the bank account that you want, you need to ask the right questions.

Questions to ask yourself before opening a bank account

ask yourself

- Why do I want to open a bank account? (*Is it because you want somewhere for your salary to be paid in, a cheque book, a place for your savings, or to be able to pay bills automatically? Or do you already have a bank account*

and want a second or third account, or an additional joint account?)
- Why do I want to change my bank account? (*Is it because you are unhappy with the one you have, you want to try one of the new providers, or you want a better rate of interest?*)
- Do I want a full cheque account or a simple savings account?
- Do I need a bank with a branch conveniently nearby? (*This is less important now that you can withdraw cash at many places.*)
- What hours are the local bank branches open?

tip

If you are dissatisfied with your existing bank, talk to someone in the branch before moving to another bank, they might be able to sort out your complaints.

tip

If you need to transfer money between two accounts at different banks, it can take up to four days for the money to arrive. If both accounts are with the same bank, a transfer should go through on the same day.

New-style banks versus traditional

The new-style banks pay good interest on savings, provide straight-forward accounts, and mostly operate by telephone with long opening hours (sometimes 24 hours a day, seven days a week).

ask Margaret

Is my money safe with a new bank account provider?
Certainly. Institutions can sell savings accounts only with authority from the Financial Services Authority. Depositors are protected under the Deposit Protection Scheme (see p.29).

Are the new bank accounts comparable with those from traditional banks?
Most of the new accounts are simple savings and loans accounts. They include instant-access savings accounts, occasionally notice accounts, often mortgages, personal loans and insurance. They exclude cheque books, overdrafts and foreign currency.

Do the new-style banks give better rates of interest than other financial institutions?

Often but not always.

How can I get cash from a new-style bank?

You can write or telephone, asking for money to be transferred to your main bank account. Supermarket banks often have cash machines at their stores, and usually you can withdraw money at the checkout.

tip

> Banks should call accounts 'instant access' only if customers can get cash over the counter or through a cash machine.

Will banks pass on my details to anyone else?

They are bound by rules of confidentiality, unless you default on a loan, in which case the information is forwarded to a credit reference agency; you want to deposit, say, £10,000 in cash, uncharacteristically, and can't explain where the money came from; a court orders the bank to disclose details of your account; or you agree to the bank passing on information.

tip

> Traditional banks sell house insurance, life insurance, personal pensions and unit trusts. You can buy all these from one source for convenience but you might get better value if you buy them separately from different companies. See the individual chapters on each subject.

Questions you will be asked when you open a bank account

ask yourself

- Can you prove that you are who you say you are? (*Banks have to satisfy themselves that you are genuine and will not use the account for laundering drug money. To prove your identity, you will need to provide at least one of the following: a current valid full UK driving licence; a current valid passport; or an employer's identity card showing your photograph and signa-*

ture. The bank will probably also ask for an up-to-date bill that proves your current address, preferably from a utility company or for council tax because these also show the bank that you pay your bills promptly. Banks won't accept birth certificates, credit cards or just an envelope addressed to you, since these do not provide sufficient proof of identity.)

- What is the name of your employer?
- How long have you worked for that employer?
- How long have you lived at your present address? (*If that is less than two years, you will be asked for your previous address as well.*)
- Where is the money coming from that will go into the account?
- Have you any outstanding debts?
- Who do you want to be able to sign your cheques? (*It might be you alone or a partner as well.*)

Cheque accounts

'Cheque account' and 'current account' mean the same.

ask Margaret

Who provides cheque accounts?

Banks, ex-building society banks, some insurance-company banks, some foreign banks, telephone-based banks, and the larger building societies.

Where can I get a cheque account?

At bank and large building society branches, from telephone-based banks, and insurance-company banks.

What can I expect from a cheque account?

With a cheque account, you can:

- pay in your salary and other money you receive
- get hold of cash
- pay regular bills by standing order or direct debit
- write cheques
- pay for goods and services by debit card
- go overdrawn
- obtain foreign currency

- send money abroad
- switch money between several accounts
- demonstrate your creditworthiness.

How many cheque accounts do I need?

Most people need one full cheque account, and maybe another as a joint account with a partner.

Can I have as many cheque accounts as I like?

In theory, yes. But some accounts require your salary or pension to be paid into them. Banks tempt you with better interest rates than their competitors pay, but they want something from you in return. The account that receives your salary is your main account and therefore the one from which the bank is likely to make most profit.

tip

> **'Free banking' means only that there is no charge for writing and receiving cheques, standing orders and direct debits into or out of a cheque account. Even with free banking, banks still charge for many other services.**

Why do banks charge for some services and not for others?

Banks could charge for all services, or charge more for some and less for others. But, as a marketing decision, they believe customers are attracted by a 'free' service.

What should I do if the bank has charged me too much?

Explain politely why you think the charges are unfair. Banks take their charges directly from your account, but they are required to warn you 14 days in advance how much they are going to deduct.

Can a bank refuse to give me a cheque account?

Yes, and the bank doesn't have to give you a reason unless it was because of a bad report from a credit reference agency, in which case it must give you the agency's name and address.

tip

> **Each time you apply for a bank account, the bank checks your credit reference agency record, whether you open the bank account or not. Next time you apply, the bank will see multiple searches on your file with no accounts being opened. It will think you have been rejected as a bad risk and possibly do the same.**

Why is my credit record relevant when I only want a cheque book?

Once you have a cheque book with 25 cheques in it, and a cheque guarantee card, you could go on a spending spree even if you didn't have enough money in your account.

If I'm planning, say, to rent a flat, can landlords check my creditworthiness?

They can make a 'status enquiry' at your bank, although the bank gives out information only with your consent. The answer comes back in broad terms such as 'respectable'.

BANK STATEMENTS

Can I ask for a statement at any time?

Probably, but there will be a charge. A few banks will fax you a statement but that is expensive. Many banks have machines at branches where you can print up-to-date statements as often as you like, free of charge. With some, you can call up a statement through the Internet.

tip

> **Check each statement as soon as it arrives. It is easier to sort out mistakes if you find and report them quickly. Keep the statements with your tax self-assessment records.**

What should I do if a statement contains an error?

Write to the branch immediately, but keep hold of the original statement.

Will the bank compensate me if it makes a mistake?

As a matter of course, the bank will reinstate any money wrongly deducted and all charges or interest wrongly imposed. But whether it compensates you for your wasted time and telephone calls depends on how serious the mistake is, on the bank's attitude to its customers, and on your determination to make it pay up.

Should I do anything if the error is in my favour?

You should tell the bank, unless you can honestly say you thought it was your money. They will find out sooner or later anyway and demand it back.

CHEQUE CLEARING

Cheque clearing is the process of transferring money from one bank account to another.

ask Margaret

Why does the bank sit on my money before letting me use it?

Banks will not release money until the end of the cheque clearing cycle.

How long does cheque clearing normally take?

The clearing cycle takes three days, because cheques are physical pieces of paper that need to be moved around the country. There are two subdivisions within the system: 'cleared for interest', when you start earning interest on the money, and 'cleared for funds', which comes later, when you can withdraw cash against the money from the cheque. If your cheque account is with a building society, you might have to wait ten days before you can withdraw money if the society uses a bank to clear its cheques.

How soon do I start earning interest?

On day two or day three, depending on your bank.

What counts as 'day one'?

The day you pay in the cheque.

When can I withdraw cash?

Usually on day four or day five.

Is there any way of getting the money faster?

A few banks allow withdrawals, from a branch but not through ATMs, on the same day that you pay in a cheque, but this is a concession and does not change the clearing cycle.

What happens if I receive a cheque that subsequently bounces?

Either your bank tries putting the cheque through the clearing system again, to see if the person who wrote it now has enough money in their account. Or it sends you the cheque saying 'refer to drawer'. The 'drawer' is the person who signed the cheque, and you have to sort out the problem with the person who owes you money.

USING CHEQUES

Banks do not like cheques because they are an expensive way of moving money around. Banks prefer debit cards – the plastic equivalent of cheques. But cheques will be with us for a long time yet.

ask Margaret

Why can't I cash cheques in the pub any more?

Blame drug dealers. Banks have to ensure they are not inadvertently laundering drug money. They issue only 'crossed' cheques, preprinted 'account payee', which can be paid only into the bank account of the person named on the cheque – the payee.

tip

> **If you are known by a nick-name that has a different initial to your full name, banks will refuse to accept cheques made out with the wrong initial. Under the money laundering rules, banks must be satisfied that the cheque is paid in to the right person's account. Before the problem arises, visit your branch, taking documents showing that you are known by another name, and ask the bank to recognise your cheques with either initial. You might have to sign an indemnity.**

Where can I get cash?

You can withdraw over the counter from bank branches, building society branches, supermarket checkouts and post offices. You can use cash machines (ATMs) at banks, building societies, at supermarkets and shopping centres, railway stations and motorway service areas, and at a few football grounds.

Can I stop someone cashing a cheque after I've paid them?

Not if the cheque was supported by a cheque guarantee card. But otherwise you can, for a fee, provided the money has not already left your account.

tip

> **To be valid, the cheque guarantee card number must be written on the back of the cheque by the person you are paying; you should not write it yourself.**

Is there an upper limit to the amount I can pay by cheque?

The most you can write a cheque for is the amount on the cheque guarantee card, if you use it; otherwise, the maximum is the amount of money in your account plus any permitted overdraft.

If I want to pay more than the amount on my cheque guarantee card, can I write two cheques for the same purchase?

You can, but the amount will not be guaranteed. However, that is the shop-keeper's problem.

How can I pay for something costing thousands of pounds, perhaps to buy a car?

You can pay by cheque, but the seller will want to know that the cheque has cleared before parting with the goods. The seller might insist on a 'bank draft' which is safer than a cheque.

How does a bank draft work?

You, as the person paying the money, must order a bank draft in advance from your bank, pay a fee and use a pre-agreed password when you collect it. The bank draft is made out to the recipient and signed by the bank manager.

tip

> **If you accept a bank draft, you still need to be careful because they can be forged. If you accept a forged draft, you cannot get your money back. Wait for your bank to confirm that the draft is genuine before handing over the goods. Be particularly suspicious of anyone producing a bank draft after the banks have closed on a Friday evening who insists on doing the deal immediately.**

If I date a cheque for, say, a week hence, can I rely on the bank holding it back before paying the money?

This is postdating a cheque and banks should honour your instructions not to pay the cheque before that date but, in reality, the staff usually do not notice. The bank where the cheque is paid in (probably not your bank anyway) will most likely push it straight through the clearing system. If this happens, and as a result you are charged overdraft fees, ask your bank to refund them.

tip

> **Some banks have tried freeing themselves from responsibility for postdated cheques in their terms and conditions. This does not absolve them of their duty not to pay too soon.**

In my attic I found an old passbook but the bank says the money has already been paid out. How can that be if I still have the passbook?

When banks moved to computer record-keeping, passbooks were replaced with computer-generated statements. Passbooks no longer had to be presented to withdraw money but not all of them were returned to the branch for cancellation.

What happens if I don't have money going into or out of my cheque account?
If no money goes in or out of your account for, say, a year, the bank will ask if you want to keep it open. The bank will hope you won't, because it is not profitable. If you fail to reply, the bank will mark the account 'dormant'; your money sits there for all time, earning a tiny amount of interest at best, and the bank stops writing to you. In these circumstances, think about closing the account and transferring the money into a better-earning account.

If I've paid the bank to hold my valuables in its safe, and something is destroyed or stolen, will the bank compensate me?
No, you should make sure your valuables are covered by your house insurance.

Can I open a bank account in euros?
Yes, although, as with other foreign-currency accounts, the minimum deposit can be high. There is nothing complicated about the euro – it is simply a foreign currency, like the dollar.

Can I open an account with a foreign bank?
There is no reason why not, if they accept you, although the minimum deposit will be high.

STANDING ORDERS AND DIRECT DEBITS

ask Margaret   **What is the difference between a standing order and a direct debit?**
With standing orders you instruct your bank to pay a fixed amount at regular intervals, often monthly. This arrangement continues until you tell your bank to stop or change the amount or payment dates. In contrast, with direct debits you authorise the organisation you owe to take whatever it needs out of your account. If the amount differs from one occasion to the next, it must inform you in advance in case you object. If anything goes wrong with a direct debit, the banks promise to refund customers and then sort out the problem for you.

tip

> WARNING: **An organisation you pay by direct debit can mistakenly stop taking payments, which leaves you owing money, perhaps on an insurance policy. Keep a check, through your bank statements, that the direct debits are continuing correctly.**

tip

> WARNING: **Be careful about paying direct debits out of your credit card account instead of a cheque account. This is called a 'continuous authority transaction' (CAT) and does not provide the same protection as paying from your cheque account. If anything goes wrong with the deductions, you have to sort it out yourself. You cannot cancel a CAT unless the company you are paying agrees; the company can take higher amounts without telling you; and, meanwhile, you cannot close your credit card account.**

OVERDRAFTS

Banks make a lot of money out of overdrafts, particularly when customers go overdrawn without permission. Make sure your overdraft is cost effective.

ask Margaret

If I go overdrawn without permission, can the bank take money from another account to repay the debt?

Possibly. If the terms and conditions allow, the bank can take money from any account that you have there, except a business account. In practice, they should tell you first.

How much will I pay if I go overdrawn without arranging it first?
Charges include:

- monthly or quarterly fee
- daily fee on top of the authorised overdraft charges
- charge for a warning letter
- charge for returning unpaid cheques
- charge for using your cash card or debit card
- vastly higher-than-normal rate of interest on the amount you owe the bank.

tip

> WARNING: **Don't go overdrawn (beyond any fixed buffer zone) without arranging it first, because the charges will be enormous. Unauthorised overdrafts are so expensive that they should be avoided at all costs.**

Overdraft questions

get the facts

- Does the cheque account include a safety margin so that I can go a little overdrawn by mistake without paying charges?
- How much can I go overdrawn in the safety margin?
- How quickly must I get the account back into credit after going in to the safety margin? (*Usually within a few days.*)
- Is there a temporary overdraft facility for the occasional emergency? (*Some accounts allow a small overdraft, charging only interest but no arrangement fee.*)
- Do I have to set up a temporary overdraft in advance, or is it automatically included in the account?
- If I want an ongoing overdraft, what are the charges? (*These can include a one-off arrangement fee, a monthly or quarterly charge, a rate of interest on the amount you are overdrawn, and a charge for every cheque you write while you are overdrawn.*)
- If I go overdrawn, repay the overdrawn amount and then go overdrawn again, do I pay the same charges? (*With some accounts you pay the arrangement fee only once; the other charges stay the same.*)
- Does it count as an unauthorised overdraft if I exceed the limit on an agreed overdraft? (*The answer to this question will be 'Yes'.*)

WHAT OTHER SERVICES DO BANKS PROVIDE?

Bank services are expanding:

- stockbroking
- investment portfolio management
- independent financial advice (through a separate subsidiary)
- house and car insurance
- health insurance
- foreign money and travellers cheques
- help with writing a will

- acting as executor to your will
- safe custody of valuables
- status enquiries
- tax advice.

tip

> **WARNING: Avoid using banks as executors; their charges can be out-rageously expensive, even for straightforward estates.**

For questions about your bank account when you marry or divorce, see p.9.

get the facts

QUESTIONS TO ASK THE BANK WHEN CHOOSING A CHEQUE ACCOUNT

- Can I have a tariff of your charges? (*All banks must publish their charges, and copies should be available in branches. If they later try to charge you for something not on the current tariff, you can refuse to pay.*)
- Do I get all the normal cheque account services that I expect, including overdraft facilities?
- How much interest do you pay on credit balances in the cheque account? (*Some banks pay a paltry amount; others a more reasonable figure. The non-traditional banks usually pay better rates.*)
- Do you pay interest on the full amount in the account? (*Some accounts pay no interest below a minimum balance.*)
- Are there any restrictions on the number of withdrawals that I can make or cheques that I can write?
- What is the maximum amount of cash I can withdraw each day?
- How quickly can I get my cash?
- Is there a limit to the number of withdrawals I can make each month?
- Must I have my salary or pension paid into this account, or pay in a mini-mum amount, each month?
- Is banking free when the account is in credit?
- Exactly which services are free?
- How high is the cheque guarantee card limit? (*Different accounts set differ-ent figures, but it is not a negotiable amount.*)
- How frequently will I get a statement? (*Some banks send them monthly, others quarterly, twice a year or when a printed page is full.*)
- Can I access my account through the Internet?
- If so, how much does it cost to communicate by computer? (*Some banks*

charge nothing, others perhaps £5 a month.)

- By what time must I pay in a cheque for it to be processed that day? (*Often by 3.30 pm, but some banks and building societies accept cheques until 5 pm.*)
- How soon can I make withdrawals after paying in a cheque?
- From what time of day can I withdraw cash from a cash machine against a cheque recently paid in? (*At the end of the clearing cycle, some banks allow withdrawals from early morning but others make you wait until midday.*)
- How soon does the money start earning interest when I've paid in a cheque?
- Are there any charges if I use my cash card in another bank's ATM? (*Often there are, but it is your own bank that makes the charge. The ATM bank can't charge you because it can't take money out of your account.*)
- Are there charges for withdrawing cash over the counter? (*If you need this facility, make sure you pick an account that does not charge.*)
- Is there a cash machine close to my home or work?
- Can I get mini-statements through an ATM?
- Is there a 24-hour lobby near my home or work where I can draw money, pay in cheques and get statements?
- What can I do if the cash machine swallows my cash card at the weekend?
- Will you pass my personal details to any other department in the bank?
- Is there a charge if I need a duplicate copy of a statement I've lost? (*Almost certainly.*)
- Can I speak to someone face to face whenever I want?
- Does your branch have its own manager?
- How long does it take to get to speak to the manager?
- How long does it take to agree a loan application?
- Can I give instructions by telephone?
- Do you have a customer helpline?
- If so, at what times is it open and how much do calls cost?

tip | **Before making your final choice, try to get an impression of the bank's staff: are they welcoming and knowledgeable, and do they seem genuinely willing to help? Does the bank seem likely to provide:**

- convenience
- accuracy
- a speedy response
- a wide range of services
- an ability by staff to discuss your account over the phone
- fast access to your money

- quick lending decisions
- good interest rates
- reasonable charges.

SWITCHING BANKS AND BANK ACCOUNTS

Never close an old bank account until the new one is safely up and running, all your standing orders and direct debits are working properly, and you have a new cheque book. Put all your instructions to both banks involved in writing, and keep copies of the correspondence.

How do I switch standing orders and direct debits?

ask Margaret

This is where most problems occur and you need to handle them differently.

For direct debits you need to complete a new direct debit mandate, which you get from the company you pay; send this to the new bank. For standing orders, give details to the new bank and cancel them with the old bank.

Ask the old bank for a list of standing orders and direct debits; there should be no charge.

Questions for the bank you move to

get the facts

- How will you help me switch from my existing cheque account?
- Will you provide all the forms I need to transfer my account? (*Some do; some don't. If they don't, you will have to contact your employer to have your salary paid to the new account, and every organisation you have standing orders and direct debits with – and don't forget the payments that go out only once a year.*)
- Will you ask my old bank for a reference? (*Banks used to do this, but today they rely more on credit scoring and checks through a credit reference agency.*)
- How long will it take to get the account up and running? (*It should be around seven days.*)
- Will you give me a free overdraft for the first few months in case anything goes wrong with payments? (*Some will; some won't.*)
- How quickly can I make withdrawals after the account is open?
- Can I keep my existing credit card when I change accounts? (*The answer*

should be 'Yes'. Credit cards are independent of your cheque account. You can start an additional credit card with the new bank as well if you like. They will certainly try to persuade you.)

Plastic cards

There are several types of plastic card that come with bank accounts.

CHEQUE GUARANTEE CARD

This guarantees that each cheque will be honoured up to the amount shown on the card – £50, £100 or £250.

tip

> **Never keep your cheque book and cheque card together, because that makes it easier for a thief to use your account. Indeed, the bank could say you had been negligent and make you repay any money stolen from your account.**

CASH CARD

This is available with most cheque accounts and some savings accounts. You key in your secret four-digit Personal Identification Number (PIN) at automated teller machines (ATMs) to withdraw cash.

ask Margaret **Can I get cash from any ATM?**
You can use ATMs owned by banks other than your own, but only those belonging to the same network – although the network is widespread. Your bank might charge you for using a competitor's machine and, as the charge is a flat fee, it can work out expensive for withdrawing small amounts of money.

DEBIT CARD

This is the plastic equivalent of paper cheques and is cheaper for banks to operate. With a debit card, you can also request up to £50 cashback at supermarket checkouts.

ask Margaret
How quickly does the money leave my cheque account when I pay by debit card?
Usually within two or three days.

Can I use a debit card in cash machines abroad?
You can, with your usual PIN, if the machine shows the same logo as on your card (such as Visa, Cirrus or Maestro).

CREDIT CARD

A credit card is convenient for buying expensive items and, if you do not have the money, for spreading the cost over a few months. You do not need to have a cheque account and credit card from the same bank. (For more on credit cards, see p.179 and p.215 (holiday money.)

CHARGE CARD

A charge card is used to pay for goods in shops but, unlike credit cards, the whole bill has to be paid at the end of the month.

LOYALTY CARD

This is issued by retailers, particularly supermarkets, to encourage you to keep visiting their store; and you earn bonus points each time you shop.

ELECTRONIC PURSE

This is a new 'intelligent' plastic card, on to which you electronically transfer money, through an ATM, from your cheque account before going shopping. You can then hand the card to a retailer, who will draw down the amount you are spending. You can top up the card again at an ATM.

REMEMBERING YOUR PIN

ask Margaret

What happens if I forget my PIN when I need money from a cash machine?
You usually have three chances to get it right, but then the machine either swallows your card or just refuses to pay out. You will have to get in touch with your bank to ask for a replacement card.

How can I remember my PIN?
Most accounts allow you to choose your own PIN when you first use the card. You can then use the same PIN for all your cards. Pick a number you find easy to remember, although preferably not your birthday or obvious numbers such as 9999 or 1234.

Can I write down my PIN at all?
If you must write the PIN down, write it in coded form – anything to disguise the real number. You can write the number backwards, or starting with the second digit instead of the first, or disguise it as a telephone number, or move the number on one digit. The problem, then, is remembering what you did!

tip

> WARNING: **If your card is misused before you tell the bank it has been lost or stolen or that someone else has discovered your PIN, you will have to pay a maximum of £50. If you write down the PIN and keep it with the card, the bank will probably decide that you have been grossly negligent and make you pay for all the money stolen from your account.**

Access to your money while abroad

What are the options for holiday spending money?

You have three choices: cash; travellers' cheques; and plastic cards (credit card, debit card, cash card and pre-paid card).

Which is best?

This depends on what suits you. Cash is convenient but a security risk. You can use a credit card, and sometimes a debit card or cash card, with your usual PIN, in overseas cash machines, to withdraw small sums as you need them. But do not rely on finding cash machines in out-of-the-way places.

Travellers cheques are secure and, if they are stolen, they will be replaced. You can face two commission payments, though: when you buy and when you encash; and you have to decide in advance how much you are likely to spend. You could take a small amount of travellers cheques for backup to cash and a plastic card.

tip

> For safety reasons, take your holiday money in two different sources so that, if one is lost or stolen, you have a fallback. You can take two plastic cards on different accounts. Always keep them separately.

Within Europe, can I use my usual cheque book?

You need a special cheque book containing 'eurocheques' which can be written in any European currency. They are convenient but expensive, and banks are anyway starting to scrap eurocheques because customers are using plastic cards instead.

Do I need euro coins when travelling in Europe?

Not yet. The countries that have signed up to the single European currency are using their original notes and coins until the new coinage is introduced in January 2002. Then there will be six months when both will be acceptable; only after that will you need to use euro coins.

tip

> Post offices sell foreign currency. And look out for banks and building societies offering special commission-free holiday money deals.

USING CREDIT CARDS ON HOLIDAY ABROAD

Credit cards are an economical way of obtaining foreign currency: you get a better rate of exchange than with travellers cheques or currency bought before you leave. You can withdraw the local money from cash machines and bank branches but, before travelling, check how much cash you can withdraw abroad each day.

ask Margaret

Can I get foreign currency in any overseas bank?

No. You have to look for one that has symbols matching the ones on your card.

Can I raise my credit limit if I need more money while I am on holiday?

You can telephone the bank from wherever you are and ask for more. This is easier with a telephone-based bank account. If you need extra credit just for your holiday, ask for a short-term increase in your overdraft limit.

Can hotels put through extra charges on my credit card after I've left and paid the bill?

They are allowed to, in case you have not declared drinks from the mini bar or telephone calls.

How can I stop a hotel charging me for something I didn't have?

If you spot a wrong deduction on your monthly statement, contact your credit card company. Keep receipts for everything and make notes of exactly when you used the hotel's facilities. This shows the credit card company that you are a methodical person and strengthens your case if you are wrongly charged.

tip

> **WARNING: Be careful if your credit card is swiped to cover the deposit for a hotel or car rental but you actually pay by a different method or with another card. Even though you have not used that amount of credit, the outlet might fail to cancel the voucher so that, even while you are still on holiday, it goes through on your account and reduces the credit available for the rest of your holiday.**

My credit card provides travel insurance when I use it to book holidays. Does this mean I don't need separate holiday insurance?

The free insurance that comes with credit cards is very restricted: it pays only if you lose a limb, are disabled or die while in the process of travelling to and from your destination.

Can I use my credit card to pay in euros?

Yes – the euro is just another foreign currency, like the dollar.

How can I pay my credit card bill if it's due while I'm on holiday?

You can telephone the card company to ask how much is outstanding and pay in advance. Or you can arrange for the credit card bill to be paid automatically by your bank every month.

tip

> **If, while abroad, you buy something with your credit card but return the item for a refund – perhaps an excursion that was cancelled or car rental you didn't use – contact the card company when you get home. The refund should come through all right, but it will be at a different rate of exchange. Card companies have promised to ensure you are repaid the same as you spent in sterling terms.**

SENDING MONEY ABROAD

Sending money abroad can be ridiculously expensive, especially for small amounts.

ask Margaret

Can I be sure the recipient pays no charges?

Many systems cannot tell you for certain. Sometimes you can pay the recipient's charges as well as your own, but it depends which bank they use.

tip

> **You do not always need to have an account with a bank to use its money transfer service.**

Could I open an account with, say, an Irish bank and write cheques in euros for transfer of money into other euro-friendly countries?

Even within Euroland, there is no euro-wide clearing system, and so another country's cheques are still treated as a foreign item.

To get the best deal, ask yourself the following questions:

- Which country am I sending the money to? (*Some cheaper schemes operate only to certain countries.*)
- Do I need the money to get there fast? (*This costs more.*)
- Do I want the money to arrive at a guaranteed time? (*This also costs more.*)

Student accounts

Many banks produce accounts especially for students, who are regarded as the profitable customers of the future. The main attraction is an interest-free overdraft, but you also want to know:

get the facts

- Is there a branch of the bank on or close to the campus?
- If it is close, how close?
- At what times is the branch open?
- Who is eligible for a student account?
- Is there an age limit?
- Is it available to mature students?
- Where is the nearest cash machine I can use?
- Is this the bank's own cash machine and, if not, would I be charged for using it?
- How big an overdraft can I get? (*Remember that banks don't treat you as fondly as your grandparents do: any money you borrow has to be paid back, maybe with interest and charges.*)
- What do I get with the account? (*As well as overdraft facilities, student accounts can include a debit card, cash card, credit card, and no-commission travellers cheques.*)
- Does the overdraft increase each year?
- Is any overdraft repayable in full immediately I finish my studies?
- If there is a delay before I have to repay the overdraft, how long is it?
- What happens if I can't repay all the overdraft within this period?
- If I want to take a post-graduate course, will I still be eligible for student terms?
- If I take a year's break from my studies, will I still qualify for student terms during the break?
- If I don't finish the course, do I have to repay the overdraft straight away?

tip

> **Arrange to open the account through a branch near your home a few weeks before going to university. Then your credit card, cheque book and overdraft should be ready when you arrive.**

For questions about bank and building society savings accounts, see p58 in Chapter 3.

The Banking Code

Banks and building societies that comply with the Banking Code promise to:

- act fairly in all their dealings with you
- ensure that all products and services, and staff procedures, comply with the code
- write and talk in plain English and explain anything you don't understand
- help you to understand the financial implications of anything you buy from them
- maintain safe, secure and reliable banking and payment systems
- correct errors and handle complaints speedily
- react sympathetically when customers face financial difficulties.

9 General Insurance

Questions to ask about insuring your possessions

General insurance – for homes, cars, holidays, possessions – pays out if disaster strikes. It provides money to put you back to where you were before the problem arose: money to replace stolen possessions; money to pay for accident repairs to your car; money to pay health charges on holiday.

But insurance can give you a false sense of security. If you do not ask the right questions, you can buy a policy that excludes the very circumstance for which you need to claim. This is avoidable if you cross-question the insurer and read the small print before you sign. At that point you might be able to change an inappropriate clause, or you can choose a more suitable policy. But it is too late to do anything if you do not discover the problem until you make a claim.

House, holiday and car insurance is sold by many companies, usually by telephone but increasingly through the Internet, which makes comparing the products straightforward if time consuming. The cheapest insurers often accept only those customers who are least likely to claim and so, if you are a safe risk, seek out the lowest prices. However, it is better to pay more for insurance and be able to claim, than to pay cheaper premiums but still be uninsured.

ask Margaret

Do I have to wait until a policy comes up for renewal before moving to a different insurer?

No. You can switch at any time. You should get a refund of any unused premiums, but you may be charged an administration fee.

tip

> When buying insurance or switching insurers through an intermediary such as a broker, ask for the name of the insurance company you are about to use. This is not always obvious, and it is easy to confuse the insurance broker with the insurance company.

Is it safe to buy through a direct insurance company?

Yes. All companies selling insurance in the UK are bound by the same rules and are tightly controlled.

I know I mustn't lie on an application form but, if I make a genuine mistake, will the policy be invalid?

That depends on how seriously you misled the insurance company. Errors come to light only when you make a claim: wrong information might make no difference; the insurance company could scale down the payout; or it might refuse to pay up altogether. To challenge a refusal successfully, you need to convince the insurance company you did not write down wrong information deliberately.

tip

> WARNING: If you have a criminal record or you have been convicted of dishonesty, or there is a case pending, you must admit it if the insurer asks, even if it means paying higher premiums. If you don't, and the insurer finds out, it is legally entitled to declare the policy void and return your premiums, leaving you without insurance.

Do I have to pay premiums all in one go?

Many insurers allow you to spread the premiums for house and car insurance over a year; some provide this as free credit but others charge interest. Check the interest rate carefully: it may be a reasonable rate but some are expensive, especially from the companies with cut-price premiums. It might be cheaper to pay by credit card.

tip
> **Check that quotations include insurance premium tax (IPT). This has to be paid on most general insurance policies, with a higher rate for all holiday insurance.**

Does my age make any difference to how much I am charged?

Yes, in some circumstances. Young and inexperienced car drivers are charged a higher premium. In contrast, once you turn 50, some insurance premiums are cheaper because you are a safer risk – ask for an age-related discount.

tip
> **Most insurance business is done over the telephone. Whenever you have a question or a claim, get on the phone. Always ask for the name of the person you are speaking to and write it down, along with the date, time, and a note of what the person said.**
>
> **And don't hesitate to get on the phone and chase an insurer if you think it is taking too long over your claim. The insurer may well be processing the claim but have failed to have kept you informed about what is happening.**

tip
> **Insurers are more likely to agree a borderline claim if you have other insurance policies with them as well.**

House insurance

There are two types of house insurance: one covers the contents of your home, and the other the structure of the building.

ask Margaret
What comes under the contents policy and what under buildings?

Mostly it is obvious: a television, a computer, clothes and jewellery are contents; walls, roof and windows are buildings. Roughly, anything you would take with you when you move counts as contents, and the rest as buildings.

What about fitted kitchen units and fitted carpets?

These should come under the buildings policy, because you leave them behind when you move. But it is a point worth checking with your insurer.

How much does a house insurance policy pay up?

You have a choice. You can buy 'indemnity' insurance, which pays the amount that the item is worth today in its worn, second-hand state; cover for this is cheaper. Or, as is more usual, you can buy 'new for old' cover, which replaces the old stolen or damaged item with a new one.

Do the policies cover everything that might happen?

You can choose to pay extra for damage to the property or its contents caused by anyone in the family (accidental cover); and to cover your possessions while they are away from the house (all-risks cover).

What counts as an accident?

Unavoidable events, such as spilling paint on a carpet or knocking a vase off a shelf.

What affects house insurance premiums?

The size of your house, any unusual construction, the building material, the age of the property (older homes are more expensive) and your postcode.

What difference does a postcode make?

Insurers can tell which areas are susceptible to subsidence, flooding and storm damage and which homes suffer more burglaries.

Who provides house insurance?

There are numerous providers:

- general insurance companies
- direct-sell insurance companies
- specialist insurance companies
- some friendly societies
- banks
- building societies
- some utility companies
- a few retailers.

Where can I buy house insurance?

You can buy:

- through insurance brokers
- at bank and building society branches

- through charities for the elderly
- by responding to direct-marketing mailings
- through advertisements
- through the Internet.

Do I have to buy insurance from the bank or building society that provides my mortgage?

No, except with some special-deal mortgages where the lender makes it a condition that you buy its own policy. Sometimes lenders let you choose from half a dozen or so insurers; or, if they allow you to buy from one not on their list, they charge you around £25.

tip

> WARNING: **If you frequently change insurer to get a better deal, be careful because your lender might charge you every time you switch.**

Are bank and building society house insurance policies good value?

Rarely – they are usually more expensive than other insurers, particularly those that sell direct. And if insurance premiums are added to mortgage repayments, you pay interest on the premiums – so make sure you pay the premiums separately.

When comparing rates, you might notice a policy from your lender that appears good value, but it might not be available to you as a borrower. Banks and building societies can sell several versions of their policies. Check the detail.

tip

> WARNING: **If you insure through your lender, take care when you pay off the mortgage. The insurance continues for the rest of the year but, after that, the lender might not remind you to renew.**

Is it better to buy a joint contents and buildings policy rather than buy them separately from different companies?

Joint policies should be cheaper than separate policies.

Will the premiums rise each year?

Possibly. Many policies link the amount you have insured to the rate of inflation, so that both the sum insured and the premiums rise accordingly.

tip

> **Keep an eye on inflation-linked increases: you can become under-insured if you improve the house or acquire extra possessions; or you might find yourself paying for more insurance than you need if you do the opposite.**

As I'm most unlikely ever to claim for the full amount of the policy, do I really need to insure for so much?

Yes. If you don't, insurers will say you are underinsured and pay for only a proportion of your loss, even if the amount insured was more than enough to cover the claim.

If I suffer a catastrophe, can I get emergency repairs done before contacting the insurance company?

Certainly, if you need repairs to prevent the damage getting worse. Do not waste time writing to your insurance company; get on the telephone. Some operate a 24-hour helpline and maintain their own register of recommended repairers.

When can I go ahead with less-than-emergency work?

If you possibly can, you should wait for the insurer to agree the claim before repairing or replacing. Some insurers insist you use their own contractors or suppliers.

When I make a claim, will the insurer send someone round to check on it?

Often they do, but not always. They employ loss adjusters, who make an appointment to see the damage for themselves, confirm that the claim is genuine and that it falls within the terms of your policy. Loss adjusters report to the insurer, and the insurer almost invariably takes their advice.

Is the loss adjuster trying to catch me out?

Loss adjusters must assume that your claim is honest. If you feel that one has treated you unfairly, complain to the insurance company.

Can I complain if I disagree with the loss adjuster's decision to refuse a claim?

Certainly. Write to the insurance company, explain why you think your claim should be paid, and provide estimates for repairs and replacements.

Isn't it true that loss adjusters always scale down a claim, so you ought to ask for more in the first place?

You should never claim for more than you have lost, even if you are convinced that everyone else does, because that is fraud. However, loss adjusters are not on your side; they are paid by, and work for, the insurance company and are naturally keen to satisfy the insurer. If you feel your claim has been unfairly scaled down, go back to the insurance company and ask for someone more senior to look at your case.

Can I get someone to put my case forward?

You can appoint a loss assessor to negotiate your claim with the insurance company, although the fee might be high. You should check a loss assessor's credentials because they are not regulated or controlled.

If a friend is helping me with repairs, and damages a neighbour's house, can I claim on my insurance?

No. Your policy would cover you, and your family who permanently live with you, if you damaged a neighbour's property – by drilling through a party wall, for instance. But it does not cover someone else working in your home.

If a tile falls off my roof and hits my car, which policy pays?

Car insurance, but only if you have a fully comprehensive policy. However, if the tile landed on a neighbour's car, the neighbour could claim against your house policy's third-party liability, although they would have to prove that you had been negligent and left the roof in a poor state of repair.

tip | Policies often become invalid if your house is empty for more than 30 days at a stretch. If you are going on a long holiday, tell the insurer in advance; you might have to pay extra to keep the house insured or the company might extend the cover at no additional cost. And you must inform your insurer if you rent out your house (whether short term or long term); you might have to buy a different, more expensive, policy.

tip | Insurers class squirrels as 'vermin' and will not pay for squirrel damage to your house. But bad publicity forced one company to change its mind. If your claim is turned down, tell your local newspaper.

HOW TO CUT THE COST OF HOUSE INSURANCE

There are a number of ways to reduce premiums:

- fit good security locks
- install a burglar alarm
- fit a smoke alarm
- join a Neighbourhood Watch scheme
- place all your insurance with one company and ask for a discount
- pay part of the claim yourself (an excess)
- pick a policy with a no-claims discount – and don't claim
- look, if you are over 50, for a policy with an age-related discount
- live in a safe area.

tip

> The insurer will ask if you have previously been rejected for house insurance. There are various reasons why you might: perhaps your situation did not fit a previous insurer's profile of risks it took on. However innocent, this could prejudice your next application, and so ask the insurer why you were not acceptable so that you can explain to the next insurer you approach.

HOUSE CONTENTS INSURANCE

ask Margaret

How much should I insure for?

Enough to replace everything you own at today's prices.

How can I work out how much to insure for?

You can walk round the house and put a price on everything (and that means everything, including pictures, suitcases, lawnmower, domestic appliances, furniture). To make the job easier, some insurers simply give you a figure according to the number of bedrooms you have.

tip

> If the value of your possessions is not standard for the size of your house, it is worth doing a long calculation as you could otherwise pay for too much or too little insurance.

Will the insurance cover particularly valuable items?

You might need an insurer that specialises in high-value items.

Do I have to get expensive pieces professionally valued or will the insurer accept my figure?

You should get them valued, and revalued at regular intervals, so there can be no dispute if you make a claim. But that costs money.

tip | It's worth photographing valuable possessions – to show to the police if they are stolen and to prove to the insurance company what you owned. Keep receipts as well.

I inherited some valuable pieces of jewellery, which have sentimental value, but I never wear them and certainly wouldn't want to replace them if they were stolen. Do I have to pay to insure them along with everything else?

You can ask the insurers if they will ignore certain items, but it is unlikely.

Will the insurer pay for a replacement when something is damaged?

No. They might insist you get it repaired instead.

When I claim for stolen items, do I have to accept a replacement item or can I ask for cash?

It depends what you are claiming for. With a television, for instance, the insurance company expects you to take a new set because the purpose of insurance is to put you back where you were before the loss. But companies appreciate that there are some items, such as jewellery with sentimental value, that cannot be replaced. Then they may let you take cash, but you will get less in cash than the replacement price.

Why is the cash payout lower than the value of a replacement?

As always, insurance companies have a plausible excuse. Because they buy replacement household goods and valuables in such large quantities, they negotiate substantial discounts with wholesalers. It costs them far less than the shop price. If you opt for cash, they will pay you only the same as a replacement would have cost them to buy.

What should I do if I've claimed for something I thought was lost, and then it turns up?

Strictly, the property belongs to the insurance company and you should report your find. In practice, for small items, the insurance company will be amazed at your honesty and possibly let you keep your possession and the replacement.

If I get a discount for having a burglar alarm and am burgled after forgetting to set it, will the insurer pay out?

Possibly not.

Will the policy pay if a burglar gets in through a window left open in summer?

It depends on the attitude of the particular insurer; it might refuse.

QUESTIONS ON HOUSE INSURANCE YOU NEED TO ANSWER FOR YOURSELF

When you call for a quote for contents insurance, you will be asked a number of questions. Have your answers ready.

ask yourself

- What is your address and, particularly, postcode?
- What is the value of your possessions?
- How many bedrooms are in the house?
- What high-risk items do you have (*televisions, video recorders, computers, cameras, etc*)?
- What individual items do you have that are high-value (*jewellery, antiques*)?
- Do you want accidental damage cover?
- Do you want to insure your possessions while they are away from the house (all risks cover)?
- How much excess do you choose to pay? (*The lower the excess, the higher the premiums.*)
- When did you last make a claim and how much was it for?
- What security devices do you have on doors and windows?

HOUSE BUILDING INSURANCE

As well as the contents of your house, its structure also needs to be insured.

ask Margaret

Do I insure for the price I paid to buy the house?

No. Buildings insurance is unconnected to the value of your property or the Council Tax band.

How much should I insure for?

Enough to rebuild your house if it was completely destroyed, including the cost of clearing the site first, at today's prices.

But total destruction is most unlikely. Why can't I insure for less?

Insurance companies will not let you. It is all or nothing.

How can I find out how much to insure for?

Insurance companies help you work it out. And the Association of British Insurers (ABI) issues a free leaflet with an index of rebuilding costs, showing how to work it out yourself, at least for standard houses. The ABI's address is given in the Appendix.

Do non-standard houses cost more?

Yes. If you want to insure a windmill, a thatched cottage, a house with a cellar, one with more than three storeys, or a stone-built house, you will have to get a special quotation.

Must I buy buildings insurance?

You do if you have a mortgage; the lender insists on it. But if you own the house outright, you can choose to take the risk. If you rent, it is the landlord's responsibility.

tip

> **If you are in rented accommodation, check that the landlord has bought insurance and ask exactly what it covers: you might not be able to claim for accidental damage to your property – say if someone in the flat upstairs let the bath overflow and the water ruins your decorations.**

If I switch insurer and, soon after, subsidence is discovered, who pays: the company that insured the house while the subsidence was happening; or the one that has now taken on the risk?

Most insurers agree that, if a claim arises in the first eight weeks after you switch, the old insurer will pay. For claims between eight weeks and one year, the new insurer handles it but they share the cost. After a year, the new insurer is totally responsible.

Do I have to tell my insurer if I have, say, a conservatory built?

You should let the insurer know about anything that changes the value of your home; premiums will not necessarily go up. Conversely, let the insurer know if you have the conservatory pulled down – your premiums might reduce.

tip

> WARNING: **If the insurance company believes that damage was caused, or made worse, because you had not maintained your house properly, it will refuse to pay a claim.**

If I buy a brand-new house, with a National House Building Council guarantee, is there any point in having buildings insurance?

The NHBC guarantee covers only defects in the building work, and only serious ones at that.

When do I start insuring the house I am about to buy?

Lenders insist that you insure your new home from the day you exchange contracts because that is the point from which you are commited to go ahead. But you should also keep the old house insured until you complete the sale in case your buyer reneges on the contract.

QUESTIONS ON BUILDINGS INSURANCE THAT YOU NEED TO ANSWER FOR YOURSELF

When you call for a quote for buildings insurance, you will be asked for details about the property. They will include:

ask yourself

- What is the address and, particularly, the postcode of the building?
- What is your home constructed from (brick, stone, wood)?
- What is its roof made of?
- What is the house's style, and how many rooms does it have?
- How much do you estimate the house would cost to rebuild?
- When was it built?
- Do you want all-risks cover?
- Do you want cover for accidental damage?
- How much excess do you choose to pay?
- When did you last make a claim and how much did it cost?
- What security devices do you have on doors and windows?

QUESTIONS TO ASK THE INSURER OR BROKER BEFORE BUYING HOUSE INSURANCE

get the facts

- How much are the premiums?
- How much is the excess?
- If the fitted carpet is damaged and a patch would look dreadful, will all the carpet be replaced?
- Is my computer covered?
- Will the insurance cover the occasional business use of my home computer and fax machine? (*This is a grey area: some insurers cover you up to a limit; others not at all.*)
- Would working from home affect my house insurance? (*Some insurers insist that you pay for business insurance, although logically it should be cheaper because you are around most of the time to deter burglars. You will certainly have to buy more expensive insurance if customers visit you at home because this adds to the risk for the insurer. If you use expensive equipment, you should insure that separately.*)
- Will the policy pay out if my decorator spills paint on the carpet?
- What if my dog knocks over the paint?
- Are my possessions insured only while they are in the home, or when I am on holiday as well? (*They are generally insured away from home only if you pay extra for 'all-risks' insurance.*)
- If I have all-risks cover, could I claim if I left my raincoat on the train?
- Does all-risks insurance include possessions stolen from my car, or do I claim on the motor policy? (*It depends on the policies you have. You might be covered by neither, and so check.*)
- Are bicycles included in the insurance? (*Usually you have to pay extra.*)
- Are the premiums index-linked?
- Is the all-risks element index-linked?
- Will my policy cover everything in the house, even when I am temporarily storing someone else's possessions?
- Will you increase my insurance, at no extra charge, to cover Christmas presents?
- If I damage an armchair in a three-piece suite and it can't be re-covered to match the rest of the furniture, will you pay for the whole three-piece suite to be replaced?
- Does the policy cover garden furniture, garden plants and garden ornaments?
- Does the policy cover the cost of metered water that leaks out?
- Is the policy valid if I rent out my house?

- How quickly does the company usually settle claims?
- Does the policy include legal expenses insurance? (See p. 243.)
- Will the insurance cover my belongings while they are in transit to my new house? (*You need to check your policy; you might be able to extend the insurance for the time your possessions are between homes. The larger removals firms offer insurance as well.*)

tip

> **If you change insurer when you move house, make sure that there is no gap between policies, particularly for the time while your possessions are in transit.**

Car insurance

Car insurance is a legal requirement.

ask Margaret

Who provides car insurance?

Insurance brokers and insurance companies, and some car manufacturers who have schemes for people driving their models.

Where can I buy car insurance?

You can compare policies:

- through insurance brokers
- from insurance companies by phone
- through national motoring organisations
- through charities for the elderly
- through the Internet.

What are the various levels of car insurance?

There are three: third-party insurance; cover against damage to third parties, and damage by fire or theft; and comprehensive insurance.

Third-party insurance is the minimum legal requirement but only drivers with a dreadful record would choose it. It pays, following an accident, for injuries you cause to another person, damage you cause to other cars or property, and any injuries caused by your passenger. It does not cover any damage to your own vehicle.

Third party, fire and theft insurance pays, following an accident or theft, for everything covered by third-party insurance, repairs or a replacement if your car is damaged by fire, a replacement if your car is stolen and not recovered, and for repairs if your car is stolen but recovered in a damaged state.

Fully comprehensive pays, following an accident or theft, for everything covered by third party, fire and theft insurance, plus damage to your own car, replacing possessions inside your car, up to a limit, and any necessary medical expenses arising from an accident.

Can I drive abroad with my UK insurance?

In most European countries, your UK motor policy covers you, but only for the local minimum level. Some insurers grant you the same level of insurance as you have at home; others do so for an additional charge. In Spain, you need to buy a bail bond – ask your insurer about this.

Do I need a Green Card?

This is not compulsory but it proves you have the minimum legal insurance required locally. Ask your insurance company to provide one.

Driving a company car for several years means I have no no-claims discount. Now I have to buy my own car, will I have to pay the full rate for insurance?

You shouldn't. Get a letter from your employer confirming your good driving record.

My spouse wants a separate car but until now has been insured on my policy and has no no-claims discount. Does someone in this position have to start from scratch?

They shouldn't, but you need to negotiate with the insurance company.

Is it possible for teenagers to get insurance at a reasonable price?

Some insurers are more tolerant than others of young drivers; phone around or ask a broker.

Is my insurance affected if my colleague pays me for a lift to work?

Your insurance is valid, provided you are not making a profit.

If my car is a write-off after an accident, will the policy pay the price on the insurance application form or today's price?

You get the current value. Insurers check the latest price in publications such as *Glass's Guide*. You may be disappointed with the company's estimate of your car's value, particularly if it had low mileage or a particularly expensive sound system.

tip

> **You do not have to accept the price that the insurance company offers for a write-off if you believe it is too low. Provide the company with your own evidence of the car's true value and be prepared to argue your case strongly and repeatedly.**

Does my policy enable me to drive someone else's car?

It does, but only for the cost of damages to a car, or person, you hit; it won't pay any repair bills for the car you borrow; the owner's own insurance might cover you for this, though.

If another driver hits my car, but doesn't have motor insurance, do I have to claim on my policy?

Contact the Motor Insurers' Bureau, whose contact details are given in the Appendix. The Bureau compensates drivers in this situation.

tip

> **Insurance companies expect you to report all accidents, even those that were not your fault and that the other party is paying for. You should also report theft from the car, even if you don't make a claim.**

If I claim on my policy even though the accident wasn't my fault, do I have to pay the excess?

Yes, although you should be able to claim it back from the other party.

QUESTIONS TO ASK AN INSURANCE COMPANY OR BROKER BEFORE BUYING CAR INSURANCE

get the facts

- How much are the premiums?
- Will you give me a discount?
- How much is the excess on the policy?
- Will you provide a replacement car while mine is being repaired following an accident? (*Some policies do and others don't. If the policy does provide this benefit, check the procedure for claiming a car and any limitations.*)

- Does the policy include legal expenses insurance? (*For more on legal expenses insurance, see p.243.*)
- If I have fully comprehensive insurance, does this insure me to drive other cars? (*Probably, assuming you have the owner's permission – but only for third-party cover.*)
- Does one insurance policy cover me to drive all the cars I own?
- If I buy insurance that allows anyone to drive my car, does that include my children? (*Probably not anyone under 25, unless you tell the insurance company and pay a higher premium.*)
- I own a classic car, which I never drive in the winter. Do I have to insure it all year round?
- Do you discriminate against any particular occupations?
- Is windscreen damage covered by the insurance? (*Often, it isn't; you have to pay extra if you want it covered.*)
- Do you charge for providing a Green Card?

HOW TO CUT THE COST OF CAR INSURANCE

- Drive a 'sensible' car with an approved immobiliser.
- Restrict the policy to named drivers.
- Do not include anyone under 25 on the policy.
- Claim a reduction if you are over 50 (but under 70).
- Keep the car in a garage.
- Work in a low-risk job, such as bank clerk or civil servant.
- Do not have accidents and do not make claims.
- Live in a crime-free, low-accident area.
- Pay a high excess.
- Take the advanced driving course; some insurers charge lower premiums if you have passed this test.
- Just tell the insurer that you want to pay lower premiums. (*It often works, if you are a good customer.*)

QUESTIONS ON CAR INSURANCE TO
ANSWER FOR YOURSELF WHEN GETTING QUOTES

ask yourself

- What is the make and model of the car?
- What is the registration number?
- What is the engine size?

- What is the vehicle's approximate value?
- Do you want fully comprehensive insurance, or third party, fire and theft, cover?
- What are the names of the people who will drive the car?
- Do all your drivers have a full UK licence and, if so, how long have they held the licence?
- What are the drivers' ages? (*This increases premiums for younger drivers but reduces them for older people.*)
- Have any of the drivers had motoring convictions (apart from parking offences)?
- When did you last claim on car insurance, and how much was it for?

Holiday insurance

ask Margaret

Who provides holiday insurance?

- general insurance companies
- specialist insurance companies
- direct-sell insurance companies
- banks
- large building societies
- a few high-street retailers and supermarkets
- the Post Office.

Where can I buy holiday insurance?

Holiday insurance is sold by travel agents (whether you buy the holiday there or not), through tour operators' brochures, from banks and building societies, direct from insurance companies, through insurance brokers, through the national motoring organisations, and at post offices.

What does holiday insurance cover?

Holiday insurance protects you against most of the problems that cost you money to put right:

- travel delays
- cancellation or curtailment of your holiday

- lost luggage
- stolen belongings
- medical expenses
- personal liability in case you injure someone or damage their property
- the costs of an accident that you yourself have.

If my house insurance covers possessions while I'm away from home, do I need holiday insurance as well?

If your belongings are insured twice, you can't claim twice and so look for a policy that lets you exclude belongings from travel insurance and pay a lower premium.

tip

> WARNING: **If you have a no-claims discount with your house insurance, ask the insurer to confirm that this will not be affected if you claim on another company's holiday insurance policy. It can happen.**

If my camera, say, is specifically covered by holiday insurance and also by my house insurance policy while I'm away, which policy do I claim on if I lose the camera while travelling?

The holiday insurer will say that, if the camera is specifically insured on the house policy, that is where you claim. In any case, travel policies usually limit the amount you can claim for any one item to £200 or £250. But check that the house insurance will accept the claim, because you could find the camera insured by neither.

Does holiday insurance cover everything that might go wrong?

No, only financial loss. It will not pay because the hotel is below standard or you do not have a sea view.

Where is the best place to get travel insurance?

Direct insurance companies are likely to be cheaper than travel agents' and tour operators' policies.

tip

> **Ask to see a copy of the policy document before you buy travel insurance. If the travel agent does not keep copies in the branch, ask for one to be sent from the insurance company. It is worth insisting.**

Can a travel agent force me to buy holiday insurance?

A travel agent can make it a condition of selling you the holiday, but it cannot insist that you buy its own insurance policy to qualify for a cut-price holiday. In other words, they can't make you pay more for a holiday just because you won't buy their insurance.

Are annual policies worth buying?

They are if you travel several times a year. Often, they include UK trips as well.

Are a travel agent's staff qualified enough to discuss details of the insurance policy?

Probably not. If you have any doubts, ask for the name of the underwriter - that is, the insurance company behind the policy and the one that decides whether or not to pay out. The underwriter will talk it through with you.

How much insurance is necessary for medical expenses?

Sensibly, £2 million if you are visiting the United States, and £1 million anywhere else abroad. (Insurance companies have almost certainly never paid out £1 million for medical expenses. The most expensive event would be an accident or illness in the United States that required a long hospital stay, in which case they would fly you home as soon as you could be moved.)

Will medical expenses cover any health problem that might happen on holiday?

As with any type of health insurance, beware the 'pre-existing condition' clause. If you need to visit a doctor on holiday about an illness that you already have, the insurance will not pay for it.

Does that mean I can't get insurance unless I have perfect health?

You can. But you should tell the insurance company about any illness before you buy the policy. It is better to pay more for insurance and be able to claim than to save money on premiums but still be stuck with a medical bill.

tip

Remember to pack enough of any medication you take on prescription; the insurance will not pay to restock if you run out while abroad.

Can I get holiday insurance if I'm pregnant?

You should disclose the fact; better policies will cover you.

Do I need health insurance if I'm travelling in Europe; surely I'd get treatment in an emergency?

You can pick up form E111 from post offices before you go, which entitles you to free, or at least reduced-price, emergency treatment in European Union countries. But such treatment might not be at the most convenient hospital to where you are staying, and it will not compensate you for cutting short a holiday or getting you home in an emergency.

Do I have to disclose my age when I buy holiday insurance?

The insurance company or broker will ask and, if you are above 65 or 70, you will find holiday insurance vastly more expensive.

Is it therefore worth lying about my age if I am over 65?

Never. The insurer could refuse to pay your claim if it found you had been dishonest about your age, even if you were claiming for lost luggage.

tip
> **For people over 50, charities for the elderly that sell insurance do not discriminate on age and are worth a look.**

Are my possessions covered immediately I buy the policy?

The policy is in force from the time you buy it (in case you have to cancel your holiday for an insured reason); your possessions are insured from the moment you leave your home at the start of your holiday until you walk back through the front door.

tip
> WARNING: **The nearer you are to taking the holiday, the less you will get back if you have to cancel. Immediately you suspect you might have to cancel, check the terms of the insurance policy. If you delay cancelling in the hope that you might be able to travel, but can't at the last minute, you could lose the whole cost.**

Am I insured while waiting at the airport?

Yes, but insurance companies expect you to keep a close watch on your luggage at all times and to take reasonable care. They can refuse to pay out if you walked away from your trolley at the airport, left your suitcases in full view in the back of a car, or even left them locked in a car boot overnight.

When you are staying in a different hotel every night, it's not convenient to carry all your bags inside every time. Can't I leave them in the car?

That is certainly inconvenient, yet it is what many insurance companies expect. Some policies cover non-valuable items left in cars overnight, as long as they are locked and hidden from sight in the boot.

tip

> To satisfy an insurance company that you have taken reasonable care, you should behave as though you had no insurance and would have to pay for losses yourself.

Does holiday insurance cover me for driving a hired car?

No. For that you need car insurance.

Is there a maximum I can claim for lost items?

Yes. If you have a particularly expensive camera, for example, you should insure it separately through your house insurance, with all-risks cover.

Will the policy give me the amount needed to replace lost items, or only their second-hand value?

Holiday insurance provides indemnity cover, which means that you get only the second-hand value.

When do I claim on a travel insurance policy?

It is important to follow the insurance company's procedures, otherwise it might refuse to pay up, so check this before you go. In particular, if something is stolen, you must report it to the police.

I tried reporting a stolen camera to the local police but the police station was in a village miles away and only open on certain days. It just wasn't possible. Won't the insurance company be understanding?

Most insurance companies say this is no excuse. If you don't report the claim, they won't pay.

Is it enough to report a theft to the holiday rep?

No. But it is worth appealing against a rejected claim, showing that you really tried to report the loss. A statement from the holiday rep and hotel staff helps.

Is it worth buying travel insurance for a UK holiday?

This is unlikely: the all-risks clause on house insurance covers your possessions and there is the National Health Service for medical problems. It is debatable whether it is worth being able to claim for cancellation or delay once you have paid the excess on the insurance policy, although excesses should be smaller on UK holidays.

Annual policies often cover UK trips as well as foreign holidays, which could tip the balance towards buying an annual policy.

QUESTIONS TO ASK AN INSURER OR BROKER BEFORE BUYING HOLIDAY INSURANCE

get the facts

- How much excess will I have to pay?
- Does the excess apply once to a claim, or does it apply to each section of the policy? (*Very probably, to each section. If it does, and you claim for lost money, clothes and delay, you can pay three excesses.*)
- When there is more than one person on the policy, does the excess apply to each one individually? (*It usually does, and this is an important point. If there were four people on the policy, and you all lost possessions, you might have to pay four excesses. And if two of you put clothes in one suitcase, which was then lost, the insurer could deduct two excesses on just one piece of luggage.*)
- Am I insured, whatever activities I get up to on holiday? (*Not all activities are covered and certainly nothing illegal is. Hazardous sports, such as white-water rafting, hang gliding and cave diving, are usually excluded; but insurers have different definitions of what is hazardous. Get confirmation from the insurer before you go.*)

Usually you pay for holiday insurance before you have the opportunity to read the policy in detail. If your situation is not standard, get assurances in writing before committing yourself.

- What if I unexpectedly get the opportunity to go scuba diving or bungee jumping while I'm on holiday? (*Insurers say that, before you put on a wetsuit or attach the bungee rope, you should telephone them for clearance. Reliable insurers are more likely to be realistic and understand that this is not always possible.*)
- Do annual policies include ski cover? (*Some do; some don't. Check the policy.*)
- Does ski cover include equipment and personal liability in case I injure someone? (*Yes, although there are limits on the amount you can claim for lost or damaged equipment.*)
- Will the insurance pay up if the friends we were going on holiday with have to cancel? (*Strictly no, but some insurers will be sympathetic.*)

- Will the insurer pay out under the policy if I cancel because someone in the family is ill? (*It should, although it might want to be assured that the relation is sick enough for you to be seriously concerned.*)
- Will the insurer pay out under the policy if I have to cut my holiday short because of a relation's serious illness? (*It should, but remember the 'pre-existing condition' clause; the insurer might refuse if the person was ill before you went.*)
- Does that mean that I can't be fully insured just because I have elderly relatives? (*If you tell the insurer beforehand and they agree to insure you, they can't refuse to pay. But it is a tricky area.*)
- Will the insurer refund the cost of the holiday if a friend I plan to stay with falls ill and I have to cancel? (*It should.*)
- If I have to cancel the holiday, will the insurance reimburse everything I've paid for, including excursions. (*It should, provided that the policy covers excursions.*)
- Will the insurer refund the cost of an excursion I've paid for if I'm not ill enough to return home but am too sick to take the trip? (*It should if the trip was pre-booked and prepaid in the UK and you are hospitalised abroad. Otherwise, probably not.*)
- Will the policy refund the (expensive) cost of opera tickets I've bought if I have to cancel the holiday? (*It should, provided that the policy covers excursions – but only if the performance was part of an excursion paid for in the UK.*)
- Will the policy pay if I set out for the airport in good time but miss the plane because of a traffic jam? (*You might have a problem claiming, because insurers expect you to listen to road reports and to leave ample time to allow for emergencies.*)
- Will the insurer pay out if I'm held up by a transport strike? (*If it is an ongoing strike, the insurers will argue that you should have known about it and made other arrangements.*)
- What if I miss a connecting flight because the first flight was delayed? (*Many policies won't compensate you if the first flight leaves on time. The same applies to connecting train trips.*)
- If I have to cut short the holiday, will the insurance reimburse the additional costs of getting home? (*Yes, provided the reason for curtailing the holiday is covered by the insurance policy.*)
- Does the policy include legal expenses insurance?

tip

If you intend buying holiday insurance, buy it as soon as you book your holiday, to get maximum benefit from the cancellation clause.

Legal expenses insurance

Legal expenses insurance gives telephone access to a legal adviser 24 hours a day, everyday. It pays the costs of taking someone to court, or defending a case, perhaps following a motor accident or a disastrous holiday.

ask Margaret

Who provides legal expenses insurance?

Legal expenses insurance is provided by specialist insurance companies and specialist intermediaries.

Where can I buy legal expenses insurance?

Through brokers, and as an add-on to car, house or holiday insurance policies.

Which legal costs are covered by the insurance?

These include:

- the solicitor's bill
- any barrister's fee
- court costs
- the other side's costs if you lose the case
- fees for expert witnesses.

What sort of legal problems can I claim for?

These may be limited by the terms of the policy, but can include:

- neighbour disputes
- property disputes
- consumer complaints
- claiming compensation if you have been injured
- claiming against your employer for unfair dismissal
- claims following a motor accident.

When won't the policy pay?
The policy is unlikely to pay: if the legal costs are covered by other insurance policies you have; if the insurer thinks that you are unlikely to win the case, except in criminal cases such as a motoring prosecution; and if you start proceedings without telling the insurer.

Will the policy pay the solicitor's fee for writing my will?
No.

QUESTIONS TO ASK THE SPECIALIST INSURANCE COMPANY OR SALESPERSON BEFORE BUYING LEGAL EXPENSES INSURANCE

get the facts

- Do I pay extra to have legal expenses insurance added to my insurance policy?
- Exactly what problems does the policy cover?
- What is the maximum payout?
- Is the maximum for each claim or over one year?
- Will the policy pay if I have legal expenses insurance with my house or car insurance policy as well?
- Will the policy pay if I sue someone?
- Will the policy pay if someone else sues me?
- How soon after the event must I inform the insurer? (*Immediately you know there is a problem, and you may be disbarred if it is more than six months later.*)
- Can I choose my own solicitor? (*You have a right to nominate a solicitor, but the insurer can recommend a specialist and that is probably preferable.*)
- Does the policy apply when I'm travelling through Europe? (*The better ones do.*)
- Does the policy include other helplines, such as finding a plumber in an emergency or a vet? (*Good ones do.*)

For insurance that covers you when you are ill, see Chapter 10.

Extended warranties on goods

Extended warranties are insurance policies, lasting usually two to four years, that insure against the cost of repairs (call-out charge, parts and usually labour) after the manufacturer's initial guarantee period (usually one year) has expired. It is also called mechanical breakdown insurance.

Typically, extended warranty insurance covers domestic appliances such as washing machines, tumble driers, dishwashers; other electrical goods such as hifi systems and computers; and cars.

ask Margaret

Who provides extended warranty insurance?

Specialist insurance companies provide it.

Where can I buy extended warranty insurance?

You can buy it:

- at the shop when you buy the goods
- from the manufacturer
- direct from insurers.

Is this sort of insurance necessary?

It can be useful, provided that the price is reasonable.

Is the price reasonable?

Occasionally it comes free, from a retailer or as an add-on to a credit card. But often the policies sold by shops are poor value.

Then why do people buy them?

The salespeople selling the goods get commission for every insurance policy they sell. Hence they can be tempted to gloss over the facts and exert pressure on customers to buy the insurance as well as the goods.

What is the alternative?

You do not have to buy extended warranty insurance through the retailer. Specialist insurance companies sell this type of insurance, and some manufacturers sell it with their own products – usually more cheaply than shops charge. You may be able to find local repair people who repair broken equipment for less than the insurance costs.

QUESTIONS TO ASK A SALESPERSON OR BROKER BEFORE BUYING EXTENDED WARRANTY INSURANCE

get the facts

- When I claim, do you pay the repair bill direct or must I pay first and then reclaim the money from you?
- How much is the excess on the policy?
- If the appliance is not repairable, will you replace it with a new one or a reconditioned one?
- Will you pay for frozen food that has defrosted if a freezer fails?
- Does the insurance cover parts and labour, or parts only?
- What happens if a broken spare part on an appliance is no longer available? (*You should get a new appliance, but some policies only give you the cost of the spare part that is now defunct.*)
- Does the insurance include damage to inessential parts of the appliance? (*Almost certainly not. If you damage trim round a door of a fridge or washing machine, say, you cannot claim.*)
- When insuring a car, is there a mileage limit?
- Do you have a 24-hour telephone helpline?

tip

> WARNING: **Ask to see a copy of the insurance policy before you buy; it is too late to complain about the small print afterwards.**

The British Retail Consortium sets down minimum standards of good practice for retailers selling extended warranties on electrical goods. The retailers must:

- draw attention to the range of extended warranties, including those available from manufacturers
- print leaflets for customers to take away, showing prices, the name and address of the insurer (or, if not insured, whoever provides the warranty), the period of cover and whether it is in addition to or inclusive of the manufacturer's guarantee, full terms and conditions of the insurance, details of what is not covered, and the complaints procedure that should be followed
- not tell lies, or mislead, about the manufacturer's warranty

- not offer an extended warranty where a free warranty is available unless it provides additional cover
- not put undue pressure on customers to buy this type of insurance
- not make misleading or exaggerated claims about the insurance
- not impose onerous conditions, such as asking the customer to keep the original packaging or return non-portable products for repair
- not impose unrealistic time limits for making claims.

Pet insurance

Pet insurance covers vet's bills if an animal is ill or has an accident, up to a set limit each year or for each incident. It also covers third-party liability if your pet injures somebody or their property.

ask Margaret

Who provides pet insurance?

Specialist insurance companies and some general insurance companies.

Where can I buy pet insurance?

You can buy it direct from insurers, through brokers and at veterinary surgeons.

Are all pet insurance policies the same?

Some include the cost of kennelling if the owner has to go into hospital; and the cost of a replacement if a pet is lost through death, theft or straying.

Do the animals covered have to be pedigree?

No, all mongrels, mutts and moggies are included – and they can be cheaper to insure as they do not suffer problems of in-breeding.

What affects the premiums?

A few policies charge more for large dogs. And your postcode can be a factor.

Can I insure all my pets?

Usually the insurance is designed for cats and dogs, but you can seek out policies for other small pets.

What about horses?

For horses and ponies, you need a specialist policy. Ask an insurance broker to find one or look for advertisements in a specialist horse magazine.

What is not generally covered?

Routine vaccinations (which, to be insured, animals must have), neutering, problems stemming from a pre-existing condition, and older animals.

tip

> **Some policies pay compensation if you have to cancel your holiday because your pet is ill.**

Lloyd's of London

You can buy insurance through insurance companies or through Lloyd's of London. Lloyd's is not a company; it is an insurance marketplace.

ask Margaret

What sort of insurance can I buy at Lloyd's?

Lloyd's is known for insuring the gigantic, such as supertankers and aircraft, and the unusual, such as a footballer's legs. In addition, ordinary people can buy general insurance for holiday, house and car cover at Lloyd's.

How do I go about buying insurance through Lloyd's?

You can buy only through Lloyd's brokers, or else insurance brokers who have an agreement with a Lloyd's broker. The insurance risk is taken by an underwriter, but members of the public can't approach underwriters direct.

Is it safe to buy a Lloyd's insurance policy?

You have the same protection as buying from an insurance company, through the Policyholders Protection Scheme (see p. 29).

What can I do if I have a complaint about a Lloyd's policy?

You can write to the Lloyd's broker or underwriter you used, or to Lloyd's Complaints Department (whose address is given in the Appendix). If you are still dissatisfied, you can take a complaint to the Ombudsman.

The ABI Code of Practice

The Association of British Insurers (ABI) sets a Code of Practice for everyone selling general insurance, whether they are independent or employed by an insurance company. Salespeople must:

- make an appointment before calling, or at least call during social hours
- immediately identify themselves, state that they want to discuss insurance, and explain who they work for
- make sure any policy they sell is suitable for the customer
- advise only on insurance matters that they know about
- treat all information as confidential
- disclose the commission they earn, if you ask
- co-operate with insurance companies investigating complaints from customers.

They must not:

- say that someone gave them the customer's name unless they are prepared to say who it was
- unfairly criticise competitor companies
- make comparisons with other types of policy, unless they make clear the difference
- add any charges to the premiums for a policy, unless they tell you how much and why you are paying the charges.

10 Life and Health Insurance

Questions to ask about insurance for looking after your family and your finances

Your earnings might dry up when you are ill or made redundant, but your bills don't go away. And yet, today, there is less support in times of hardship for fewer people: state help is shrinking; more workers are self-employed, with no company to look after them. If you would face financial difficulty if you lost your job, you need to buy insurance to protect your income.

You can buy insurance to cover more or less any eventuality, but there is no one policy that covers it all. No one knows what setbacks lie ahead but, because only the wealthiest can afford to buy all the insurance they might need, you have to guess what you are most likely to suffer.

You might need insurance to:

- replace your wages if you are too ill to work
- provide a lump sum if you lose your job
- pay out if you contract a serious disease

- meet your mortgage and credit repayments
- pay for private hospital treatment
- pay care home fees
- provide money for your dependants when you die.

Term insurance

There are two broad types of life insurance: one is designed to pay as much as possible to your family when you die; the other is intended mainly as an investment. This section deals only with life insurance to provide your family with money when you die. It is called 'protection' or 'term insurance'. For questions about life insurance as an investment, see Chapter 4.

ask Margaret

Who provides life insurance?

Insurance companies, banks, large building societies, friendly societies, and some retailers.

Who gives advice on life insurance?

Independent financial advisers, and company salespeople, but only on the products sold by the company they work for.

Where can I buy life insurance?

You can buy it through insurance brokers and independent financial advisers, from insurance company salespeople, direct from insurance companies by phone, at bank branches or from banks by phone, from friendly societies and the large building societies, by responding to advertisements and mailshots, through some retailers, and through the Internet.

Do I need life insurance?

Life insurance pays out when you die. If anyone depends on your earnings – perhaps your children, elderly relatives or business partners – you should buy life insurance. If no one is financially dependent on you, you do not need life insurance.

Who buys the insurance? Me or the person who needs my income?

Insurance is taken out on the life of the person whose income is vital. You can buy insurance on your own life, or someone else can buy it on your life; but you can take insurance out only on the life of someone with whom you have a financial connection.

How does term insurance operate?

You decide the number of years for which you want to be insured and buy term insurance to cover that period (or 'term'). If you die at any time during those years, the insurance policy pays a pre-agreed amount of money to your family. If you survive the term, the policy comes to an end and you receive nothing.

Wouldn't it be better to buy a type of life insurance that always pays out something?

It comes back to deciding whether you want protection or investment from life insurance; and policies that always pay something are more expensive.

Why might I need term insurance, which is in force for only a limited time, as I don't know when I'm going to die?

You might want term insurance:

- until your youngest child has finished at university
- for the seven years you need to survive to escape inheritance tax after giving assets away
- for the length of your mortgage, if you do not have an endowment policy
- until your pension starts, if your partner depends on your earnings.

How many years can I buy insurance for?

You could buy it for just one year – or whatever number of years you need.

Will the premiums go up each year?

Generally, they stay the same.

Could the insurance company cancel the policy if I became very ill?

No. Once you buy term insurance, it continues until the date agreed, assuming you keep paying the premiums.

Do insurance companies contact my doctor when I apply for life (or health) insurance?

Not usually, but they might, depending on your age, how much insurance you are buying, the type of policy you want, and your answers to the medical questions on the application form. Even if your doctor is contacted, few applicants are charged higher premiums or turned down.

Will I know if the insurer contacts my doctor?

Yes. Your doctor will not pass on any medical details without your consent. And your doctor might charge you a fee.

Might I have to take a medical test?

Possibly, but very few applicants do.

Do insurers ask questions about Aids?

They ask only whether you have had an Aids test that showed positive.

Can the insurer take my family's health history into account or ask for genetic testing?

Only recently has genetic testing made it possible to predict your chances of contracting an inherited disease. This is valuable knowledge for insurance companies in their assessment of applicants for policies that pay out when you become ill, but less so for life insurance, where they calculate your chances of dying early. For the foreseeable future, insurers will not ask policyholders to undergo genetic tests. And, if the application is for life insurance to go with a mortgage up to £100,000, insurers do not ask about previous genetic test results. See also the ABI Code of Practice on Genetic Testing, given at the end of this chapter.

If I'm turned down for life insurance, will the company tell me why?

Not usually, although the company's chief medical officer would give your GP a reason.

Does life insurance pay out if the person insured commits suicide?

Yes, although some will not pay if the policyholder commits suicide within, say, a year of buying the insurance.

Do insurance companies pass on information about me to anyone else?

The Data Protection rules ban insurers from revealing sensitive information to anyone outside the company without your consent. However, they do share information on a central register to combat potential fraud.

What happens if I can't afford to keep paying the premiums?

You will probably be given a month's period of grace, in case something had gone wrong with your bank account, but then the insurance stops. The insurer, though, should be in touch with you before then.

If I buy insurance on someone else's life, and they die, does the money go to their estate or to me?

The money comes straight to you.

tip
> When you buy a policy written on your own life, you should have it written 'in trust' for your dependants, so that the money goes directly to them and not into your estate first. See the section on life insurance as an endowment in Chapter 4.

Do joint life insurance policies pay out when the first person dies or the second?

You choose. If you want a cash sum for the survivor, perhaps to repay a mortgage, pick a 'first life' policy that pays when the first dies. If you want money for your beneficiaries or to pay inheritance tax, choose a second life policy. You have to decide at the time you buy the policy; you can't change the conditions later. But joint policies are generally cheaper than buying two separate policies.

tip
> Term insurance pays out a lump sum. If you want your beneficiaries to receive an income, you can buy 'family income benefit', which is structured like term insurance but, when you die, it pays regular amounts in the years left until the end of the term.

tip
> You can buy term insurance with your personal pension and receive tax relief on the premiums. Normally there is no tax relief on life insurance premiums.

QUESTIONS YOU NEED TO DECIDE WHEN BUYING TERM INSURANCE

ask yourself

- Do I want to be insured for the same amount throughout the period? (*This is called 'level' term insurance.*)

- Do I want the amount I'm insured for to go up over the years? (*This is 'increasing' term insurance.*)
- Would I prefer to increase the amount I'm insured for from time to time rather than every year? (*You need 'increasable' term insurance.*)
- Do I want the amount of insurance to reduce steadily, as the debts it covers go down? (*This is 'decreasing' term insurance.*)
- Might I want to switch from term insurance into a policy that includes investment? (*You would need 'convertible' term insurance. But be careful: you have to buy an investment policy with the same insurer, and sometimes insurers who are good for term insurance are not best for investment.*)
- Might I want to keep the policy going after the end of the term? (*There is either 'extendable' term insurance, where you can add a few years at the same premiums; or there is 'renewable' term insurance, where you buy another policy, at higher premiums because you are older, but without answering any questions about your state of health.*)

tip | **Every option you add makes the premiums more expensive.**

- How much should I insure for? (*To replace your lifetime future earnings, you should insure for between 10 and 20 times your current gross income.*)
- How long do I want to insure for?
- Do I want a policy that pays a lump sum or a regular income?
- Do I want the policy written in trust?

tip | **If you smoke, or have a dangerous occupation, term insurance premiums are likely to be more expensive.**

QUESTIONS TO ASK THE INSURER OR ADVISER BEFORE BUYING A TERM INSURANCE POLICY

get the facts
- How much are the premiums?
- Can I opt to have the premiums paid if I lose my job or fall sick?
- When the insurance comes to an end, can I renew?
- Can I choose a policy that pays more, or less, each year?
- Can the premiums go up during the term of the policy?

Insurance to provide money when you are ill

There are different types of insurance for different circumstances, which provide money when you are ill.

- Income protection insurance, which pays a monthly amount to replace some of the income you lose if you become too ill to work. It is also called permanent health insurance (PHI), long-term disability insurance, income replacement insurance, disability income insurance, or personal disability insurance.
- Loan protection insurance, which meets your loan repayments for a limited time if you cannot work through accident, sickness or unemployment. This is also called accident, sickness and unemployment insurance, creditor insurance, or payment protection insurance. It includes mortgage payment protection insurance.
- Critical illness insurance, which provides a lump sum if you suffer certain sorts of serious illness.
- Long-term care insurance, which provides money towards the cost of nursing care or a residential home.
- Private medical insurance, which pays the cost of care in a private hospital or in a private NHS ward.
- Health cash benefit, which pays cash for every day you spend in hospital.
- Dental plans, which meet dentists' bills.

ask Margaret

How ill do I need to be before any of these policies pay out?
This is a contentious question. Disputes over a claimant's ability to work cause enormous arguments with insurance companies and a great deal of bitterness.

Some insurers say you must be too ill to continue your own usual occupation. Tougher policies will not pay unless you are unable to work at anything suited to your education, training and experience. The worst type will not pay if the insurer believes you could do some work of some kind.

tip

The cheaper the premium, the more restricted the policy will be. Read the terms and conditions carefully before you buy, because it is too late to change the policy once you fall sick.

Income protection insurance

Income protection insurance pays a regular income if you cannot work as a result of an accident or illness. This is unnecessary for employees who are paid while they are off sick, but important for the self-employed. You pay regular premiums and the insurance company cannot refuse to renew the policy unless you move to a high-risk job.

ask Margaret

Who provides income protection insurance?

It is provided by insurance companies and friendly societies.

Where can I buy income protection insurance?

You can buy it:

- from insurance company salespeople
- direct from the insurer
- through insurance brokers
- through independent financial advisers.

Why does the job I do make a difference?

You have to be employed to buy the insurance, except with friendly societies' policies. In some jobs, you are more likely to have an accident, so premiums are higher:

- very safe: accountant, librarian, secretary, barrister
- fairly safe: baker, dog breeder, postworker, midwife
- fairly risky: teacher, gunsmith, plumber, farmer
- high-risk: bricklayer, plasterer, timber merchant, landscape gardener
- Uninsurable: airline pilot, motorcycle messenger and footballer.

tip

The policy will not pay out if your employer keeps you on full pay while you are sick.

Will the policy pay out the whole time I am off sick?

Payments continue for as long as the insurance company believes you are unable to work. They expect regular reports from your GP, and someone from the company might visit you. Policies usually stop paying if you are still off work at the official retirement age.

Does the policy start paying immediately I am ill?

No. Most kick in only after a number of weeks. You choose how long you want to wait, say 4 or 13 weeks. The longer you have to wait, the cheaper the premiums.

If I'm off sick for a long time, will the payments rise to keep up with inflation?

You can choose a policy that pays out more each year, perhaps 3 per cent, or is fully linked to inflation, but premiums are more expensive.

How much do the policies pay out?

Payouts are based on your actual salary and are unlikely to pay more than 75 per cent of your gross earnings less state benefits. This is to make sure you have an incentive to return to work.

How can I estimate my earnings if I am self-employed?

This is difficult, but often the insurance company averages your earnings over, say, three years.

What happens if I am made redundant?

The policy does not pay out and insurance cover stops, unless you are claiming at the time.

Will I get any money back when I stop the policy if I haven't made a claim?

Policies differ. Some include an element of investment, when you should get a small repayment; others return nothing. Sometimes, any growth in value is used to offset higher premiums as you grow older.

Can I keep the policy if I go to work abroad?

With some, you can; with others, you cannot.

Are premiums the same for everyone?

Not at all. Women pay more than men because insurance companies' statistics show women are more likely to fall ill.

Can I buy income protection insurance for my partner who looks after the children and the home? It would be expensive if we had to pay someone else to do the work.

Some insurers sell 'houseperson' policies, although the maximum allowed is usually low.

What if I can go back to work but, because of the disability I now have, I can't earn as much as I did before?

Many policies continue to pay a proportion of the benefit in these circumstances.

Will I have to pay tax on a payout?

No – unlike your salary.

QUESTIONS TO ASK BEFORE BUYING INCOME PROTECTION INSURANCE

get the facts

- What are the premiums?
- Can the premiums rise?
- Is there a ceiling on the amount the policy pays out?
- Do I have to continue paying premiums at the same time as receiving benefit?
- How does the insurer define 'unable to work'? (*Some pay as long as you cannot return to your usual job; others stop paying if they believe you can do some sort of work.*)
- Is there an investment element?
- Will I get any money back if I don't make a claim?

Loan protection insurance

Loan protection insurance pays towards your loan repayments for a limited time if you cannot work through illness or, usually, redundancy. Loan protection insurance is different from income protection insurance, which replaces some of your income if ill health – but not redundancy – stops you earning.

Who provides loan protection insurance?

This type of insurance is provided by insurance companies, banks, building societies and the Post Office.

Where can I buy loan protection insurance?

You can buy it:

- through insurance brokers
- from banks and building societies
- through retailers
- through your credit card company
- from companies selling products such as double glazing and fitted kitchens on credit.

Can one loan protection insurance policy cover all my debts?

No. You need a separate policy for each loan – mortgage, credit card bill, store cards, and each personal loan.

Does the policy start paying immediately I am off work?

That varies. Cheaper policies include a waiting period before paying.

How long do policies keep paying?

Usually for a maximum of one year.

Can contract workers buy this type of insurance?

Only if they have reasonably long contracts and can show these have already been renewed several times. If you are in this situation, get confirmation from the insurance company that the policy would pay out before you buy the insurance.

Can self-employed people buy loan protection insurance?

Possibly, but check the policy carefully. The insurer won't pay up if you have no income simply because your business hits a bad patch and might insist that you become bankrupt before paying out.

tip

> **The self-employed and contract workers should read through loan protection insurance contracts particularly carefully to ensure that the policy meets their needs.**

Do I have to buy the insurance from my lender?

Not at all. You can buy a standalone policy from an insurance company, and you should certainly compare a few before choosing.

Does loan protection insurance pay the whole amount due on the loan each month?

It may pay a set percentage of your outstanding debt or just the minimum you have to pay. Policies designed to go with your home loan should cover whatever you usually pay each month for your house, possibly up to a limit: mortgage capital and interest; life insurance premiums; and house insurance premiums.

Can I start the insurance after the mortgage has been running for a few years?

Yes.

Won't Income Support cover my mortgage if I'm off work?

If you bought your mortgage, or remortgaged, after September 1995, you get no Income Support for mortgage costs until you have been out of work for nine months. You can buy cheaper mortgage protection insurance to cover just the nine months while you have to wait for Income Support.

tip

> **There are several different types of insurance available with mortgages, which is confusing. Mortgage payment protection insurance, a type of loan protection insurance, meets your monthly outgoings for up to 12 months. You might also be offered mortgage protection insurance, which is a form of term insurance and pays off the whole loan if you die; and be required to pay mortgage indemnity insurance (for which see p.51 in Chapter 6).**

MINIMUM STANDARDS OF PROTECTION

The Association of British Insurers (ABI) and the Council of Mortgage Lenders (CML) together set down minimum standards for mortgage payment protection insurance. These are:

- policies pay out after a maximum of 60 days
- policies pay out for at least 12 months after the excess period

- there are fewer exclusions for medical conditions such as pregnancy complications and backache
- there must be a minimum of six months between changes to the terms of a policy
- contract workers can claim under the policy for unemployment, provided that they have worked for the same employer for at least a year
- self-employed people can claim under the policy, provided that they have informed the Inland Revenue that they have involuntarily ceased trading and registered for Jobseekers Allowance.

QUESTIONS TO ASK A SALESPERSON OR BROKER BEFORE BUYING LOAN PROTECTION INSURANCE

get the facts

- What are the premiums?
- Can the premiums go up? (*They might change as your mortgage repayments change.*)
- Do the premiums include insurance premium tax?
- Do I pay the premiums in one go or by regular instalments?
- How much does the policy pay out?
- How long will it pay out for?
- Is the cost of payment protection insurance added to the amount I'm borrowing? (*If it is, you will be paying interest on the cost of premiums.*)
- Can I cancel the policy if I want to?
- How much of my monthly loan repayments will the insurance meet?
- Will the policy pay twice if I claim, go back to work, but then need to claim again?
- Does the policy start paying immediately I'm off work? (*Few policies pay for the first two or three months. Often you can't claim at all if you are made redundant within perhaps a year of taking out the policy, although this does not apply to mortgage payment protection.*)
- Do I have to keep paying the premiums while I'm off work and the policy is paying out?
- Will the policy pay if I'm made redundant, or only if I'm ill?
- Can I buy this insurance if I'm a contract worker?
- Can I buy this policy if I'm self-employed?
- If I repay the loan early, will I get any insurance premiums refunded? (*This is a subject that causes many complaints; insurance companies differ in their approach.*)

- When might the insurer refuse to pay out on the policy? (*It may refuse if you have a pre-existing medical condition, stress or mental problems, back problems, or a pregnancy-related disability.*)
- Can I see a list of exclusions?

tip

> **Get several written quotations and read them through in your own time. If you buy through a retailer, do not be pressurised by a salesperson suggesting the goods will cost more unless you buy loan protection insurance on the spot. Even if that were true, it is better to pay more for the goods than buy insurance that fails to pay out when you need it.**

Critical illness insurance

Critical illness insurance provides a lump sum if you suffer a serious illness. You can use the money for any purpose you choose, such as repaying a mortgage, paying for medical care or household bills. A critical illness is defined as a serious illness from which you might die or become severely disabled.

ask Margaret

Who provides critical illness insurance?
Insurance companies and friendly societies.

Where can I buy critical illness insurance?
You can buy critical illness insurance from insurance company salespeople, from insurance companies direct, from friendly societies, and through insurance brokers.

Do the policies pay out for any critical illness?
No. Each policy clearly states which illnesses are covered, and they vary. They include:

- cancer
- heart attack
- stroke

- multiple sclerosis
- coronary artery bypass surgery
- kidney failure
- major organ transplant
- permanent total disability (PTD), which means permanent and total unfitness for work not covered by any specified illness.

tip

It is important to understand which illnesses are included and excluded in any policy you might buy. Study the wording carefully to see whether it provides adequate protection for your likely circumstances.

How are premiums calculated?

They become vastly more expensive as you get older and are higher for women because, statistically, women are more likely to contract a critical illness.

Who decides if I'm ill enough to be paid?

The insurer, based on evidence from your doctors. If your claim is rejected, you can appeal to somebody senior in the insurance company.

If I claim because I suffer, say, a heart attack, will the policy continue and pay again if I then contract cancer?

No, the policy pays out only one lump sum.

Does the policy pay anything on my death?

Most critical illness policies are combined with life insurance and pay out either when the illness is diagnosed or when you die, whichever comes first. Standalone critical illness policies will not pay on death.

If I were to die some years after the illness was diagnosed, would my dependants get a payout from combined life insurance?

Not under most policies: the money is paid on an either/or basis. Some, though, pay, say, 60 per cent when you are diagnosed and the remaining 40 per cent when you die.

What might I need money for at the time a critical illness is diagnosed?

A fair question, and one that you should think through carefully. You might want money simply to enhance your quality of life.

But, if it is to replace lost income, an income protection policy would be more appropriate; if you become severely disabled, a long-term care policy might be more useful; and if your life expectancy has been cut short and you are worried about your dependants, you should have bought life insurance.

The problem is that you don't know in advance what is going to happen to you.

Can I insure my spouse as well?

You can buy joint policies, whether married, unmarried or have a same sex partner.

QUESTIONS TO ASK AN INSURER OR SALESPERSON BEFORE BUYING CRITICAL ILLNESS INSURANCE

get the facts

- Which illnesses does this policy cover?
- How much will the policy pay out?
- Can I increase the amount I am insured for later on if I want?
- Does it include life insurance?
- What payout might I get?
- How does the insurer define 'unable to work'?

Long-term care insurance

'Long-term care insurance' is a general expression covering the help that elderly people need with day-to-day living: in their own home with cleaning, shopping and paperwork; at home with washing and feeding; and in a residential home or nursing home for full-time care.

Do not buy long-term care insurance for services that are provided free by social services or a health authority.

ask Margaret

Who provides long-term care insurance?

Some insurance companies.

Where can I buy long-term care insurance?

You can buy it from specialist financial advisers, independent financial advisers, insurance brokers, and insurance company salespeople.

Should I buy long-term care insurance before I need to go into a nursing home, or wait until the time arrives?

You can buy either type of policy.

Buying the insurance in advance (a pre-funded policy) should be cheaper, and you can subscribe in regular instalments. But, if you never need to go into care, the premiums go to waste. If, on the other hand, you wait until you need the care before buying a policy, you will have to pay a substantial lump sum immediately, which might mean selling investments or your home.

Can the insurer change the terms or definitions after I've bought the policy?

Some policies guarantee the benefits they pay; others might review the terms after five or ten years.

How infirm must I be before the policy pays out?

There are recognised standards, called Activities of Daily Living (ADLs). These include: feeding, mobility, dressing, toileting, washing and continence. Policies show how many failed ADLs trigger a payment, and they usually pay out when you fail three. Sometimes half benefits are paid if you fail fewer. More expensive policies pay if you suffer dementia.

Is there a cooling off period in case I change my mind?

You can pull out of the policy within 14 days of signing the agreement.

Will I get any money back if I want to cancel the policy, or can't afford it, after it has been running for a few years?

Only if the policy includes an element of investment.

Does the policy pay anything when I die?

Not usually.

Will the benefits affect my entitlement to state benefits?

Yes, for means-tested benefits.

Is there a compensation scheme if the insurance company fails to pay up?

Long-term care is not regulated under the Financial Services Act, but you are covered by the Policyholders Protection Act if the insurance company goes bankrupt. See p.29.

Will I have to pay tax on the benefits I receive under a long-term care policy?

There is no tax to pay, whether the money is paid direct to the provider or to you in cash.

tip

> WARNING: **If you are thinking of selling your home, or remortgaging, to pay for long-term care, discuss this with a solicitor before signing the contract. Make sure that your relatives know if you buy long-term care insurance and tell them where you keep the policy. Also tell your GP.**

Is long-term care insurance worth buying?

It depends on your attitude. If you eventually did need nursing care, without insurance you might have to sell assets to pay for it, which would leave less for your beneficiaries to inherit. Some policies combine long-term care benefits with investment so, if you do not need nursing care, there is some money left for your beneficiaries.

What can I do if I need to pay for long-term care but haven't bought insurance?

You have several options. You can buy an 'immediate needs' insurance policy: an actuary decides how long you are likely to live and calculates a single premium you have to pay to obtain lifetime cover. This guarantees the cost of your care however long you live. You can buy an annuity to provide regular income (see p.144 in Chapter 5). Or, you can use the equity in your home (see 'When you are retired' p.168).

Without insurance, what help can I get with paying for long-term care?

The local authority pays the fees for care, within limits, when your assets fall to several thousand pounds. Until then, if you do not have enough money in savings to pay the fees, you will have to sell your assets – the things you own.

Do I have to sell my home to pay for care?

The value of your house is included in your assets, unless your spouse or a dependent relative is living there. If you live alone, you would have to sell the house only if you could not afford the fees any other way.

Would the house be excluded from my assets if I gave it to my children in advance?

Your local authority can say that you deliberately deprived yourself of an asset to claim benefit, and it can then refuse to pay your nursing home fees.

What if I give the house away several years before needing care?

That is no protection. If you made the gift within six months of moving to a nursing home, the local authority can demand that the recipient of your gift pays the fee out of that money. If more than six months pass, the council can behave as though you still owned the asset and leave you to pay the bill.

QUESTIONS TO ASK YOURSELF BEFORE BUYING LONG-TERM CARE INSURANCE

ask yourself

- Would I rather pay for long-term care in advance, even though I might never need it, or pay for care when the time comes?
- Am I prepared to sell the family home to pay for my long-term care?
- Do I want insurance just for myself, or for my spouse as well?
- Will I be able to afford the premiums after I retire?

QUESTIONS TO ASK THE INSURER OR SALESPERSON BEFORE BUYING LONG-TERM CARE INSURANCE

get the facts

- Do I pay in one go or by regular premiums?
- How much are the premiums and for how long do I pay?
- Will the premiums go up after I retire?
- What happens if I can't continue paying premiums?
- How much have premiums for this policy increased each year for the past five years, and how does that compare to the rate of inflation?
- If premiums continue rising at the same rate, how much will they be in five years time?
- Is there any limit on how much premiums can go up?
- How much will the policy pay out?

tip

> WARNING: **It is important to understand that the policy will provide money that goes towards the cost of long-term care; it is most unlikely to be enough to pay all the bills.**

- When will the policy start to pay benefits?
- Is there a limit on how long it will continue to pay out?
- Is there a limit on how much it will pay out in total?
- Will the policy pay for me to be looked after at home or only if I go into a nursing home?

- Are the benefits paid to me or directly to the care home?
- If care costs go up while the policy is paying me, will the payout also rise?
- Does the policy pay anything if I die without claiming on it?
- If it is an investment-linked policy, what investment performance is required to meet the care costs?
- With an investment-linked policy, what are the insurance company's charges? (*Charges can be high.*)
- Are there charges to pay when I die?
- What is the claims procedure? (*It is worth being clear about this well before you need to claim.*)
- Is there a telephone helpline for the policy? (*This is the minimum back-up you need. Many include a support service, with people who visit you, at no extra charge.*)
- What support services are there?
- Will someone visit me at home regularly?
- Will they help adapt my home so I can continue living there?
- How does the care system work? (*This reveals whether the salesperson understands the subject or is interested only in selling policies.*)

tip

When you buy long-term care insurance, arrange for someone you trust to have enduring power of attorney at the same time. They will not do anything until you need help, but then they can make decisions for you.

Private medical insurance

A fully comprehensive private medical insurance policy pays every cost of private medical treatment: hospital room, surgeons' fees, drugs, out-patient charges, home nursing, and private ambulance. This is extremely expensive. At the other end of the scale, a budget version pays for fewer expenses - hospital bed, surgeons' fees, drugs and dressings – and pays only if you would otherwise have to wait, say, six weeks for NHS treatment. You can choose various levels in between.

Who provides private medical insurance?

It is provided by specialist insurance companies, direct insurers and friendly societies.

Where can I buy private medical insurance?

- direct from insurance companies
- through insurance brokers
- from independent financial advisers
- through charities for the elderly
- possibly as an employee benefit.

What treatment does private medical insurance pay for?

Treatment for acute conditions such as hip replacement, varicose veins, impacted wisdom teeth, cataract removal, heart bypass operation, tonsil removal; but not anything connected with terminal, chronic or long-term illnesses.

Will Private Medical Insurance pay all the cost of treatment?

All treatment is covered by the policy, but watch out for limitations on some: they may say they give a full refund of costs but then say it is a full refund only up to a certain amount. This can be a problem if you choose a particularly expensive consultant.

Why should I pay for private medical insurance?

With private medical facilities, you are likely to be treated sooner, you can choose when to have the operation, and you will probably get more privacy.

Will Private Medical Insurance pay for out-patient treatment?

Some, but not all, policies do.

Will private medical insurance pay for treatment for illnesses I'm already suffering?

No. Private medical insurance pays only for treatment for conditions you don't yet know you have.

tip

WARNING: **If you need to claim soon after buying a policy, the insurer will examine your claim particularly carefully. It will not pay if it suspects you had the problem beforehand, even if you had not needed treatment any earlier. But don't put off seeing your doctor just because it might affect your health insurance policy.**

Will I have to fill out a long questionnaire?

That depends on the insurer. Some insurers want you to answer a long list of questions. They might agree to pay for treatment for a pre-existing condition, which the questionnaire will reveal, but you will probably pay higher premiums. Other insurers use a 'moratorium' system. Here, there is no lengthy form to fill out but you are insured only on the basis that, for the first two years of the policy, the insurer will not pay for treatment for an illness you had perhaps in the five years before the policy started.

Can I choose where I have treatment?

You must use a hospital that is on the insurer's list.

Can I see a list of the hospitals where I can be treated?

The insurer provides the names of the hospitals it uses. Some insurers divide these into different grades, called 'bands'; you choose which level you want to pay for.

Am I guaranteed that I'll get into the hospital of my choice?

Nothing is guaranteed. It depends what is available at the time.

Could I be sent somewhere more luxurious than I've paid for?

In an emergency, you could.

Would I have to pay extra?

Probably, although some policies allow a little leeway – called an 'out-of-band' benefit.

Can I choose the grade of hospital accommodation I have?

Policies usually offer a choice of quality: the more you pay, the greater luxury you can demand.

Is the hospital obliged to provide a room like the one pictured in the brochure?

Brochures must not be misleading, but there is no guarantee that you will get the same degree of comfort they show in the marketing literature, nor even a room to yourself or en-suite bathroom.

Will the insurance include nursing at home after an operation?

It should, although only for a few days.

Once I've turned 60, can I still buy private medical insurance?

Yes, but it is more expensive.

When I retire, what happens to any policy I've already got?

Premiums rise sharply. A 70-year-old can pay twice as much as a 50-year-old.

Will the policy pay for whatever treatment I have?

No. It probably excludes:

- 'alternative' therapy
- check-ups
- normal pregnancy, although there might be a cash lump sum
- cosmetic surgery
- long-term care
- incurable illnesses
- mental or psychiatric illness
- minor surgery at your GP's surgery.

Can I get private treatment for stress-related problems?

This depends on the policy you buy and exactly what your problems are.

Will the policy cover me if I'm taken ill abroad?

Almost certainly not. For this you need travel insurance.

Is there any point taking out private medical insurance when I would probably have the operation on the NHS?

Some policies give you cash if you have NHS treatment.

If I have an accident, and tell the ambulance driver I have private medical insurance, will I be taken to a private hospital?

Not even if you are knocked down outside the private hospital gates.

tip

> WARNING: **It could happen that, in an emergency, you are taken to an NHS hospital but the consultant tries to persuade you to pay through your private medical insurance. Don't be bullied into this, unless you want more luxurious surroundings.**

Will the premium provide insurance for my whole family?

Policies can be for just yourself, or they can include either your partner or the whole family, usually at a special family rate. But be aware that a no-claims discount is lost for everyone if any member of the family claims.

Is there any way of reducing the premiums?

You can limit the types of operation permitted, the hospital you would be admitted to, and the overall maximum payout.

tip

WARNING: **Some policies place a limit on how much you can spend each day; often it applies to the standard of accommodation but you need to be careful if the restriction also applies to treatment: if complications arise after private treatment starts, your policy might not pay enough to meet the bill.**

Can I switch from one private health company to another later on?

Yes, but be careful. If you have developed a health condition since starting the policy, the existing policy covers you for treatment but a new one probably will not.

If I make a claim, is the money sent to me or to the hospital where I was treated?

With some policies, you pay the hospital bill and reclaim the money from the insurer. With others, the insurance company pays the bill direct, which is preferable.

If there is a dispute between the insurer and hospital over the hospital's charges, could I finish up paying?

You might have to make up a shortfall.

Once I've signed up, can the insurance company change the terms?

Yes, because this is an annual contract.

Can the company refuse to continue insuring me?

Not as long as you keep paying the premiums, unless you leave the country. But it can raise the premiums hugely or exclude a particular illness.

My employer provides private health insurance as a perk. Is there any point in buying more?

No. But check whether your company scheme extends to your spouse and children.

Is the private medical insurance I get through my employer likely to be exactly the same as I could buy myself?

Not quite. Employers' schemes give no choice over the precise terms; and your employer might decide to cancel the perk. An individual policy continues for as long as you pay the premiums.

What happens if I resign from a firm that has an employer's scheme for private medical insurance?

That depends on the policy: some insurers let you continue paying the premiums yourself, but it will not be on the same favourable terms.

What happens to an employer's scheme when I retire?

You can probably continue with the same insurer but as an outside individual, not an employee.

Is there an age after which I can't start buying private medical insurance?

This varies between companies but can be as low as 64.

Is there tax relief on private medical insurance premiums?

There was for a few years, for people over 60, but no longer.

QUESTIONS TO ASK AN INSURER OR SALESPERSON BEFORE BUYING PRIVATE HEALTH INSURANCE

- How much are the premiums?
- Do the premiums include insurance premium tax?
- Will the premiums go up each year? (*Beware: they are likely to increase each year by more than the rate of inflation.*)
- Are there any limits on how much premiums can rise each year?
- How much do premiums go up when I reach 65?
- Is there an age at which you will stop insuring me?
- Is there a no claims discount?
- Is there a long questionnaire or a moratorium? (*See earlier in this section.*)
- What choice of hospitals do I have?
- What is the excess I have to pay on any claim?
- Will the policy pay all the specialists' fees?
- Will the policy cover all treatment in a private hospital?
- Do I pay the hospital bill or does the insurance company pay it?

tip

> WARNING: **Some companies calls their customers 'members'. Do not be deceived into thinking you are joining an exclusive club – you are buying a commercial product.**

Health cash plans

Health cash plans are low-priced insurance policies that reimburse money you have to pay out in connection with your health, such as laboratory tests, physiotherapy, and dental costs. They also give you cash for every night that you spend in hospital.

ask Margaret

Who provides health cash plans?
Specialist insurance companies.

Where can I buy a health cash plan?
You can buy one from the insurer, through advertisements or through mailshots.

Do the plans pay only if I go into a private hospital?
No, they pay whichever hospital you are in.

What if I have hospital treatment during the day but don't stay overnight?
You get no money.

How much cash do they pay?
It depends on how much insurance you have paid for, but it is a modest amount. You can spend the money on whatever you want (perhaps travelling costs for the family to visit you).

Dental plans

There are two schemes.

With dental insurance policies you pay premiums according to how much insurance you want to buy each year; then you claim on the insurance to pay your dental bills, but if the bills exceed the amount of insurance you bought, you have to pay the extra. You can buy the policies independently of your dentist.

With capitation plans, your dentist signs up with a provider; your dentist decides how much dental work you will need in the future, and how much this will cost in the coming year – the price varies from one dentist to another. Then you pay one-twelfth of that amount each month. If the work costs more, you have nothing extra to pay. The plan organiser takes around 10 per cent of your monthly payments.

ask Margaret

Who provides dental plans?

Insurance companies provide this type of cover.

Where can I buy the plans?

You can buy them direct from insurers, as well as through insurance brokers and dentists. Dental plans can be included with private medical insurance or hospital plans. And it may be an employee benefit with your job.

Are dental plans cheaper than paying the dentist as work is done?

That is difficult to say; it depends how much dental work you would otherwise pay for. Either way, the worse your teeth are, the more it costs.

Do the premiums stay the same each year or go up?

Apart from increases for inflation, it depends on the state of your teeth. With the insurance policy approach, you decide how much you want to insure for and can pay more, or less. With capitation plans, in theory – and assuming you follow your dentist's oral-hygiene advice – your teeth and gums should need less work but any improvement is likely to be offset by higher dental costs.

Can I stop the policy if I want?

You agree the premiums for only one year at a time, but you might need to give notice to terminate a plan.

Does the policy include the whole family?

Rarely, because children are treated free on the NHS. Premiums for children would be low, but the policy would exclude expensive work such as having their teeth straightened.

Will the policy cover all the dental work that I might need?

No. Capitation plans cover normal treatment, such as fillings, crowns and bridges, as well as visits to the hygienist; but you still pay for laboratory work, braces, having wisdom teeth removed in hospital, cosmetic dentistry and dental implants. Insurance policies also have exclusions.

Will a dental plan cover emergency treatment?

Yes, and some plans pay for work if you are abroad at the time.

tip **Check any private medical policy or health cash plan you have, because it might include an element of dental work.**

The ABI Code of Practice on Genetic Testing

Insurers have agreed to abide by the Association of British Insurers' Code of Practice on Genetic Testing, which states that:

- applicants must not be asked to undergo a genetic test in order to get insurance
- if an application includes a genetic test result, the underwriter must consult the insurance company's chief medical officer on the matter
- insurers can take account of existing genetic test results only if relevant to the insurance product
- any decisions must be clearly recorded
- insurance companies can decide to refuse insurance because of a genetic test result, although they should try to offer reduced terms instead.

tip **Anyone selling term or health insurance is bound by the Association of British Insurers' Code of Practice for selling general insurance – see the last section in Chapter 9.**

Appendix

Where to find more information

There are more sources of information available today than ever before, and increasingly so through the Internet.

- all national daily and Sunday newspapers write about personal finance, usually on one particular day of the week
- many local papers write about personal finance, some in more depth than others
- specialist weekly and monthly magazines range from those aimed at sophisticated investors to general magazines for novices
- regular radio and television programmes, and occasional television series, are broadcast
- trade associations provide information packs
- individual companies, trade associations, some ombudsmen and regulators publish booklets and have websites
- Ceefax and Teletext publish information
- online information about share dealing is available through computer programs
- software packages help organise your finances and fill out tax returns.

Addresses

**Adjudicator for the Inland Revenue
(also Customs & Excise and
Contributions Agency)**
Haymarket House, 28 Haymarket,
London SW1P 4SP
tel: 0171 930 2292
fax: 0171 930 2298
e-mail: adjudicators@gtnet.gov.uk

Association of British Insurers (ABI)
51 Gresham Street, London EC2V 7HQ
tel: 0171 600 3333
fax: 0171 696 8996
www.abi.org.uk
free leaflets on many insurance subjects

Association of Friendly Societies
Royex House, Aldermanbury Square,
London EC2V 7HR
tel: 0171 606 1881
fax: 0171 606 0794
e-mail: info@afs.org.uk
free booklet

**Association of Investment Trust
Companies (AITC)**
Durrant House, 8–13 Chiswell Street,
London EC1Y 4YY
tel: 0171 282 5555
fax: 0171 282 5556
brochures and factsheets tel:
0171 431 5222
e-mail: info@aitc.co.uk
www.aitc.co.uk

Association of Policy Market Makers
Holywell Centre, 1 Phipp Street, London
EC2A 4PS
tel: 0171 739 3949
fax: 0171 613 2990
e-mail: apmm@dircon.co.uk

**Association of Private Client Investment
Managers and
Stockbrokers (Apcims)**
112 Middlesex Street, London E1 7HY
tel: 0171 247 7080
fax: 0171 377 0939
www.apcims.co.uk
free booklet and list of members

**Association of Solicitor Investment
Managers (Asim)**
Chiddingstone Causeway, Tonbridge,
Kent TN11 8JX
tel: 01892 870 065
fax: 01892 870 160
e-mail:
heather_martin@compuserve.com

**Association of Unit Trusts and Investment
Funds (Autif)**
65 Kingsway, London WC2B 6TD
tel: 0171 831 0898
fax: 0171 831 9975
www.investmentfunds.org.uk
free leaflets

Bank of England Gilts Register
Registrar's Dept, Southgate House,
Southgate Street,
Gloucester GL1 1UW
tel: 01452 398 080
fax: 01452 398 098
publications hotline tel: 0800 818 614
www.bankofengland.co.uk

Banking Ombudsman
70 Gray's Inn Road, London WC1X 8NB
tel: 0171 404 9944
fax: 0171 405 5052
www.obo.org.uk

Benefits Agency
DSS Pensions,
Newcastle-Upon-Tyne
NE98 1BA
pensions leaflets: 0345 313 233
(8am–10pm)
www.dss.gov.uk

British Bankers' Association
Pinners Hall, 105–108 Old Broad Street,
London EC2N 1EX
tel: 0171 216 8889
fax: 0171 216 8811
leaflet order line tel: 0171-216 8801
www.bba.org.uk
www.bankfacts.org.uk
free leaflets

**British Insurance and Investment Brokers'
Association (Biiba)**
14 Bevis Marks, London EC3A 7NT
tel: 0171 623 9043
fax: 0171 626 9676
e-mail: enquiries@biiba.org.uk
www.biiba.org.uk

Building Societies Association
3 Savile Row, London W1X 1AF
tel: 0171 437 0655
fax: 0171 734 6416
www.bsa.org.uk

Building Societies Ombudsman
Millbank Tower, Millbank, London SW1P
4XS
tel: 0171 931 0044
fax: 0171 931 8485
e-mail:
bldgsocombudsman@easynet.co.uk

Council of Mortgage Lenders
3 Savile Row, London W1X 1AF
tel: 0171-437 0075
enquiry line: 0171-440 2255
fax: 0171-434 3791
e-mail: info@cml.org.uk
www.cml.org.uk

Equifax Europe (credit reference agency)
Dept 1E, PO Box 3001, Glasgow G81 2DT
tel: 0141-951 1100

**Ethical Investment Research Service
(Eiris)**
80–84 Bondway, London SW8 1SF
tel: 0171 840 5700
fax: 0171 735 5323
e-mail: ethics@eiris.win-uk.net

Experian (credit reference agency)
Consumer Help Service, PO Box 8000,
Nottingham NG1 5GX
tel: 0115 976 8747

Financial Services Authority (FSA)
25 The North Colonnade, Canary Wharf,
London E14 5HS
enquiry unit tel: 0845 606 1234
publications tel: 0171 676 3298
fax: 0171 676 1099
www.fsa.gov.uk

IFA Promotion
2nd Floor, 117 Farringdon Road, London
EC1R 3BT
tel: 0171 831 4027
tel for names of local IFAs:
0117 971 1177
www.ifap.org.uk

Inland Revenue leaflets
orderline: PO Box 37, St Austell,
Cornwall PL25 5YN
tel: 0645 000 404
fax: 0645 000 604
e-mail: saorderline.ir@gtnet.gov.uk
www.inlandrevenue.gov.uk

Inland Revenue Self-Assessment
evening and weekend helpline:
0645 000444

Institute of Actuaries
Staple Inn Hall, High Holborn, London
WC1V 7QJ
tel: 0171 632 2100
fax: 0171 632 2111
e-mail: institute@actuaries.org.uk
www.actuaries.org.uk

Institute of Chartered Accountants in England and Wales
PO Box 433, Chartered Accountants'
Hall, Moorgate Place,
London EC2P 2BJ
tel: 01908 248090
fax: 0171 628 1791
e-mail: comms@icaew.co.uk
www.icaew.co.uk

Institute of Chartered Accountants in Scotland
27 Queen Street, Edinburgh EH2 1LA
tel: 0131 225 5673
fax: 0131 225 3813
www.icas.org.uk

Institute of Financial Planning
Whitefriars, Lewins Mead,
Bristol BS1 2NT
tel: 0117 930 4434
fax: 0117 929 2214
e-mail:
enquiries@institutefinplan.demon.co.uk
www.financialplanning.org.uk
list of fee-charging financial planners
and leaflet

Insurance Ombudsman Bureau
City Gate One, 135 Park Street, London
SE1 9EA
tel: 0845 600 6666
fax: 0171 902 8197
e-mail: complaint@theiob.org.uk
www.theiob.org.uk

Investment Ombudsman
6 Frederick's Place, London EC2R 8BT
tel: 0171 796 3065
fax: 0171 726 0574

Investors Compensation Scheme
Cottons Centre, Cottons Lane, London
SE1 2QB
tel: 0171 367 6000
fax: 0171 367 6001

Law Society of England and Wales
www.lawsociety.org.uk

Law Society of Northern Ireland
Law Society House, 98 Victoria Street,
Belfast BT1 3JZ
tel: 01232 231 614
fax: 01232 232 606

Law Society of Scotland
26 Drumsheugh Gardens,
Edinburgh EH3 7YR
tel: 0131 226 7411
fax: 0131 225 2934

Lloyd's of London
Complaints Department, One Lime
Street, London EC3M 7HA
tel: 0171 327 6385
fax: 0171 327 5225
www.lloydsoflondon.co.uk

Money Management Register of Fee-based Advisers
for names of local fee-charging
advisers: 0870 013 1925

Motor Insurers' Bureau
152 Silbury Boulevard, Central Milton
Keynes MK9 1NB
tel: 01908 831 001
fax: 01908 671 681

National Savings
Sales Information Unit
Freepost BJ2092, Blackpool FY3 9XR
tel: 0645 645 000
www.nationalsavings.co.uk

Occupational Pensions Advisory Service (OPAS)
11 Belgrave Road, London SW1V 1RB
tel: 0171 233 8080

Pension Schemes Registry
PO Box 1NN, Newcastle upon Tyne,
NE99 1NN
tel: 0191 225 6393

Pensions Ombudsman
11 Belgrave Road, London SW1V 1RB
tel: 0171 834 9144
fax: 0171 821 0065
e-mail:
pensions.ombudsman@iclweb.com

Personal Insurance Arbitration Service (PIAS)
Chartered Institute of Arbitrators, 24
Angel Gate, City
Road, London EC1V 2RS
tel: 0171 837 4483
fax: 0171 837 4185
e-mail: 71411.2735@compuserve.com
www.arbitrators.org

PIA Ombudsman
Hertsmere House, Hertsmere Road,
London E14 4AB
automated enquiries tel: 0171 712 8700
helpline: 0171 712 8937
fax: 0171 712 8742

ProShare
Library Chambers
13 Basinghall Street, London EC2V 5HU
tel: 0171 394 5200
fax: 0171 600 0947
www.proshare.org.uk

Safe Home Income Plans (SHIP)
4th Floor, Tolworth Tower, Ewell Road,
Surbiton, Surrey KT6 7EL
tel: 0181 390 8166
fax: 0181 399 3461

ShareGift
24 Grosvenor Gardens,
London SW1W 0DH
tel: 0171 761 4501
fax: 0171 761 4479
www.sharegift.org.uk

Society of Trust and Estate Practitioners (Step)
PO Box 13272, Eagle House,
110 Jermyn Street, London
SW1Y 6ZH
tel: 0171 839 3886
fax: 0171 839 3669

Stock Exchange
Public Information Department, London
EC2N 1HP
tel: 0171 797 1372
fax: 0171 410 6861
www.londonstockex.co.uk

Index

ABI, *see* Association of British Insurers

accountants 16, 20, 44, 45, 54–5, 148

and tax returns 17, 18–19

accumulation and maintenance trust 27

accumulation units 68

Activities of Daily Living (ADLs) 266

actuaries 107, 148

additional pension 125, 127

Additional Voluntary Contributions 131, 133, 134–6, 150, 151, 152

Adjudicator for Inland Revenue, Customs & Excise and Contributions Agency 29, 279

affinity cards 181

age-related pension 125

Aids 253

AITC 279

allocation rate 118

all-risks cover 222, 231

all-share index, *see* stock

market index

Annual Percentage Rate (APR) 183, 186–7

annuities 37, 56, 135, 136, 141, 142, 144–9

APCIMS, *see* Association of Private Client Investment Managers and Stockbrokers

appointed representatives 34

appropriate personal pension 127

APR 183, 186–7

ASIM 279

Association of British Insurers (ABI) 229, 249, 261, 277, 279

Association of Friendly Societies 279

Association of Investment Trust Companies (AITC) 279

Association of Policy Market Makers 279

Association of Private Client Investment

Managers and Stockbrokers (APCIMS) 50, 279

Association of Solicitor Investment Managers (ASIM) 279

Association of Unit Trusts and Investment Funds (Autif) 279

ATMs, *see* automated teller machines

AUTIF 279

automated teller machines (ATMs) 62, 202, 203, 211, 213, 214

AVCs, *see* Additional Voluntary Contributions

bail bond 233

bank accounts, *see* current accounts, savings accounts

Bank of England 100, 279

Banking Ombudsman 28, 279

banks 95, 98, 223, *see also* credit cards, current

accounts, savings
accounts, mortgages
bare trust 26
behaviour scoring 192
benchmark 46, 51–52, 53
Benefits Agency 6, 150,
  280, see also Department
  of Social Security
Bermuda 90, 92
bid price, definition 67
Biiba 280
bonds 61, 71, 83, see also
  investment bonds
bonus, life insurance
  108–9, 113, 116
British Bankers'
  Association 280
British Insurance and
  Investment Brokers'
  Association (Biiba) 280
British Retail Consortium
  246
broker funds 36
brokers, see stockbrokers,
  discount brokers, insurance brokers
building societies 83, 95,
  223, see also credit
  cards, current accounts,
  savings accounts,
  mortgages
  Building Societies
  Association 280
Building Societies
  Ombudsman 28, 280
buildings insurance, see
  house insurance

capital gain 68
capital gains tax 12, 13, 14,
  17, 20, 45, 119
capital shares 78
capital, definition 59
  car insurance, see motor
  insurance
cash card 211, 214
cashback with mortgage
  157–8
CAT standards 84, 85–6
changing your mind, see
  cooling off

charge cards 178, 185, 212
charges, see also commis-
  sion, fees
  investments 39, 42, 43,
  53, 76, 85
  life insurance 107, 117
  pension 138–9
  unit trusts 67–8, 70, 71
  charities 27, 179, 181,
  223, 232, 239
cheque accounts, see
  current accounts
cheque guarantee cards
  203–4, 211
cheques 60, 203–5
Child Support Agency 10
children 138
  investing for 7–8, 62–3,
  95, 122
  tax 24, 26
churning 44
CIFAS (Credit Industry
  Fraud Avoidance System)
  193
Citizens Advice Bureau 24
client agreement letter 36
co-habiting couples 24,
  132, 134, 138, 265
collective investment,
  definition 67
commission 35, 36, 39, 42,
  43, 49, 56–7, 79
  discounts 38
  investments 67, 68, 79
  pensions 137, 138, 139,
  149
  stockbrokers 50, 53
company pensions 28, 30,
  125, 128–34, 139, 150,
  151, 152
company salespeople
  33–34, 35, 42, 48–49,
  149
compensation schemes
  29–30, 69, 74, 92, 125,
  178
complaints 27–9, 45, 51–2
compulsory purchase
  annuity 146–7
computers 30–2, 40, 44,
  51, 278

and tax returns 17, 19
Consumer Credit Act 178,
  194
contents insurance, see
  house insurance
continuous authority transaction 206
Contributions Agency 29,
  279
cooling-off periods
  insurance 266
  investments 59, 70, 105,
  122
  credit 177, 188
  pensions 137, 147
corporate bond funds 71,
  73, 82
Council of Mortgage
  Lenders 261, 280
council tax 10, 12
county court judgements
  189, 190, 192, 193
credit 176–95
credit cards 11, 31, 177,
  178, 179–184, 185, 192,
  212, 220
  add-ons 245, 260
  on holiday 214, 215–6
Credit Industry Fraud
  Avoidance System
  (CIFAS) 193
credit record, poor 168,
  190, 192–4
credit reference agencies
  177, 188–90, 198, 200
credit repair 194
credit scoring 191–2
Crest 97–9
critical illness insurance
  256, 263–5
current accounts 9–11, 28,
  29, 196–218
  by computer 30, 31, 32
Customs & Excise 29, 190,
  279

data protection 40, 253–4
deadlines for tax returns
  17, 19, 20–21
death in service benefit 134
debit cards 199, 203, 212,
  214

dental plans 256, 275–7
Department of Social
 Security (DSS) 8, 127,
 128, 150, *see also*
 Benefits Agency
deposit accounts, *see*
 savings accounts
Deposit Protection Scheme
 29, 197
direct debits 30, 199, 200,
 205–6, 210
direct mail 40
discount brokers 56–7
discounts on investments
 38, 56–7, 67
discretionary trust 27
distribution bonds 120–1
distribution units 68
distributor funds 91
dividends 67, 68, 76–7, 93,
 94, 98
 and tax 12, 14
divorce 10–11, 153–4
DSS, *see* Department of
 Social Security
Dublin 73, 90

early retirement 151–2
early settlement rebate 194
Eiris 4, 5, 280
electronic purse 212
Electronic Version of the
 Return (EVR) 17
endowment life insurance
 56, 104, 105, 106–114, 115
endowment mortgage 105,
 158–60, 166, 171, 172
environmental funds, *see*
 ethical investment
Equifax Europe 280
equities, *see* shares
ethical investment 3–5, 37,
 142
Ethical Investment
 Research Service (Eiris)
 4, 5, 280
euro 66, 70, 162, 205, 214,
 216
excess 226, 241
execution-only 40, 47, 50,
 52, 54

executors 208
expatriates 37
Experian 280
extended warranties 245–7

fact find 35, 47, 150
family income benefit 254
fees for advice 35, 42, 43,
 50, 54, 55
final salary pension 128,
 129, 152
financial advice 33–57,
financial advisers, *see*
 independent financial
 advisers, company sales-
 people
Financial Services Act 30,
 33, 36, 44, 48, 76, 98,
 266
 complaints 27–29, 114
Financial Services
 Authority (FSA) 36, 42,
 280
Financial Services
 Ombudsman 28
Financial Times 51
fines for late tax 17, 19, 21
fixed-interest 62, 71, 173,
 see also gilt-edged stock
Footsie (FTSE 100 index)
 see stock market index
foreign currency 93, 197,
 199, 214–7
free-standing additional
 voluntary contributions
 (FSAVCs) 134–6, 150
friendly societies 121–2
FSA, *see* Financial Services
 Authority
FSAVCs, *see* free-standing
 additional voluntary
 contributions
FTSE100 index, *see* stock
 market index
fund, definition 66
funerals 24
futures 88

GAIN (Gone Away
 Information Network) 193
general insurance 29,

31–2, 219–49, *see also*
 house, holiday, motor
 insurance
genetic tests 105, 253, 277
gilt-edged stock 71, 82, 93,
 94, 100–2, 141, 146
Glass's Guide 234
gold card 182
Gone Away Information
 Network 193
graduated pension scheme
 125
grandchildren 7–8, 62–3
Green Card 233
green funds 4
guaranteed equity bonds
 88-90
guaranteed income and
 growth bonds 56, 116,
 119–20
guaranteed stock market
 bonds 88–90
guaranteed sum assured
 105
Guernsey 90, 92

health cash benefit 256,
 275
health insurance 44,
 250–77
hire purchase 177, 187–8
holiday insurance 12, 31,
 215, 236, 243, 248
holiday money 214–6
home income plans 37, 170
Home Responsibilities
 Protection 126
house insurance 12, 31–2,
 157, 198, 221–232, 237,
 243, 248

IFA Promotion 34, 280
ill health pension 134, 151
impaired life annuity 146
IMRO (Investment
 Management Regulatory
 Organisation) 28
income drawdown 152–3
income protection insur-
 ance 256, 257–9, 264
income shares 78

income support 167, 261
income tax 8, 12–24, *see also* individual savings products, life insurance and pensions
income withdrawal 152–3
indemnity 222, 240
independent financial advisers 28, 33–48, 67, 79, 149
index funds, *see* tracker funds
Individual Savings Accounts (ISAs) 3, 39, 57, 74, 76, 79, 81–8, 98
by computer 31–2
for retirement 6, 140, 144
tax 13, 65
inheritance tax 9, 12, 24, 26, 45, 91
and trusts 25, 27, 123, 138
Inland Revenue 13–8, 19, 21–5, 81, 91, 190, 262
addresses 279, 280, 281
pensions 137, 139
Institute of Actuaries 281
Institute of Chartered Accountants in England and Wales 281
Institute of Chartered Accountants in Scotland 281
Institute of Financial Planning 34, 281
insurance broker 220, 241–3,
Insurance Ombudsman 28, 281
insurance premium tax (IPT) 12
insurance-company banks 196, 197–8
interest rates 16, 111
questions 59–60, 62, 63, 119, 183, 184, 196, 220
intermediary, definition 56
Internet 30–2, 53, 59, 181, 196, 219, 278,
investment advice 33–57
investment bonds 57, 104
investment clubs 96

Investment Management Regulatory Organisation (IMRO) 28
Investment Ombudsman 28, 281
investment trusts 31, 73, 74–81, 82, 94, 95, 98, 135, 144
advice 44, 50
Investors Compensation Scheme 29–30, 51, 98, 137, 281
IPT (insurance premium tax) 12
ISA, *see* Individual Savings Accounts
Isle of Man 90, 92

Jersey 90, 92
joint accounts 9–11, 29, 180, 181
joint tenants 9–10
junk bonds 71

key features 36, 137

Law Society of England and Wales 281
Law Society of Northern Ireland 281
Law Society of Scotland 281
legal expenses insurance 243–4
life insurance, investment 3, 11, 29–30, 32, 91, 103–23, 198,
advice 42, 44
commission 56, 57
in trust 27, 123
Individual Savings Accounts 82–6
life insurance, protection 11, 29, 32, 264–5
in trust 27, 123
Individual Savings Accounts 82–6
lifelong individual savings accounts (LISAs) 144
life-rental trust 26
LISAs 144

Lloyd's of London 28, 248–9, 281
loan protection insurance 12, 256, 259–63
loans 11, 31, 32, 177, 178, 185–7, 197
London Stock Exchange 50, 80, 94, 282
shares quoted on 70, 73, 75, 95, 96
long-term care insurance 256, 264, 265–9
loss adjusters 224–5
loyalty card 212
lump sum investments, 67, 76, 88, 104, 112
Luxembourg 73, 90

market maker 56
market value adjustment 117–8
marriage and money 9–10, 24, 27
Mastercard 182, *see also* credit cards
Maxwell, Robert 125
Money Management 34, 281
money purchase pension 128
moratorium 271
mortality rates 146
mortgage indemnity guarantee 161, 165, 166
mortgage payment protection insurance 256, 261
mortgages 3, 10, 28, 31, 123, 155–75, 197
and house insurance 223, 229
endowment 105, 107, 109, 253
motor insurance 12, 31–2, 225, 232–6, 240, 243, 248
Motor Insurers' Bureau 234, 281

National House Building Council (NHBC) 230
National Insurance

contributions 12, 125–6, 127, 130, 151
National Savings 35, 64–5, 82, 83, 100, 282
net asset value (NAV) 77
new for old 222
NHBC 230
no claims discount 226, 233, 236
nominee accounts 52, 53, 56, 76, 95, 97–9
non-qualifying life insurance 106, 113, see also single-premium policies
nursing homes 26, see also long-term care insurance

Occupational Pensions Advisory Service (OPAS) 29, 130, 134, 282
occupational pensions, see company pensions
oeic, see open-ended investment companies
offer price, definition 67
Office of Fair Trading 189
offshore investments 90–3
ombudsmen 28–29, see also under separate ombudsmen
on-line information, see computers
OPAS, see Occupational Pensions Advisory Service
open-ended investment companies (oeic) 66, 73–4, 82, 91
open-market option 142, 145
options 88
ordinary shares, see shares
overdrafts 177, 197, 199, 206–7

partners, see joint accounts
part-time workers 133
Pay As You Earn (PAYE) 13, 15, 21, 23, 154

penny shares 96
pension mortgage 172
Pension Schemes Registry 6, 150, 282
pensions 6, 13, 66, 124–53, see also company, personal, and state pensions, investing for retirement
Pensions Ombudsman 28–29, 145, 282
PEP, see Personal Equity Plans
performance tables 31, 68, 69
perks for shareholders 53, 95–6, 98–9
permanent health insurance, see income protection insurance
persistency record 45
Personal Equity Plans 3, 73, 79, 81, 83, 84, 86–7, 98
Personal Identification Number (PIN) 181, 211, 212, 213
Personal Insurance Arbitration Service (PIAS) 282
Personal Investment Authority (PIA) 28
personal pensions 3, 28, 125, 130, 131, 136–43, 150, 151, 152, 198, 254
advice 37, 39
by computer 32
commission 57
offshore 91, 92
pet insurance 247–8
phased retirement 152–3
PIA Ombudsman 28, 282
PIAS 282
PIN, see Personal Identification Number
Policyholders Protection Scheme 29, 89, 248, 266
pooled investment, definition 67
portfolio, investors 32, 51
post offices 64, 100, 214, 236

postal accounts 60, 61
Private Investor Index 51
private medical insurance 12, 256, 269–75
probate 9, 24, 92
property 12, 141
as investment 6, 140, 162
ProShare 96, 282
protection schemes 29–30
purchased life annuity 147

qualifying life insurance 106, 113, see also endowment and whole life insurance

reason why letter 137
Registry, Pension Schemes of 6
regular saving, 48, 67, 76, 104, 108
regulated financial products 48
Rent-a-Room 169
repayment mortgage 170–1
retailers and banking 196, 197–8
retirement age 126, 127, 133, 139–40, 151–2
retirement planning 6, 37, 148, 150, 168–70
risk 100, 107, 109, 137, 141–2
collective investments 68–9, 70, 74, 79
roll up funds 91

Safe Home Income Plans 170, 282
savings accounts 3, 24, 28, 29, 30, 58–64
joint 9–11
offshore 91, 93
savings schemes, investment trust 75, 76
second-hand policies 112–4
Section 226 pension 138
secured loans 188, see also mortgages
securities 94

self assessment 13–22, 40, 281

self-employed 126, 154, 158, 231, 257, 260, 262

separation, *see* divorce

Serps (State Earnings Related Pension Scheme) 125, 127–8, 141

SETS 99

settlement for shares 97

share account, definition 63

share certificates 97

share exchange schemes 70, 80, 95

shared appreciation mortgages 169–70

ShareGift 95, 282

shares 3, 44, 66–7, 71, 73, 88, 93–9, 100
  and tax 12
  by computer 31–2
  ethical 3, 4
  Individual Savings Accounts 82, 83

simple trust 26

single premium policies 89, 104, 105, 116–7, 121, 138

single price 68, 73, 85

Society of Trust and Estate Practitioners (Step) 27, 282

solicitors 34, 44, 55–6, 148

split capital investment trust 77–8, 80

spread, definition 67

stakeholder pensions 143–4

stamp duty 12, 95

standing orders 30, 199, 200, 205–6, 210

state benefits 8, 126, 266, *see also* state pension

State Earnings Related Pension Scheme (Serps) 125, 127–8, 137

state pension 6, 28, 125–8, 150, 151
  and tax 15, 23

status enquiry 201

Step *see* Society of Trust and Estate Practitioners

Stock Exchange Electronic Trading System (SETS) 99

Stock Exchange, *see* London Stock Exchange

stock market 3, 51, 88–9, 94, 100, 108, 125
  index 70, 71, 75

stock markets, world 70, 104

stock transfer form 51, 95

stockbrokers 31, 44, 66, 82, 93, 94, 95, 97, 100
  for financial advice 50–4

stocks 93–4, *see also* gilt-edged stock

store cards 184, 260

students 177, 217–8

subsidence 229

sum assured 106, 108

supermarket banks 196, 197–8

surrender value, pension 140

surrendering life insurance 107, 111, 112

tax 10, 11–25, 221, 267, *see also* inheritance tax and under the various types of savings
  and life insurance 106, 113, 116–7, 121, 142, 254
  and mortgage interest 161
  and pensions 135, 136, 137, 140, 142, 147, 154
  friendly societies 121–2

tax advice 12, 18–19, 20, 44, 53

Tax Exempt Special Savings Account (TESSA) 81, 87–8

tax investigation 14, 15–16

tax office 15, 22–23

tax return 13–19, 21, 23, 91

taxman, *see* Inland Revenue

tenants in common 9–10

term insurance 142, 251–5

TESSA 81, 87–8

tied advisers, *see* company salespeople

tour operators 236, 237

tracker funds 68, 70–1, 89

traded policies 112–4

transfer value 140

travel agents 236, 237–8

travel insurance, *see* holiday insurance

travellers cheques 214

trustees 25–27, 69
  pension 129, 130, 132, 133–4, 136

trusts 17, 25–7, 92, 123, 138, 254

umbrella funds 73

unit trusts 3, 28, 30, 36, 65–73, 76, 77, 91, 94, 198, 144
  advice 34, 42, 50
  by computer 31
  commission 56, 57
  ethical 3, 4, 5
  Individual Savings Accounts 82, 83

unit-linked bonds 116, 118

unit-linked life insurance 82 104, 107, 109–110, 121

value added tax (VAT) 12

Visa 182, *see also* credit cards

waiver of premium 106, 141

warrants 78

whole life insurance 104, 105, 113, 114–5, 172

will trust 26

wills 7, 9–10, 11, 44

withdrawal questions 61–2, 63, 90, 116

with-profit bonds 117–8

with-profits life insurance 56, 82, 104, 121
  bonds 116, 117–8

yield 101

zero shares 78